THERAPEUTIC PHOTOGRAPHY

of related interest

Exploring the Self through Photography
Activities for Use in Group Work
Claire Craig
ISBN 978 1 84310 666 1
eISBN 978 0 85700 191 7

Inspiring and Creative Ideas for Working with Children
How to Build Relationships and Enable Change
Deborah M. Plummer
ISBN 978 1 84905 651 9
eISBN 978 1 78450 146 4

The CBT Art Activity Book
100 illustrated handouts for creative therapeutic work
Jennifer Guest
ISBN 978 1 84905 665 6
eISBN 978 1 78450 168 6

Toxins and Antidotes
A Therapeutic Card Deck for Exploring Life Experiences
Bonnie Thomas
Illustrated by Rosy Salaman
ISBN 978 1 78592 763 8

Art Therapy and Creative Coping Techniques for Older Adults
Susan I. Buchalter
Part of the *Arts Therapies* series
ISBN 978 1 84905 830 8
eISBN 978 0 85700 309 6

The Handbook of Art Therapy and Digital Technology
Edited by Cathy Malchiodi, PhD
ISBN 978 1 78592 792 8
eISBN 978 1 78450 774 9

Portrait Therapy
Resolving Self-Identity Disruption in Clients with
Life-Threatening and Chronic Illnesses
Susan M.D. Carr
ISBN 978 1 78592 293 0
eISBN 978 1 78450 605 6

THERAPEUTIC PHOTOGRAPHY

Enhancing Self-Esteem,
Self-Efficacy
and Resilience

NEIL GIBSON

Jessica Kingsley *Publishers*
London and Philadelphia

First published in 2018
by Jessica Kingsley Publishers
73 Collier Street
London N1 9BE, UK
and
400 Market Street, Suite 400
Philadelphia, PA 19106, USA

www.jkp.com

Library of Congress Cataloging in Publication Data
Names: Gibson, Neil, 1973- author.
Title: Therapeutic photography : enhancing self-esteem, self-efficacy and
  resilience / Neil Gibson.
Description: London ; Philadelphia : Jessica Kingsley Publishers, 2018. |
  Includes bibliographical references and index.
Identifiers: LCCN 2018006132 | ISBN 9781785921551 (alk. paper)
Subjects: | MESH: Psychotherapy | Photography | Self Concept | Resilience,
  Psychological
Classification: LCC RC455.4.A77 | NLM WM 450.5.P5 | DDC 616.89/1656-
-dc23 LC record available at https://lccn.loc.gov/2018006132

British Library Cataloguing in Publication Data
A CIP catalogue record for this book is available from the British Library

ISBN 978 1 78592 155 1
eISBN 978 1 78450 421 2

Printed and bound in Great Britain

For Kirsi, Coen and Harris

Contents

INTRODUCTION

Photographs and photography can be a powerful tool. A photographer aims the camera at a certain subject, presses the shutter at a certain time, and immortalises a scene – frozen in time for all to see. The photograph is then printed, possibly after editing in a darkroom or on a software package, and then revealed to interested onlookers for a message to be conveyed and interpreted. The image can be passed around, reproduced in many formats, and may facilitate discussion and comment. The *power* behind the final image is rooted in numerous steps preceding the finished product, but can this power be therapeutic?

In 2004, I visited a refugee centre in Belgium for three months. During my time there I wanted to work with a group of asylum seekers and run a project with them. I had with me an old Nikon F100n film camera and several spools of 35mm black and white film, so I decided to run a photography club in the centre and asked volunteers to meet me one afternoon.

A variety of participants with different cultural backgrounds attended and I explained the purpose of the group – to have fun with the camera, to take pictures of life in the centre, and to select images for display within the centre. Each day the participants would book out the camera and document their lives.

When I developed the images I expected to see a multitude of bleak, stark photographs of the cramped conditions, the unsanitary dormitories, and the oppressive atmosphere, but instead there were lots of smiling people. The participants spoke about the images and identified positives in their environment, which included a sense of community (albeit temporary), and the support they gleaned from one another. The images were displayed during a community open day and the participants wrote captions for each one explaining why they had captured that particular image.

Years later, the intervention still sticks in my mind. This was my first foray into using photography with clients, and my last for over ten years. From my practice experience I noted that within statutory UK services the work tended to be procedural and system driven. There seemed to be little opportunity to allow clients to creatively express and explore their situations, and the dominant method when working in adult services was the one-to-one interview, which relied solely on verbal information.

However, I did encounter pockets of practice where photography was being used: a day-care service for adults with a learning disability had set up a photography group; a young female in residential care was able to express emotions through photographs of seascapes in various weather conditions she had pinned to her bedroom wall; and care managers were engaging with photograph albums when conducting assessments. When I asked practitioners why they used photography there appeared to be no definitive reason, only that it seemed to be effective in engaging the client.

And so this was the starting point for my interest in therapeutic photography. I wanted to find out if photography could assist the caring professions, and initial research led me to the practice of therapeutic photography which appeared to underpin the pockets of practice I had encountered. Since then I have been involved in the design and delivery of therapeutic photography programmes with a wide variety of clients, including those with substance use issues, carers, people with mental health issues, young adults with employability issues, and adults with autism. This led to the writing of a PhD entitled 'Is there a role for therapeutic photography in social work with groups?' from which material has been used to write this book. The programme has also been adopted by a number of organisations and incorporated into practice.

This book brings together the theorists who underpin the approach, the theories to assist in understanding the dynamics, and the practicalities of delivering therapeutic photography interventions. Included in the Appendix is the full programme, which was designed to be delivered over a six-week period, but it is anticipated that the reader can use this as guidance for initiating their own projects to adapt and design appropriate therapeutic photography approaches to use with their own clients.

What's in the book?

In Chapter 1, the concept of therapeutic photography is introduced and explanation offered as to how it can be used. In doing this, the practice of phototherapy will also be discussed, drawing parallels and distinctions between the two approaches. The intended outcomes of using therapeutic photography as an intervention will also be explored within this opening chapter.

Chapter 2 moves on to look at how therapeutic photography can actually be used in professional settings, drawing on the previous application of the approach within the field of research. Concepts of control and power dynamics between the facilitator and participant are introduced and the chapter examines who can benefit from this creative approach. Focus is given to the concept of identity and a three-stage model of exploration is suggested as a result of using therapeutic photography.

Chapter 3 looks at the dynamics of using therapeutic photography and discusses the advantages of the approach, as well as the challenges, which include ethical and legal considerations. Within the chapter, the structure of delivery is analysed and ways in which a facilitator can focus attention on specific areas of concern are presented. This uses a systems-based approach, as originally proposed by Bronfenbrenner (1986, 1992, 2009), and uses the structure of his micro-, meso-, exo- and macrosystems to consider where pressures may be presented in the lives of participants.

In Chapter 4, the focus is on using therapeutic photography to explore the self. This includes consideration of self-portraiture, "selfies", and other ways of creatively representing the "self". It is often a useful starting point in any therapeutic intervention to ascertain how a person perceives themselves and this chapter recognises this, exploring issues of self-concept and self-esteem. Within this chapter, the reader is also introduced to some key psychoanalytic and psychodynamic theorists who aid in the understanding of the self and how perception may manifest through conversation, and through the photographs.

Humans are social beings and do not function in isolation, and Chapter 5 discusses how therapeutic photography can be used to identify and analyse relationships – both supportive and problematic. Focus begins by looking at the primary experience of relationships and the formative nature of these experiences which are shaped by the family. This may involve using existing photographs and family images as a catalyst for conversation about the dynamics within the family, or it may involve the exploration of new images that creatively represent issues or people within family units. The reader is introduced to object relations theory and how this may be used to understand how participants or clients internalise past experiences and use these to shape expectations of relationships.

There is recognition when using therapeutic photography that it is not always easy or possible to photograph certain concepts that relate to issues in the lives of clients. Chapter 6 identifies this and discusses ways in which participants can be encouraged to creatively represent things they wish to focus on. In order to do this, attachment theory is introduced as it offers further guidance about how to understand and interpret relationships, both within and outwith the family unit. This is linked to working with emotions, and ways in which clients can pictorially explore emotions are introduced.

When clients are in a professional setting, the concept of loss and change is often dominant as a person has to deal with a significant alteration in their circumstances. Chapter 7 looks at the theory behind loss and change and how issues might manifest within photographs. There is also discussion of how a person may cope with transitions, and how photographic memories may be a source of comfort and support, but equally may prevent someone from taking steps to embrace change.

Chapter 8 moves to consider external drivers on behaviour, attitudes and actions, and looks at routines, narratives and perspectives. Focus is directed at using photography to elicit life stories and as an aid to communication. In order to do this, concepts such as stigma, labelling and societal attitudes are considered in line with the production of images and how these issues might manifest. The concept of self-efficacy is also discussed as this underpins the intervention in that clients are producing images and recognising that they are able to facilitate change in their lives.

In Chapter 9, the concept of using therapeutic photography to further explore societal issues, and then work to address these issues, is introduced. This is largely underpinned by the practice of photovoice and the key theorists are discussed, alongside ways in which this approach can be incorporated into work with clients, specifically in group work. The work of Paulo Freire is also explored, as his writings suggest links into how and why using photography to explore issues can be such an effective approach. Within this chapter, the feminist perspective is explored, alongside the concept of empowerment, as these both align with the practice and delivery of photovoice.

Chapter 10 presents a case study where all of the approaches in the preceding chapters are incorporated and applied to a group of young adults living with a diagnosis of autism. Using actual images, observations and focus group transcripts, the author demonstrates how theories were applied as the group engaged with various exercises and used the photographs to explain and explore their personal circumstances.

In Chapter 11, current practitioners who are using therapeutic photography in their professional practice present short summaries of their experience in order to highlight the flexibility and impact of the intervention. This chapter aims to give the reader further inspiration for how they might be able to incorporate and adapt therapeutic photography into their own practice.

Throughout the book there are suggested exercises, examples from groups, and points that require the reader to critically think about issues that have been presented.

A note about the images

Within the presentation of this book there are examples from real-life practice, including photographs that have been taken by participants. Permission was sought to use the images, and, where possible, they are presented in their original format, illustrating the point which was intended by the photographer. Even though all of the participants signed a release form, consideration has been given to the use of the images produced. Pink (2013) suggests that the publication of photographs within research should be an ongoing collaborative process between researcher and participant, and discussion should take place to decide which photographs should be included. Certainly, the participants were asked for permission to include their images at the end of the group process, but the researcher did not maintain contact after this to discuss the ongoing inclusion. Pink (2013) goes on to suggest that the author should give consideration to exclude certain images if they reveal the identity of the participant, stating, "absence in such cases can be equally evocative as visual presence" (p.181), and this was an issue for a number of the images as the participants included themselves in their photographs. Ethical frameworks emphasise the need to respect confidentiality and anonymity, which posed an issue for the author when presenting these images. As well as omitting the images, the researcher considered obscuring the images by using pixelating software to blur features, or by placing a black stripe across eyes to hide identity, but these approaches created a dilemma in that the participants had been exploring their identities, and a large part of that involved a sense of self.

Wiles *et al.* (2008) explored the rationale for including the original, participant-produced image within research and outlined two main reasons for doing so. First, they believe that the inclusion of visual images adds value to the text and by excluding images, an author may be denying a full exploration of identity. Second, they indicate that obscuring an image through pixilation or black stripes results in objectifying the person in the image and stripping away their identity. As one of the primary goals of therapeutic photography is identity exploration from each participant, the anonymising of the image appeared to be counterproductive. They also suggest that the approach of anonymisation can compound feelings of labelling and stigma because of the negative connotations attached to such images, relating the approach to anonymising photographs of criminals, or victims of crime.

A solution, they propose, is to present visual data in its original state, and make no attempt to anonymise the participants. With the exception of a small number of images, the author made the decision to do that with the photographs, but all names have been anonymised. Where the author has edited the image, this has been noted in the text and has been done so because the original image could have directly identified the individual.

■ Chapter 1 ■

WHAT IS THERAPEUTIC PHOTOGRAPHY?

This chapter introduces the reader to the concept of therapeutic photography and outlines a number of applications for which it can be used. This will include some history on the development of the practice, as well as acknowledging some of the key authors who have laid the foundations for this approach. An overview of phototherapy will also be given so that a distinction can be made between the practice of using photography in counselling as a trained professional, as opposed to using therapeutic photography, which does not demand a formal qualification in counselling or psychotherapy. The intended outcomes of using therapeutic photography will also be highlighted.

Therapeutic photography – an introduction

For a pastime or activity to be therapeutic there has to be an element of healing or treatment, or benefit for the user. Therefore, for photography to be therapeutic there must also be an intended outcome that should benefit the user, but can photography be *therapeutic*? Certainly, if a person engages in an activity that makes them feel good then it could be defined as therapeutic, but the problem with this is that the positive feelings may not have been intended, and are only evident because the person has a talent or flair for that particular activity. For an activity to merit the term "therapeutic", there have to be clearly defined outcomes for the end user so that they are not arriving at the benefits accidently.

To this end, an activity can be defined as therapeutic if it is utilised in a structured manner to produce end results for the participant. The nature of the activity itself will also impact on the therapeutic nature of the outcomes, and attempts to harness the therapeutic benefits of photography date as far back as the 1850s.

The first recorded use of the use of photographs in "therapy" was by Hugh Welch Diamond who was an early adopter of William Fox Talbot's photographic processes and who decided to use his new-found interest within his work at the Surrey County Lunatic Asylum (Drinkwater, 2008). He worked at the female wing of the unit as the resident superintendent and stated that his photographs could document and highlight different strains of mental illness which stemmed from his belief in the pseudoscience of physiognomy, the revelation of character through a person's physical appearance. In 1856, he presented a paper to the Royal Society of Medicine, entitled *On the Application of Photography to the Physiognomic and Mental Phenomena of Insanity*, which included the following abstract:

> The position of the author, as Medical Superintendent of the Surrey Lunatic Asylum, has enabled him to make the peculiar application of Photography, of which he gives an account in the present communication. He points out the advantages to be derived from photographic portraits of the insane, as faithfully representing the features of the disease in its different forms, or its successive phases in the same patient, and as affording unerring records for study and comparison by the physician and psychologist. In the course of the paper frequent reference is made to the series of photographic portraits of lunatic patients with which it was accompanied. (Diamond, 1856, p.117)

He used his images to record the patients he worked with, but he also used them in treatment and presented the photographs to his patients so that they could view themselves as others viewed them. It is not clear what the intended outcome of this technique was. Perhaps his intention was to shock the patient out of their malady, but this appears to have had limited effect. However, Diamond's interest in photography has left a lasting legacy of images documenting female mental health in the mid-19th century, and led to him being a founding member of the Photographic Society of London.

The therapeutic benefits of Diamond's approach are questionable, but since his time the potential for using photography to improve lives has been explored by many. Following the Second World War, servicemen recovering from injuries and trauma used photography largely for recreation, and the therapeutic benefits of the activity were noted. Later, the use of photography was adopted by civilian hospitals to aid recovery in physical and psychiatric illnesses (Glover-Graf & Miller, 2006; Perchick, 1992). In more recent years, photography within therapy has been used with a large variety of clients, including those in recovery, coming to terms with a disability or facing terminal illness (Gibson, 2017; Stevens & Spears, 2009; Perchick, 1992). Fryrear (1980) noted that the use of photography within a therapeutic setting enabled clients to explore their emotions, use the images to assist with expressing verbal information, and as a means of self-confrontation, with the added benefit of allowing clients to be creative at the same time.

It might be assumed that to engage in an intervention that is "creative" might require talent and ability, yet aspects of talent and creativity do not appear to be barriers as they might be within other interventions, such as art therapy. Indeed, Kopytin (in Loewenthal, 2015) points out that the potential for using photography within formal art therapy with trained therapists is underestimated. Perhaps this is down to the perception of photography and the fact that it has become so popular and accessible as technology has developed, that it is viewed as a tool for everyman, rather than an expressive art form. In essence, this availability has led to the democratisation of photography, but this relationship with cameras and photographs may also be the reason why it can be utilised successfully within a therapeutic setting.

Sontag (1977) noted the rising popularity of photography decades before image capture devices were embedded within mobile phones and other technologies. Nowadays, the ability to capture an image is effortless, but Sontag (1977) foresaw the attraction of photography for the masses and attributed this to a striving for information. She argued that the wealth of images that exist means that there is a sense that the world has been photographed in its entirety, and therefore photographers try to capture our attention by exaggerating features, directing our attention, and educating us on what we should be observing. Within this, the viewer of images learns how to decode what they are observing through repeated exposure to visual information. Sontag (1977) stated that this gives the viewer a sense that they can learn about the world around them through this anthology of images they hold within their heads.

■ CRITICAL THINKING

What Sontag (1977) identifies is the importance of recognising the cultural significance of photographs and photography, as well as the importance of visual information and learning.

Think about the number of visual images you have been exposed to today. These may be in magazines, newspapers, adverts, food packaging, TV, textbooks...the list goes on. If you were to attempt to document the images you have been exposed to on a daily basis, chances are you would be into three figures (at least).

With this in mind, consider how you have learned to "decode" the images you have been exposed to. How does a photojournalist awaken emotions within you by publishing a certain image? How does an advertiser entice you towards their product through visual communication?

There is no immediate answer to these questions, but when using therapeutic photography within a group setting, the participants may well be communicating considerable information through their photographs that they cannot put into words, and others will be able to recognise those messages through their ability to culturally decode the image.

Sontag (1977) expressed concern because the democratisation of photography moved the practice away from an artistic pursuit, towards one in which people took photographs to "possess" pieces of the past (p.9). This act of searching for possession places the photographer in a position where they are invariably seeking knowledge which, as a consequence, also places them in a position of power, as Sontag notes: "photography has become almost as widely practiced an amusement as sex and dancing…it is mainly a social rite, a defense against anxiety, and a tool of power" (1977, p.8).

She surmised that photography also has the ability to connect people to their communities, and their families because the collected images enable a construction of a narrative which underpins an individual's connectedness to others. In her writing, she appeared to despair about the cultural phenomenon of productivity which saw the camera as a tool for collecting experiences that could be utilised by tourists so that, even when away from their jobs, they still had a task to collect and document their leisure time. But it is this element of productivity which also enhances the therapeutic experience of photography, for if it allows us to set ourselves a task which involves placing distance from the world around us, our lives and our interactions and then capturing them in an image where they can be studied, discussed and analysed, then the experience need not be one of a visual collector, but one of a visual scientist.

Where Sontag was concerned with the act of taking photographs, Barthes (in Barthes & Howard, 1987) recognised the power of the visual image itself and attempted to provide an explanation as to why the medium of photography has such appeal. He identified two elements within a photograph which he termed *studium* and *punctum* (Barthes & Howard, 1987, p.146). Studium is the element of a photograph which provides interest for the viewer, draws them in, and helps them engage with the image. Like Sontag (1977), Barthes believed this was assisted by the inclusion of cultural cues which allows the viewer to glance at an image and know instantly what is happening in the picture, and what the photographer was attempting to convey. To illustrate his point, Barthes discusses how press photographers convey messages quickly to the reader through codes and conventions within their images – a photograph can be glanced at and the meaning becomes immediately apparent through a facial gesture, clothing, landscapes and actions. Studium helps us understand an image, and assists us in engagement so that we can decide that we *like* the image. However, if our reaction to the image goes deeper than a simple recognition of liking it, if it holds our attention and draws us in, then Barthes stated that the punctum of the image was responsible. For photographers, punctum is difficult to produce because it is often an unintended quality within the image which emotionally resonates with the viewer of the image. It might trigger a memory, or even a chain of thought, which reminds the viewer of a forgotten time, but for each and every viewer, the emotional response will be different based on lived experiences. Therefore, punctum changes the *like* of studium into something deeper, perhaps even *love*. It is often accidental as the emotional responses of others are difficult to predict, but Barthes recognised the power of photographs not only to inform, but also to evoke.

■ CRITICAL THINKING

Do Barthes's *studium* and *punctum* resonate with you?

Look through some of your favourite images and see if you can recognise aspects within the photographs that you might be able to attribute to the studium of the image. This will involve an element of decoding the image as you look for things within the picture that give you cultural cues – perhaps items of clothing on a person give you an idea of the country they are from and the era in which they live. Perhaps the appearance of someone's face will give you an indication of gender and age, and therefore you may be able to associate with that person.

Now try to find the punctum in an image that you love. This might be easier as you are looking for the element of the picture which gives it impact.

The mass appeal of photography, the ease of access and understanding, and the associated power have contributed to the rise of the use of photography within therapeutic settings. But there is clearly more at play than Barthes's studium and punctum as this only benefits the viewer of an image, not the photographer themselves. And, although Sontag recognised the feelings of power within the photographer when gathering images, this is only one beneficial aspect of taking photographs and talking about them. In order to truly define therapeutic photography, we have to understand how it is currently being used and what the reported outcomes are.

Therapeutic photography or phototherapy?

Since the early part of the 21st century, the therapeutic use of photographs has fallen under two different labels – *phototherapy* and *therapeutic photography*. Judy Weiser (1984, 1999, 2001, 2004), perhaps the matriarch of modern-day phototherapy, offers a simple distinction between the two approaches. She states that phototherapy is the name given to the structured use of photographs in a formal counselling or therapy session, usually led by a trained counsellor, therapist or mental health professional. Therapeutic photography refers to photo-based activities that can be initiated by the self, or conducted in groups, the main difference being the lack of input from a professional counsellor or therapist (Weiser, 2016). However, there is a fine line between the two disciplines, and it is therefore worth delving a bit deeper into these distinctions.

Phototherapy

Weiser (1984) was the first practitioner who attempted to give structure and clarity to the practice of phototherapy so that others could introduce the concept within their formal counselling and therapy sessions. She views it as a set of techniques to assist in sessions where non-verbal and visual communications are considered to be as important as verbal communication. She goes on to explain that clients enter therapy because they wish to grow, change, develop confidence and form better relationships with others, all elements which are underpinned by communication. Weiser views photography as an *expressive* activity, and as such, believes it can be used as an expressive therapy. Creative expressions are seen by Weiser as projections of ourselves and can be used to explore psychosocial development through the way in which an individual perceives, stores, retrieves and puts forth information. How we then go on to express this information can assist the therapist in understanding how we internalise the world around us.

Phototherapy attempts to allow the client to creatively express their internal make-up (i.e. thoughts, feelings and beliefs), where the therapist guides conversations to elaborate meaning from personal photographs and make links to the psyche. Because of the emphasis on identity exploration, phototherapy appears to be rooted in the psychoanalytic theories of writers such as Freud (2001), Fairbairn (1952) and Winnicott (1965) (Hills de Zárate, 2012; Marxen, 2009; Yerushalmi & Yedidya, 1997), while incorporating the Jungian approach of assisting the artistic expression of emotional disturbances and unconscious thought processes (Stevens & Spears, 2009; Graf, 2002). Ziller (1990) also notes that self-concept is developed in the process and this can be explained through the work of writers such as Mead (1934) and Cooley (1902).

Weiser (2004) believes that a photograph in itself can never be read like a book or deconstructed to reveal hidden inner codes or secrets. A photograph is unique to its creator, and equally unique to the viewer of the image. Weiser states that nobody can be trained to therapeutically decode a photograph because photographs only *suggest* meaning. Therefore, participants who use photographs therapeutically will construct their personal version of reality, bringing with them their own unique and subjectively accurate interpretation (Barbee, 2002; Weiser, 1999). This means that specialised training in using photographs within these settings is not required, simply the ability to recognise the photograph as a communication tool to elicit information (Stevens & Spears, 2009; Hammond & Gantt, 1998).

Phototherapy sessions tend to be structured around one of five different strategies: using photographs taken by the client; using photographs taken of the client; using self-portraits or photographs taken by the client to represent "the self", with the client having been in control of taking the image; using family photograph albums; and using "photo-projectives" (Weiser, 1999, p.3), which involves taking a phenomenological stance to explore perceptions and emotional responses as a result of looking at, and talking about, photographs to uncover meaning (Loewenthal, 2013).

Because there can be deep memories and emotions attached to personal photographs, the recommended approach is to engage phototherapy with the involvement of a trained counsellor or therapist to provide a protective counselling framework so that containment and resolution of issues which surface can be dealt with in good time (Glover-Graf & Miller, 2006). By contrast, therapeutic photography does not have to be facilitated by a trained therapist or counsellor and therefore lacks this protective counselling framework. Weiser (2004) argues that if clients become involved in a less structured form of intervention such as therapeutic photography and engage with the material on their own, or as part of a group, this might precipitate the need for formal therapy sessions with trained staff. Equally, therapeutic photography offers outcomes that might negate the need for formal therapy or counselling. She states that although therapeutic photography is not "therapy", there are mutual similarities between the two practices of phototherapy and therapeutic photography.

Therapeutic photography

Therapeutic photography is the term used for photographic practices in situations where the skills of therapists or counsellors are not needed, yet for a practice to be truly "therapeutic" there should be benefit to the end user in terms of deepening understanding of the self with an aim to reduce inner conflict and enhance coping strategies (Borden, 2000). An extensive description of therapeutic photography includes the application of photography to increase self-knowledge, awareness, well-being, relationships, and to challenge societal issues such as exclusion, isolation, intercultural relations, conflict, social injustice, as well as informing research (Weiser (J.), 2015).

The primary difference between phototherapy and therapeutic photography appears to be in the formal involvement (or not) of a counsellor or therapist, but Weiser (2004) suggests it is easier to view the two practices as being two opposite ends of a continuum: one is "photography – during – therapy" while the other is "photography – as – therapy" (p.35); one requires a trained counsellor or therapist to guide (and contain) the process and has the sole aim of *therapy*, whereas the other is about the enjoyment of *photography* with the added bonus of finding out information about yourself and others on the journey. However, she concurs that there will be a natural overlap where the two practices intersect. Although Weiser (2004) believes that the practice of therapeutic photography does not need a professionally trained counsellor, Halkola (in Loewenthal, 2013) states that phototherapy and therapeutic photography are very similar, and both benefit from having professionals guiding sessions. She goes on to explain that there may be specific outcomes within therapeutic photography that include self-expression, rehabilitation, healing and empowerment, and, because of the nature of issues that may arise from the exploration of these concepts, each session should be facilitated by a professional who has experience in health, education or social work.

For some, viewing photography as a tool for therapeutic interventions requires a shift in thinking. The organisation known as Photovoice explains that photography is typically seen as a pastime or hobby, an activity for simply recording holiday snaps and memorable moments in life, or as a means of capturing celebrity lifestyles through paparazzi intrusion to be enjoyed as images in the media. So much is involved in the taking of a photograph, which extends from the initial thoughts about the decision to take a photograph, composing the image, pressing the shutter, through to the production of a tangible image. The photographs we produce are informed by looking at other pictures, editing photographs, discussing photographs, presenting photographs, using photographs in online blogs and social networking. All of this collectively contributes to how photographs can enable dialogue and communication about who we are, what we are and where we come from. For a number of clients, photography can help explore self-identity and it can act as a distraction to help forget about problems; for others, it can help create order within their lives as those engaging with photography are forced to move away from spontaneity and consider a more structured approach. Because photography objectifies the photographed subject, holding an image can provide distance between the subject and the service user. The photographer naturally has to put distance between themselves and the subject to capture it in an image, which can encourage them to become a "contemplative 'quasi-outsider,' which…invites deeper reflection and more meaningful interpretation of events and circumstances" (Dennis *et al.*, 2009, p.468). This suggests that sensitive subjects can literally be discussed *at arm's length*, where the use of images could actually assist in the process of socialisation by becoming a protective factor in the process of exploring self-concept. Sharing photographs also encourages storytelling and dialogue, which can help build bonds and friendships; in minority communities, common issues can be identified through photography to bring isolated members of the community together (Wang & Burris, 1997, 1994).

Using artistic techniques as a therapeutic tool is, however, not a new concept. As previously noted, the practice of art therapy would appear to be a profession which could readily incorporate the use of photography, yet its use is relatively rare in this domain, and this is perhaps due to the fact that photography requires specialised equipment and, because of the planning that goes into capturing an image, spontaneity is curtailed and this in turn impacts on emotional expression (Kopytin, 2004). However, the rise of camera phones, budget digital cameras and online photo sharing sites (or social networking sites) now makes photography one of the most accessible art forms available to the general public (Loewenthal, 2013; Van Dijck, 2008).

The process of taking photographs has been described as therapeutic in itself as it can encourage the photographer to be reflective, mindful and task orientated (Huss, 2012; Kopytin, 2004). Because the skillset to participate in therapeutic photography is minimal it offers up an opportunity to engage in a medium that is widely recognised within society and creates a potentially powerful form of communication between the photographer and the viewer of the image (Griebling *et al.*, 2013; Loopmans *et al.*, 2012), not least a professional worker intent on building a meaningful dialogue with a client. Through this dialogue, a new awareness can emerge as issues are explored and people learn from each other, and the theoretic base for the practice appears to be holistic in terms of acknowledging the impact of psychosocial theories, but also theories that define how culture and society impact on self-esteem and self-efficacy. Indeed, many writers feel that the technique is underpinned by the writings of Paulo Freire (1970, 1998) and his philosophy, which aims to educate and empower marginalised individuals and communities by exploring the environment and working in groups to identify issues that can be collectively challenged (Griebling *et al.*, 2013; Ozanne *et al.*, 2013; Duffy, 2011; Catalani & Minkler, 2010; Carlson *et al.*, 2006; Carr (E.S.), 2003; Dietz, 2000).

There appears to be a fine line between the intended outcomes of phototherapy and therapeutic photography. Loewenthal (2013) explains that photo-based interventions can assist in the expression of emotions, exploring behaviours that are acceptable and unacceptable in society, elucidating experiences that may be problematic to verbalise, enhancing self-esteem and self-efficacy through exploring self-image, assisting the exploration of memories, and strengthening relationships through sharing and communication. The therapeutic aspect also includes the client taking the photographs themselves and then using Weiser's (2004) photo-projection technique to provide a narrative for the image; the photographs are not the *treatment*, but they are a useful supplement to therapeutically enhance communication (Cosden & Reynolds, 1982).

Because of the distinguishing factor of the involvement of a trained counsellor or therapist, the domain of phototherapy appears to be out of the reach of the average professional worker who is not ordinarily qualified to be a therapist or counsellor within the education they receive. Therefore, to utilise photography within professional interventions but without formal counselling or therapy, it is the practice of therapeutic photography that professions must look to, but with an appreciation of the intended outcomes.

What are the outcomes?

The engagement with therapeutic photography should have a purpose for the client. As future chapters in this book will highlight, different techniques can be utilised and different theories considered, so some of the outcomes can be shaped by initial conversations with the client to see what they wish to achieve from engagement. What will also be highlighted as the book progresses will be consideration of whether a practitioner who is using the techniques of therapeutic photography does so with groups, or with individuals. These decisions will influence the outcomes which, in general, fall into four categories: control/self-disclosure, self-efficacy, self-esteem, and empowerment.

Control/self-disclosure

Therapeutic photography is a form of visual communication. Therefore, when a client is asked to explore or investigate an issue through the use of photography they first have to think about what they want to focus on, then what to photograph, then how to photograph it, then, if they take a number of images, which image to use, and finally, they have to decide what to say about the image when presenting it to another person. Every step of this process involves decision-making, which puts the client firmly in control. This often creates a new dynamic within a therapeutic relationship between the professional and their client, as many forms of professional interventions will have the control and power firmly in the hands of the professional. Within therapeutic photography, the professional is giving the client a theme to study, but they have little control over what the participant chooses to capture or what they choose to reveal. This can be challenging for the professional and moves their position from one of a knowledgeable expert to one of a curious learner. Of course, once the narrative has been explored by the client, the professional can engage with their skillset to advance the therapeutic relationship and begin to discuss solutions to the situation.

The act of taking a photograph and then holding the image at arm's length also creates therapeutic opportunities. Newbury and Hoskins (2011) used photographs within a study they conducted to elicit views of people who had problematic substance use issues and they noted that when photography was introduced, the communication between the person being interviewed and the interviewer changed. Instead of conversations being conducted face to face across a table, people sat side by side and the focus (and eye contact) was on the photograph. This appeared to make conversation more "comfortable" (p.1068) because the body language from the interviewer was not scrutinising, and the participant was in control of the information they chose to share.

Stevens and Spears (2009) again highlight close ties with art therapy approaches and recognise the work of Carl Jung underpinning the work in both fields. Jung believed it was often easier to deal with emotional disturbances if they were given shape and form, rather than simply discussed in linguistics. Once they are expressed through art or photography they are given a concrete, objective form which is easier for the client to work with than abstract thoughts alone. This has proved useful when working with clients who might not be honest in their answers when being interviewed; the use of visual images can help to bypass denial and rationalisations by placing a concrete image into the hands of the client and directly discussing the problem presented in the photograph (Graf, 2002; Chikerneo, 1993).

In effect, the problem has been externalised, and placing it at a safe distance (literally *at arm's length*) means that it becomes safer to talk about, but Loewenthal (2015) states this poses a risk that the client reveals "too much, too soon" (p.13) because they become heady with the control and excited because someone is actively listening to their story. However, Burnard and Morrison (1992) argue that the act of self-disclosure can, in itself, be therapeutic. They explain that individuals who self-disclose to others may have been through an experience which they have found to be transformative, and that by sharing information about themselves to others they are coming to terms with their own experiences. Self-disclosure is a natural part of forming friendships and by sharing and receiving information about ourselves and others there is a process of reciprocation taking place. In essence, professionals who are concerned with the risks of clients making self-disclosures too quickly should consider whether there is a real risk to the client, or if it is down to professional insecurities in being unable to deal with too much information at once.

AN EXAMPLE FROM PRACTICE

Once, when I was running a therapeutic photography group for people with mental health problems, we were doing an exercise called "a day in the life of..." (see Appendix). In the exercise, participants were asked to document a typical day using ten photographs. One participant was exploring his typical day and had explained how he liked to keep his house clean so that, if he could outwardly present as being organised, he might begin to feel more organised internally. After a few seconds' hesitation, he then showed this image:

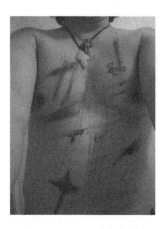

My instinct as a facilitator was to ask him to move on to his next image quickly, but I realised that he had pondered about whether to show it, so I let my initial fears dissipate and he began to explain the image. He spoke about self-harm and why he did this to himself if he felt he had upset anyone during his day. Because this was in a group setting, other participants empathised with him and spoke about their own experiences with regards to self-harm. It was an image that offered him a considerable amount of support from the group, and it had taken courage to show it.

Later, I spoke with another professional and she explained that this participant had spoken about self-harming on a one-to-one basis with his counsellor, but never with his peers. Using the photograph, he was able to explore this with people like himself and make self-disclosures, while taking control of the information he chose to share.

Self-efficacy

Self-efficacy is the belief in the personal ability to achieve and Bandura (1977) identifies self-efficacy as one of the main factors which underlies behavioural change. He states that those with good levels of self-efficacy are able to believe in their ability to make and maintain change. This is closely tied with self-esteem because human beings not only derive a sense of self from the reaction of others, but from self-evaluations of how actions and consequences of behaviour impact on self-development (Gecas & Schwalbe, 1983). For self-efficacy to be effectively developed, the power dynamics of a therapeutic relationship need to be considered. If the power balance is too unequal and the person trying to develop self-efficacy is at the lower end of that power scale, then they will look for positive feedback from the person who holds the power and then use this positive feedback to enhance self-efficacy. If the power dynamics are balanced, then the person developing self-efficacy may still be motivated by the feedback from others, but there should also be motivation from recognising the outcomes of their actions and how this can effect change in their life (Gecas & Schwalbe, 1983).

Bandura (1982) identifies four areas of experience in which self-efficacy is developed: enactive mastery (building confidence and skills), vicarious experience (seeing others overcome challenges), verbal persuasion (positive feedback from others) and physiological arousal (understanding emotions and the consequences of them). Ultimately, how an individual cognitively appraises and integrates these experiences will determine levels of self-efficacy.

Professionals need to consider self-efficacy when planning interventions. This should involve an assessment of the task in hand, as well as the individuals' personal resources and constraints, and careful management of interventions can facilitate a positive change in self-efficacy (Gist & Mitchell, 1992). Bandura (1982, 1977) also recognises that self-efficacy involves outcome expectations and therefore it is important to consider motivation alongside self-efficacy. He believes that outcome expectations are impacted by the environment, and Gecas (1989) also suggests that, from a sociological perspective, individuals are actors within their own environments but need to take an active and creative view of themselves so that they can appreciate that they have a role in shaping and creating the world around them as well as being created by it. Bandura *et al.* (2001) recognise that cultural differences will affect self-efficacy beliefs, and Gecas (1989) also identifies that self-efficacy will be affected by social structure, gender, social stability and change, as well as development over the life course, but that any work to enhance self-efficacy has beneficial and therapeutic consequences. If an intervention can facilitate identification and discussion of cultural impacts then this suggests that poor self-efficacy could be redressed.

Gecas and Schwalbe (1983) believe that self-efficacy can be viewed as an extension of self-identity, but underpinning this is the motivation to behave in a certain way, and the consequences of that behaviour, which also define the self. They believe this defines an "active self" (p.79), which is affected by Bandura's (1982) categories for building self-efficacy.

Kasabova (2014) also believes that motivation underpins self-efficacy, but for this motivation to affect the self there needs to be a realisation that changes in behaviour result in consequences.

Therapeutic photography encourages participants to use their own photographic devices to capture images, be they cameras, camera phones, or tablet computers, so participants approach the tasks with a degree of knowledge about their own photographic tools. Feedback can be offered after participants share their images (which is particularly effective in a group setting), and this can affect physiological states. It is common for participants to be nervous at the beginning of the experience, but quite quickly people tend to build up trust in facilitators and other participants, and confidences grows, an element of using photography which was also noted by Duffy (2011) where she observed participants moving from doubt at the outset, to efficacy and pride by the end. Cosden and Reynolds (1982) highlight that because photography is accessible, requires relatively little skill and produces quick results, it is a medium particularly suited to building self-efficacy.

Therapeutic photography groups also produce a large number of images throughout the duration of courses and when these are either printed off and spread out on a table, or displayed as a digital slideshow, the participants witness the volume of images they have produced in a short timescale. This gives further opportunities to reminisce on the activities, and for further feedback to be sought, but it also directs the conversation to the next steps for the participant or groups. There may be a desire to display the images to a wider audience and, for some, an interest in pursuing their photography skills further. Stets and Burke (2000) believe that self-efficacy aligns with the "behavioural enactment of identities" (p.233), as opposed to self-esteem, which they believe is more attuned to identification with other individuals within a group, but perhaps the exploration and enactment of identities through photography is enhanced by the fact that self-esteem is also addressed, and the familiarity of the group experience assists the development of self-efficacy.

Self-esteem

Enhancing self-efficacy is often viewed as being linked to the development of self-esteem, which has been highlighted as an important point for professionals to recognise as task-based interventions can effect change in both areas (Donaldson, 2005; Bednar *et al.*, 1995). Rosenberg *et al.* (1989) believe that self-esteem underpins human motivation in that every person wants to achieve self-maintenance or self-enhancement, and this is gained through three different sources: from observing and interpreting responses of others, from self-perceptions, and from social comparisons. If an individual feels appreciated by other people, if they feel that their actions are effective and productive, and if they feel that they compare favourably to others, then self-esteem will be enhanced (Verhaeghe *et al.*, 2008; Gecas, 1989).

Rosenberg *et al.* (1989) stress the importance of feeling that you are likeable and that people appreciate what you do, that you believe you can achieve what you set out to do (self-efficacy) and that you compare well against others. Verhaeghe *et al.* (2008) found that this latter point was important within peer groups and that this linked directly to bolstering recovery and maintenance of positive self-evaluations. Indeed, Gecas and Schwalbe (1983) also state that, although the perceived views of others are important in forming a sense of self, this is enhanced when these perceptions are based on the views of peers. This underpins the value of using therapeutic photography within a group setting so that peers can offer support which impacts on self-efficacy and self-esteem; as positive changes take place in one area, changes in the other two areas will also be effected when doing group work.

Empowerment and resilience

Within professional practice the terms "empowerment" and "resilience" are often used to generalise strategies which enable people to move on from situations where they may feel entrenched. It is important to understand these concepts as they can help professionals understand barriers, analyse where strengths can be drawn from, recognise where information is required, and ultimately, involve clients in capacity building and decision making (Payne, 2014). Gutierrez (1994) believes that the process of empowerment involves an individual moving through four different stages which begins with building self-efficacy, then developing the Freirean concept of critical consciousness (which will be discussed in Chapter 9), then reflecting on previous actions, and finally using these reflections to inform future strategies whilst learning and identifying with others who have experienced similar issues.

Braye and Preston-Shoot (1995) explore the concept of empowerment from the perspective of agency provision and highlight a number of considerations which need to be incorporated in order to empower clients. They highlight that, from the outset, clients need to be involved in the process and understand what is being offered to them and what the intended outcomes are; there must be a choice in participation – not compulsion; there should be flexibility throughout the process; encouragement of equity in participation and openness to advocacy; and there should also be an appreciation of individual and group perspectives. Trevithick (2012) emphasises the importance of considering these perspectives as many agencies are limited in the resources they can offer. In order to facilitate empowerment with the clients they work with, there must be an appreciation of how far these concepts can effectively be met. If these are limited, then the question has to be asked whether offered interventions are truly "empowering"?

"Resilience" is also a concept which requires definition in the context of therapeutic interventions. Gilligan (2000) describes resilience as the ability to bounce back from adversity whilst continuing to function through challenging times. The concept encourages reflection on areas were strengths can be drawn from and recognises the influence of both nature and nurture on coping strategies. Daniel and Wassell (2002) attempted to categorise the domains of resilience in children and suggested that strengths can be drawn from 6 core areas which are:

1. A secure base – Acknowledging the impact of upbringing and formative relationships and how they influence adult relationships.

2. Education – Academic achievement is viewed as a means of progression into employment, and therefore financial security.

3. Friendships – Recognising the wider support networks out with the family.

4. Talents and interests – Creativity, activity and other pursuits which benefit mental health and wellbeing.

5. Positive values – Linked to upbringing, this domain recognises the impact of how people negotiate through everyday life experiences using the beliefs, culture, and attitudes ingrained within them.

6. Social competencies – Appreciating how nurture impacts on interactions with people in the wider environment.

Daniel and Wassell (2002) highlight that not all of the 6 domains need to be entirely positive for people, but an understanding of where strengths lie can assist when challenges are encountered. It is also a factor in identity exploration as Baldry and Kemmis (1998) found when they used these domains to inform a study of looked after children in a UK city and found that a lack of personal items, including photographs, were linked to deficits within the secure base resulting in the children experiencing difficulties in exploring these formative relationships.

Both empowerment and resilience are concepts which can be incorporated into therapeutic interventions as they require an ability to explore challenges and adverse experiences, whilst recognising strengths and supports. These approaches can often be enhanced through group work and Rappaport (1995) highlights the benefits of incorporating narrative approaches when working with groups as it can encourage individuals to sustain change if they receive collective support from people they consider to be peers in order for a collective narrative can be developed and applied. Although the impact of working to directly impact an individual's sense of empowerment and resilience is difficult to quantify, a working knowledge of the principles of these can facilitate dialogue and the raising of critical consciousness. The result of this is that problems can be identified and recognised, and then knowledge gained from reflection and peer support can be applied to address them.

Arriving at a definition

As this chapter has explored, therapeutic photography is different from phototherapy, yet also has a number of similarities. This book will go on to look at the application and theoretic underpinning of therapeutic photography to help clarify exactly what this approach entails, but in order to do this, a definition of therapeutic photography is offered:

Therapeutic photography is the structured, guided, engagement with the creative intervention of photography in order to produce images for exploration with clearly defined outcomes for the participant.

Conclusion

This chapter has outlined the historic perspective of the therapeutic use of photographs and has presented some of the main principles of the approach. It is an intervention that can be used without a formal qualification of counselling or therapy, yet its use certainly benefits from the understanding of psychodynamic and sociological perspectives, and the subsequent chapters will elaborate on a number of these.

In short, therapeutic photography should be fun and accessible. It places the familiar tool of a camera (or other photographic device) into the hands of a person to facilitate exploration and communication and appeals to all ages from all walks of life. The potential for discovery is strong, both for the participant and the facilitator, and should be approached with a sense of curiosity and interest.

Chapter 2

HOW CAN THIS BE USED IN PRACTICE?

The potential applications of therapeutic photography are wide ranging. The approach can be used with anyone who can operate a camera, and the democratisation of photography will be discussed here. The practice has been used with primary school children, through to dementia care patients, and the disciplines using therapeutic photography include social work, mental health, nursing, teaching, occupational therapy and art, to name but a few. The approach has commonly been used by researchers to elicit views from their subjects and this chapter will detail the different approaches and applications of therapeutic photography.

Who can use therapeutic photography?

The implications for the effective use of therapeutic photography in professional practice are growing, and the evidence base is building to suggest ways in which disciplines can harness this intervention. As a communication tool, it is a useful method of eliciting views from people who may not be so forthcoming when we rely solely on linguistics. This means that the potential for the use of therapeutic photography in professional practice is large.

Language skills develop from birth onwards, but it is not until around the age of approximately 4 years old that the brain starts to process and sequence linguistic learning (Gerhardt, 2006). This means that visual learning is dominant in young children, and this knowledge can be utilised when considering the use of therapeutic photography. Alexander *et al.* (2014) wanted to research the importance of play for young children so they used the medium of photography and asked children to capture anything that represented "play" to them, both inside and outside their homes, and then used the images to discuss play with the young participants. Cappello (2005) used a similar method to investigate perceptions of the classroom environment with young children, asking them to talk about the environment using pre-selected photographs to initiate conversations. Cappello's rationale for doing this was that it made the children feel more relaxed and challenged their preconceptions about adults in the classroom as being the ones who held all the power because the children controlled the information they shared, prompted by the images. Popa and Stan (2013) used a similar approach, but asked the pre-schoolers to take the photographs so that their perception of the classroom environment could be investigated. Therefore, the potential to elicit views from children through photography exists, and this is an opportunity that could be harnessed by teachers, support workers and other professionals involved in the education system in order to obtain the views of the pupils. Clearly, permissions need to be considered, and any therapeutic photography would need to be discussed and approved by parents and guardians.

The power dynamics raised by Cappello (2005) are an important consideration across a number of disciplines, and if this might be a barrier to accessing information within your profession, then therapeutic photography has advantages. Within social work, professionals often work within marginalised and oppressed communities and this may result in clients who are suspicious or mistrusting of authority figures. An intervention such as therapeutic photography puts the client in control of the information they share and allows them to highlight the issues that are important to them. DeCoster and Dickerson (2014) looked at the use of therapeutic photography within mental health social work practice and concluded that "therapeutic photography's predominate client-directed, client-centred approaches, embracing experiential and interpretive diversity, cultural sensitivity, with clients as the experts, shows to be an excellent fit within the social work paradigm" (p.15). Research also points to the application of photographic approaches with clients who have learning disabilities, those who are carers, and those who are offenders or experience problems with substance use, which would be applicable to a wide variety of professional contact social workers have in their day-to-day practice (Anderson & Overy, 2010; Arendt, 2011; Aubeeluck & Buchanan, 2006; Glover-Graf & Miller, 2006; Graf, 2002; Loewenthal, 2015; Newbury, 1996).

The main focus of this chapter is how therapeutic photography can enable an understanding of the identity of a person, and this makes the approach particularly relevant if that person is dealing with a change, coming to terms with its impact, and trying to interpret the new identity they have gained from the experience. Professionals dealing with clients who have been through significant changes may well find this approach useful. Using this technique in the professional practice of medicine and health care has advantages as the power dynamics in this relationship are typically always in the hands of the professionals, yet Oliffe and Bottorff (2007) found that using photography to gain insights into the experience of men recovering from prostate cancer was enlightening and empowering for the participants, and they describe the information gleaned as "unique and unanticipated" (p.850). Sitvast and Abma (2012) highlight the benefits when working within mental health nursing, while Smith *et al.* (2006) recognise the implications of using photography with patients who have type 1 diabetes so that narratives can be better understood by medical professionals. This also underpins the application for associated health professionals, such as occupational therapists and physiotherapists, who need to work with clients to put supports in place when someone is discharged from hospital or coming to terms with a change in circumstance. The ability of a client to visually document their own situation, highlighting areas where they incur difficulty alongside areas where they can function with relative ease, provides the professional with valuable, personalised data to help shape appropriate support.

Coming to terms with a new identity will be an area encountered by a large number of professionals, including counsellors, therapists, midwives, health visitors, support workers and the police, yet the implications of therapeutic photography extend beyond the caring professions. The nature of the outcomes allows the approach to be utilised by organisations to assess the impact of change, or for institutions to ascertain views of workers – as self-disclosure, control and empowerment are primary drivers this applies to many walks of life. As we shall go on to discuss, identity applies to us all, in all areas of our existence.

Who can benefit from therapeutic photography?

As Chapter 1 outlined, the intended outcomes of therapeutic photography are to enhance self-esteem, self-efficacy and empowerment, while enabling self-disclosure and control throughout the process. When thinking about who could benefit from this intervention, the challenge lies not in selecting participants, but in justifying why a certain group of people cannot participate.

The mechanics of participation are not difficult – if someone can use a camera, operate their smartphone, or capture images via a tablet computer, then they have the ability to participate. However, even if someone cannot operate these devices themselves, support could still be provided so that someone else could be guided by a participant with limited abilities to capture an image through instruction. The ethos of therapeutic photography is that it is an intervention which should be available to anyone. The spirit of the intervention encourages empowerment while working to challenge oppression – if there are barriers to participation, then an intervention cannot be empowering. The important thing to then consider is not who can participate, but who could benefit.

To decide this, the outcomes have to be kept in mind, but the process of engagement also needs to be considered. Therefore, we need to look at the mechanics of involvement. Therapeutic photography is an activity that can be conducted one to one, or within a group, but both approaches ultimately involve the discussion of an image, and the resulting narrative which derives from this interaction. Harper (2002) highlights that when two or more individuals discuss photographs they have taken, a new meaning can emerge between participants, and in a mapping exercise of projects utilising photography and narrative he found that identity was a common issue to emerge, with other themes being family and society, history, and culture. It is this theme of identity which appears to be the vital element when working with therapeutic photography, and an area that professionals need to consider.

An exploration of identity

Certainly, conducting therapeutic photography with a group has distinct advantages when you are working to explore identity. The work of Cooley (1902) may offer insight into how the group element impacts on identity. Cooley (1902) wrote that the self and society were intertwined, and that the self could only develop through interactions and feedback from society. He famously coined the phrase "looking-glass self" (p.179) to describe the concept that identity formation is influenced by our perceptions of what we think others think of us. He describes the process of identity formation as akin to regarding one's image in a mirror and assessing the result, but instead of a mirror, the individual uses reactions of others around them to gather feedback. He explains that this is a three-step system where:

1. We imagine how we appear to others.

2. We imagine how others judge us based on our appearance.

3. We gain an emotional response from that judgement (e.g. pride or shame).

Burns (1984) explored the application of the looking-glass self principle to group working and stated that, depending on the interactions between members, the timescale and lifespan of the group, and the levels of intimacy between members, there is potential for the principle to have considerable impact on identity formation and group association. It may be that the mechanics of working with photography in a group setting creates the atmosphere where a "therapeutic gaze" (Martin, 2009, p.42) is permitted. Martin uses the term to describe the relationship between a phototherapist and a client, but in essence the term refers to working in a way that encourages an individual to create a meaningful image for themselves, and then explore the narrative behind the image in a manner which is non-judgemental, encouraging and trusting, in an environment which is safe and accepting. Instead of the phototherapist providing the therapeutic gaze, this is provided by the peers and facilitator.

THERAPEUTIC GAZE

The concept of a safe space for exploration has been identified by other theorists, using differing terminology. Winnicott (1971), who will be discussed later in this chapter, came up with the concept of a *holding* environment, which describes the didactic relationship between a developing child and the caregiver. This relationship should meet the needs of the child, thus addressing dependence, but also encourage independence by being emotionally available so that the child knows there is always a safe place to return to as they explore.

Bowlby (2008), who we will look at in Chapter 6, also described a similar concept known as the *secure base* which arises from a *secure attachment*, and it is these concepts that underpin the therapeutic alliance between a worker and a client. This alliance recreates an atmosphere where the client should feel they are being emotionally "held" and have a safe space in which they can explore concepts, thoughts and feelings. The worker recreates a *secure attachment* in terms of the feelings of trust and security the client feels, and this is often termed "earned secure" (Gibson & Gibson, 2016).

Therefore, what Martin (2009) calls a "therapeutic gaze" may be termed something different in your profession, but, in essence, we are looking at providing a non-judgemental, empathetic environment for exploration.

Social identity

The presence of peers appears to facilitate self-exploration in therapeutic photography, therefore it is worth acknowledging the concept of social identity and the role this plays in these groups. Described by Zhang *et al.* (2010) as a "social-psychological theory that focuses on membership in a social unit and intergroup relations" (p.68), social identity theory describes the process of individuals enhancing identity formation through perceived membership of social groups (Tajfel & Turner, 1979). Learning about the self can become strengthened through identification with other group members and similarities can reinforce a sense of identity. Conversely, the differences between group members and non-group members can also reinforce identity (Turner *et al.*, 1987). The advantage to individuals in enhancing social identity is threefold:

1. It assists individuals in understanding the social environment so that they can map their roles within situations.

2. It assists in the ability to define other people and, according to their social identities, predict how they might behave, which helps understand how the world functions.

3. And shared social identities provide unity and safety, aiding in the long-term survival of the group (Zhang *et al.*, 2010).

As an individual learns from a group, they activate their identity (a concept known as *salience*) in order to fit in and to direct the overall behaviour of the group (Oakes, 1987). In essence, salience is about becoming visible and having the confidence to start to reveal aspects of your character and personality. Within therapeutic photography groups, the participants develop confidence over the duration of the intervention and are guided by each other in terms of information sharing and task participation. However, Turner *et al.* (1987) also state that de-personalisation can occur on development of a social identity within groups, and this results in individuals strongly identifying with the other members to the point where individualisation can be diluted. This is a risk when doing any kind of group work, but within therapeutic photography groups this is an aspect of social identity theory that is rarely observed. This might be due to the fact that each individual normally goes through the process exploring issues from a personal perspective, and then once objectified in a photograph, bringing these issues to the group for discussion. This does result in identification with others, but the initial exploration stems from a personal perspective rather than a collective decision.

■ SOCIAL IDENTITY

In one group, the concept of social identity theory was revealed when participants were asked to explore the concept of "safety". They did this from a personal perspective, but as they shared the photographs with one another, similarities kept occurring.

These two images were not the only ones to capture closed curtains, and as participants spoke about shutting the outside world out and feeling cocooned inside the house there was recognition from all of the participants. Each one admitted that they did this when their mental health was poor, yet each one did not know the others also did this – they thought they were alone in feeling this and experiencing the strategy of self-isolation, yet through their images they found that they were not alone.

A consideration of identity theory

Stets and Burke (2000) explain that identity formation is a reflexive process wherein an individual will objectify themselves, compare themselves against others, and define themselves into categories. Because of this process, social identity theory should also be considered alongside identity theory as the two approaches, although different, have many similarities that can assist in understanding how identity is formed. Identity theory also takes the premise that society influences individual behaviour, but where social identity theory is primarily concerned with group membership, identity theory tends to focus more on roles within society (Stryker & Burke, 2000). By self-categorising into a role, an individual is potentially telling others that they identify with the societal expectations demanded by their role position. This often becomes evident as participants share their images and narratives – often people will want to explain their roles within their own family and this might include the role of parent, sibling, or child; others might want to explore roles they have in the community and how this can result in other people viewing them as important in their lives; others might want to explore hobbies or pastimes that give them a sense of purpose and being. Often, therapeutic photography groups are brought together by a common theme or trait (such as a group for people with mental health issues, or a group for people with substance use issues), but it is important to allow self-initiated exploration of *other* roles people have, rather than the role of client (or service user). Groups appear to prefer exploring other avenues of their identity, and themes such as family, reminiscence, isolation and culture are often noted ahead of their socially imposed labels.

▓ IDENTITY AND ROLES

In a group which was conducted with unpaid carers, all of the participants used the experience to explore other aspects of their roles, rather than their caring role. One participant was a man in his early 70s and he cared for his wife. He did mention her a few times during the sessions, but his narratives largely focused on his son.

It transpired that he had a 17-year-old son and he was clearly very proud of him, yet recognised that this was a role he had that most other men in their 70s did not have. Most of his photographs were used to give him an opportunity to mention his son, including his self-portrait.

He used a local museum and asked permission to sit in one of the displays which recreated a household scene from the 1950s, an era he remembers growing up in. He describes the atmosphere and the memories of other family members, which he terms a "reassuring ghostly presence", but in describing how he took the photograph he explained that his 17-year-old son stood behind the cake stand and pressed the shutter. He jokes that his son was worried that people would think he ate all the cakes. When he mentioned this, the other participants became aware of his role as a father to a teenager, a role that has societal connotations, but differences for him because of his age.

The medium of photography also directs participants to explore identity. Musello (1979, in Ulkuniemi, 2007) looked at the use of family photographs and believed they could be categorised into four distinct areas in terms of how they are used:

1. To document events (and preserve memories).

2. To demonstrate unity (which suggests the influence of social identity theory in finding commonality with others).

3. To facilitate interaction (which might be to illustrate interaction in the image, or to use the image to interact with others).

4. To build identity through investigating the self, status, and to relive experiences through the photograph.

Although he was writing specifically about family photographs, these four aspects are replicated in therapeutic photography groups during the exploration of all images, and this might be because these four categories encapsulate the cultural norms of using photographs, therefore participants unconsciously know how to use images – a process known as *implicit relational knowledge* (Stern *et al.*, 1998). This describes the ability of individuals to access procedural knowledge which directs behaviour in terms of how to act, how to think and how to respond emotionally in certain situations, primarily within a therapeutic setting where relationships between participants and facilitators can reach a productive plateau because of these unconscious norms.

■ CRITICAL THINKING

Implicit relational knowledge is about knowing how to "be" with other people. It is a mixture of nature and nurture as we build up our knowledge of the world around us, and relationships we experience, through our own growth and development. It is about being emotionally in tune with other people we come into contact with, but also about knowing what is culturally and socially appropriate, and responding appropriately.

Think about your interactions with people you work with – can you recognise actions that you engage which you believe stem from implicit relational knowledge?

Therefore, although the individuals may not directly speak about the identity which brings them together as a group, the implicit relational knowledge can provide each one with an acceptance of the reason, while also guide them in terms of the rules of using photographs and directing narratives in terms of social acceptability. This allows participants to explore individual identities with the function of the photographs having an "established discourse" (Brookfield *et al.*, 2008, p.481).

The exercises set out in this book are designed to facilitate one-to-one and group discussions so that identities can be explored and roles can be clarified. The Appendix has a suggested format for a six-week group programme and the latter exercises ask participants to document a day in their lives, and also to explore the environment to look for positives and negatives, and these are akin to reflexive photography and photo novella (Loewenthal, 2013; Parker, 2009). Reflexive photography is a research term that sees participants taking photographs about a particular topic, and then discussing the meaning of them with the researcher; photo novella is also a research term and, in a similar method to reflexive photography, seeks the views of participants through photography but is a method usually targeted at a minority community to investigate issues and to explore how empowerment can be achieved – it is akin to photovoice, which will be discussed in Chapter 9. Clark-Ibanez (2004) broadens this concept and believes that the practice of photo elicitation is a more accurate description of facilitating narratives through images. Again, photo elicitation is a research method and relies on visual means to initiate a response – in this respect, the response does not have to be verbal and the emotional and physical reactions to a photograph are also accounted for.

Similar to the photographic categories offered by Musello (1979, in Ulkuniemi, 2007), Clark-Ibanez (2004) points to the work of Harper (2002) in order to classify photographs produced for photo elicitation. Harper (2002) presented three approaches:

1. Photographs to provide an inventory of important things (such as objects, people and pets).

2. Photographs to explore events that have meaning and are usually linked to common cultural norms such as holidays, birthdays or school life.

3. Photographs that intimately connect the photographer to society, history or culture.

All three of these approaches explore identity and suggest that every single photograph produced can also give insight into identity, yet Clark-Ibanez (2004) states that "there is nothing inherently interesting about photographs; instead, photographs act as a medium of communication" (p.1512). What this suggests is that categorising images using Harper's (2002) or Musello's (1979, in Ulkuniemi, 2007) approach appears to be a secondary issue, and the main focus should be on how the photograph is used to aid communication – more specifically, how the photograph is used as a *catalyst* to explore identity.

By using photographs to identify, explore and externalise issues the participants are able to collectively discuss aspects of their identities which emerge. Any group should be conducted in an environment which is understanding so that each person can be guided by the group in terms of how much information they can share about each issue. In this way, social identity theory contains the group's actions. Identity theory then allows the participants to look at their roles, but instead of looking at the role which brings them together as a group, aspects which also define identity can be brought to the fore and areas such as creativity, family and history can all be discussed. Within these discussions, a further aspect of identity emerges, that of personal identity, and it is this third aspect of identity exploration to which we now turn.

Personal identity

Exploration of social identity adopts an ethnographic approach wherein the culture associated with "being human" is explored. Using this analogy, an interpretive phenomenological approach gives insight into how the participants determine personal identity. In essence, interpretive phenomenological analysis is a way of researching the phenomenon of "being human" – therapeutic photography encourages participants to engage with images and become researchers on themselves, with their focus being their own identity. Smith *et al.* (2009) explain that Husserl, one of the founding fathers of phenomenological inquiry, was driven by a desire to find a way of enabling people to understand their own interpretation of a phenomenon and, if this were possible, the essence of the experience could then be shared and understood by others, thus impacting on the way in which others personally interpret the phenomenon. They go on to explain that Husserl focused on the conscious nature of inquiry, that which a participant brought into their consciousness and objectified, which he believed demonstrated an intentionality on the part of the subject to define a relationship with the object of attention which was worthy of exploration.

▓ PHENOMENOLOGICAL ANALYSIS

Simply put, interpretive phenomenological analysis (IPA) is an approach in psychology and research that sees a researcher trying to make sense of how their subject tries to make sense of a particular situation or phenomenon. To do this, the researcher uses their own knowledge and experience to help them relate to how their subject is feeling, while at the same time recognising that they have had very different life experiences from their subject and, therefore, may have a different interpretation of the situation or phenomenon.

If this is applied to the process of a participant within a therapeutic photography group then we can see the objectification occurring within the production of a photograph. The *intentionality* might not have been conscious initially, but by committing a thought, idea or emotion to an image, the participant externalises it, creates a tangible item and objectifies a part of their own identity which they bring to their own consciousness, and can then explore this. It is through the act of reflecting where understanding emerges, and using photographs encourages the photographer to explore why the image was captured, what the meaning behind it is, and what that reveals about the identity of the photographer.

This interpretive phenomenological approach gives deeper insight than ethnographic social identity theory and appears to reveal identity formation as an ongoing, evolving experience, much as Sartre (2008) did when he stated "existence precedes essence" (p.652). Merleau-Ponty (1962) believed that the phenomenon of being human was driven by the knowledge that, as individuals, we were different from everything else in the world, and this difference was our identity. The philosophy of Mead suggests a useful connection in how participants using therapeutic photography explore their identity. Mead (1934) recognised that identity was born from interactions with society but identified two different components of identity, the "I" and the "me". Burns (1984) explained that the "I" relates to the impulsive nature of the identity which revels in its uniqueness and asserts differences in order to define itself, whereas the "me" is the part of the identity which learns social acceptability, rules, norms and behaviours in order to interact with others and survive in situations that demand conformity. Mead believed that the key to exploring identity was communication, so that the relationships between the self and society could be understood.

▨ CRITICAL THINKING

Can you define your own "I" and "me"?

As the "me" focuses on social acceptability and norms of interacting with others, think about you when you are out at work or in mixed company to define your "me". Maybe this is the polite, public face of you.

As the "I" looks at impulsivity, uniqueness and differences, think about how you behave in the privacy of your own home, or in the company of your closest friends to define your "I". Maybe this is the comfortable, at ease you.

Within therapeutic photography groups, participants routinely explore relationships with two forms of communication: visual and verbal. Mead wrote that identity relies on social communication and that individuals learn from the responses they get from people around them and he refers to this as a conversation of gestures wherein language emerges. It is within this conversation of gestures that Mead describes a triadic structure emerging where a person chooses to initiate communication, a receiver responds to the communication, and meaning emerges from the response. When this triadic relationship is applied to participants of therapeutic photography groups, the initiation of communication takes place when a participant displays an image and explains the meaning behind it. Eye contact is usually focused on the image and fellow participants usually lean in to see the image, thus body language is non-threatening and the participant relies on verbal feedback from which they extract meaning. It is the extraction of meaning that provides some of the therapeutic value. Burns (1984) explains that the exploration of "I" and "me" occurs in children as they experiment through play, then learn the rules of the game, and this could be applied to therapeutic photography groups too in that the participants have fun in the "play" of capturing images and interpreting each task, and are then guided by each other in terms of the "rules of the game" when it comes to sharing information with each other. What this allows the participants to see is the "I" at play; they are all able to engage their impulsive, curious and creative selves in the company of each other.

Self-concept

In turn, this appears to allow exploration of self-concept – an aspect of identity about which Carl Rogers (1951, 1959) wrote in his development of group work – to look at issues pertaining to self-awareness and emotional understanding. At the core of his work was phenomenology and he used this to try to understand how each individual learns to function in their own subjective worlds (Rogers, 1959). He believed it was the perception that individuals built up about themselves which influenced interactions with the social world, and this was a continual process which aimed to achieve actualisation.

According to Rogers (1951), the process of self-concept is threefold and consists of:

- developing a view of the self

- then developing value

- and then striving to achieve an ideal version of the self.

The view of the self is the starting point for therapeutic intervention and in Chapter 3 we explore how to structure exploration with therapeutic photography. Appendix 1 contains a suggested format to use when conducting therapeutic photography groups, which allows the participants to share information in the *pick a picture* exercise, the *self-portrait* exercise, and the *photographs with meaning* exercise, capturing elements of their identity which they feel safe to share (such as cultural ties, family, interests and roles). As the programme continues, the participants are encouraged to use the safe environment to delve deeper and explore more issues, receiving feedback from one another, which Rogers terms *positive regard*. Positive regard from others can result in positive self-regard within individuals, which equates to enhanced self-esteem, one of the main outcomes explored in Chapter 1. Rosenberg *et al.* (1989) view self-esteem as a basic human motive in that there is a natural drive towards self-enhancement which is defined by a perception that you are liked, you can achieve, and you are as good as those around you (Verhaeghe *et al.*, 2008).

However, Burns (1984) warns that if individuals are too reliant on feedback from others to enhance their self-esteem they may unconsciously work to protect their self-concept from changing and deny or distort positive regard from others. If self-esteem is enhanced then the self-concept is positively rewarded and directs behaviour towards maintaining this new feeling, which Rogers (1951) believed was a move towards self-actualisation, striving towards the ideal version of the self. He stated that this was an ongoing procedure and the self-concept would only influence a drive towards the ideal self rather than dominate it, but in defining self-concept Rogers underpins the importance of looking at the perception people have of themselves, and how it impacts on their behaviour and motivation.

A self-concept exercise

An interesting pictorial exercise to do with participants is to get them to think about their future, and in particular, their primary hopes for the future. I ask them to take one photograph to represent something they want to happen in their lives once they have finished the course. When this image has been produced, I ask them to think about what the photograph represents, and where this might place them on Maslow's hierarchy of needs model.

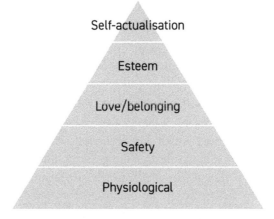

Figure 2.1: Maslow's (1943) hierarchy of needs model

At the base we find *physiological* needs, which define our requirements for basic survival – without these there will be improper functioning of the human body. Items found in this domain might include food, shelter, warmth and clothing.

Next, *safety* needs are considered and these incorporate physical, mental and economic safety. It is not unusual for children or adults experiencing domestic abuse, neglect or other forms of fear to be preoccupied by this stage.

Love and belonging is next on the hierarchy and this emphasises a need to form relationships, and to feel protected by these relationships. They include friendships and intimate relationships, but also look at intra-familial relationships and the need to find a role within the unit. Without the security of relationships, people risk being exposed to isolation, loneliness and depression.

Esteem recognises that humans need to feel respected and valued by their family, peers and society. Sometimes this can involve membership of a club or organisation where participants strive to better themselves and achieve skills that others may not possess.

Finally, at the top of the pyramid, we find *self-actualisation*, where a person has realised their full and true potential and Maslow believed that this required mastering all previous stages.

▣ MASLOW'S MODEL

By using the photograph to think about what they wish to achieve and where they might be on this model, participants can get a sense of what is important to them at the moment, and how far up Maslow's model they actually are. One participant produced this image during a group project.

What this represented to her was the need to be in a loving relationship. She stated she was very good at being a single mother, but wanted another relationship where she could feel loved by another person, recognising the stage of *love and belonging* on Maslow's model.

Self-perception

The value of considering self-perception as a starting point for any therapeutic intervention has been highlighted by Weiser (1999) who states that self-portraits can be used as a stimulus to explore self-narrative, and if this is done by a professional then the result could be that the subject learns more about themselves. Weiser was writing from the perspective of a phototherapist, as opposed to a therapeutic photographer, which means that the professional in mind would be a counsellor or therapist. Milford *et al.* (1984) recognised the value of using self-portraits to objectify oneself in order to visually confront the image presented and stated that this could instil a fight or flight response, but that if this was conducted within a group setting, the atmosphere of mutual support should provide an environment where flight would be resisted and visual confrontation could take place. In turn, this might produce a strong arousal resulting in heightened anxiety, but Milford *et al.* (1984) believed that this was the precursor to therapeutic interventions because it opened people up to exploring more "mature ego mechanisms" (p.227).

When considering identity exploration in therapeutic photography, the work of Donald Winnicott is also helpful to understand the dynamics at play. We will look at Winnicott's writings in more detail in Chapter 4, but at this stage it is useful to note that he was a psychoanalyst who recognised the importance of a therapeutic alliance between the worker and the client, and the resulting benefits which transpired from this partnership.

There are three areas within the exploration of personal identity which potentially align with the work of Winnicott (1971). The first of these areas relates to his identification of a holding environment, a therapeutic environment first identified in the parent–child relationship, but professionally adopted to represent a milieu wherein empathy and understanding are provided to a service user in order to facilitate safe exploration of problematic issues. This might allow the participant to express controversial thoughts, explore emotions or test out new ideas without being judged and criticised for doing so, and in terms of the therapeutic photography groups, participants commonly use the experience to disclose information and seek advice in a safe space, a space which could also be termed a *holding environment*.

Within this holding environment, we then witness the second area of Winnicott's (1965) work – the exploration of the false self in relation to the true self. Harwood (in Honess & Yardley, 2003) explains that Winnicott's true self refers to an identity that has been exposed to a healthy balance of experiences which lead to a sense of "aliveness and…feelings of realness" (p.57), but that if an individual strives to please other people, and adapts their behaviour in ways to meet the needs of others, then a false self can develop and a preoccupation occurs which sees the true self subsumed by the survival instincts of the false self. Winnicott (1965) described the false self as a defensive structure to protect the true self and viewed its function on a continuum, with the highly problematic false self dominating all behaviours and interactions at one end, and a healthy functioning false self at the other end informing social graces, interactions and competencies within society, "the gain being the place in society which can never be attained or maintained by the True Self alone" (p.142). Dominant false selves are impacted by a number of issues such as roles, families and societal pressures. Exploring these, then objectifying them through photography, helps individuals to confront the false self and enhance the true self through learning, and, if this is done with a group, social influences can be identified and attributed to possible feelings of oppression.

There is also a third area where Winnicott's work may be applied to therapeutic photography, and that is in its use as a transitional object, a concept that has been identified by a number of other researchers and practitioners (Riedel, 2013; Hills de Zárate, 2012; Young, 2004).

■ CRITICAL THINKING

Transitional objects are items that provide a level of psychological comfort and are traditionally associated with children's comfort blankets or soft toys to assist them through stages of change where they move from total dependence on the caregiver, to relative independence. Winnicott went on to explain that the transitional object need not be a tangible object – it may be a phenomenon such as religion, or cultural identification – but whatever it was assisted a person through a period of change by giving some comfort.

Think about your own experiences of transitional objects – do you still have them? Or rely on them?

Given a camera's ability to document change, could that be termed a transitional object?

This viewpoint assumes that the image can assist in the transition from one state to another, but Winnicott (1971) believed it was the transitional *space* that was as important and underpinned this stance by illustrating that children learn through play, and it is the process of becoming lost in play and accessing imagination and creativity which can aid a therapeutic transition and learning. This is akin to Mead's "I" at play (as described by Burns, 1984); being immersed in the transitional space can trigger emotions that may have been lost or buried in the unconscious, and reminding an individual that these emotions exist may be welcome respite from the reality of existence, which may well be enough to initiate positive change.

Summary

Stets and Burke (2000) state that "to establish a general theory of self, we must understand how group, role, and person identities are interrelated" (p.228), and with the use of photographs, these three levels of identity can be explored by participants in therapeutic photography groups, as summarised below.

■ THREE-STAGE EXPLORATION

1. *Social identity theory* – participants share images and build a therapeutic milieu, guiding each other on the appropriate level of disclosure and forming a bond through an interest in photography (which might be a welcome distraction from other aspects of life).

2. *Identity theory* – participants identify roles, cultural ties and reminiscences, which facilitates group bonding and asserts identity and commonality.

3. *Self-concept* – the images are further explored to see if the issues identified align with the purpose, ambitions and hopes of the individual.

Given that the social element of interaction serves to facilitate exploration, the catalyst that is photography could be described as the instrument of social transaction. It has been suggested by some that learning within human relations stems from transactions between individuals, and this relies on relationships which can be utilised for this purpose (Stetsenko & Arievitch, 2004; Freedman & Combs, 1996). These transactional processes do not need to be pure discourse between individuals; they can also be participation, practices and products of group interactions, which can impact on development. The photograph, in this respect, is used to encapsulate a concept, an idea or an issue, and then as a tool for discussion. It is externalised, objectified and then held at arm's length for others to see, but this distance between the photographer and the image appears to facilitate dialogue within the safety of the therapeutic space, and between individuals who demonstrate mutual understanding and respect.

Structuring the delivery of therapeutic photography appropriately also aids the exploration of relationships, and in Chapter 3 we will look at using a socio-ecological approach (as influenced by Bronfenbrenner, 1992) to underpin delivery of the intervention. This approach guides participants to explore their relationships with self, families, routines, environment and society, but by doing this in a group environment, exploration can also be conducted within the new relationships formed between members of the group. It is within these relationships where some suggest the work of Mead (1934) illustrates again how the *therapeutic* aspect of learning through interaction begins, and that discoveries made can assist an individual to move to a more mature acceptance of identity in viewing the self in a societal context (Fishbane, 2001; McGoldrick & Carter, 1999; Orlinsky *et al.*, 1994). Fishbane (2001) highlights that therapeutic work is collaborative because an individual needs to understand themselves but also feel that they are understood by others. In using photographs, the groups can utilise the established cultural norm of taking and viewing photographs to facilitate collaboration.

■ Chapter 3 ■

ADVANTAGES AND CHALLENGES

There are a number of services using therapeutic photography for the benefit of service users and clients, but delivery tends to be unstructured. This chapter introduces the reader to Bronfenbrenner's (1992) socio-ecological model and discusses the importance of using this to underpin the various techniques within therapeutic photography. It will propose that the practice involves exploring relationships, either with the self, others, environment or society, and knowing what is to be explored can guide you into the appropriate approach. The chapter will also look at the value of adding visual elements into traditional oral approaches, and at issues of confidentiality and how to practise safe therapeutic photography.

Advantages

When working with a photograph, the photographer has a real and tangible object in their hands, be it the photograph or a viewing screen with the digital image, and this allows attention to be focused on that object. When the photographer talks about the content of the image and the meaning behind it, they can look directly at the photograph, and anyone listening to this narrative will also direct their gaze at the image. This often involves leaning in closer to see what is in the photograph, and the dynamics of conversation change at this point; the body language between the photographer and listener is close and unguarded, the eye contact is non-threatening as the direction of this will ordinarily be at the photograph. There is also a sense that the photographer is truly being listened to because they can bring their narrative to life through the added element of the visual image.

Sometimes words alone do not, or cannot, paint the desired picture. With the addition of visuals, the meaning behind communication takes on a new form and there is a sense of shared experience between the photographer and the viewer. Consider, for example, someone explaining that they have a pet – you might get a sense of the kind of animal they have, but if you are presented with an image of the animal you, as the viewer, know immediately what kind of pet that person has and the significance of the animal through the depiction and positioning in the image. It also gives the photographer a tool to provide more specific detail about the animal by highlighting elements within the photograph. In essence, the photograph can speed up the process of learning by utilising the visual elements of communication.

For some, verbal communication might be difficult. It may be that schooling was absent and this has caused a deficit in language; it may be that a learning disability has affected the ability to communicate; or it may be that a physical illness or episode has impacted on speech. Incorporating a visual element to enable the expression of ideas, interests, emotions and memories takes the pressure off relying on words and language alone. The production of a photograph also requires some thought and planning, so it forces the photographer to slow down and think about what they want to capture, or what they wish to represent, within an image. It gives permission to stop and think about what is important, or what you value, before trying to form a pictorial representation of your thoughts. In searching the environment for an appropriate image, the photographer takes in what is around them and notices features about them which may not ordinarily warrant observation.

▪ MINDFULNESS

The art of slowing down and becoming aware of our surroundings is actually a significant part of mindfulness practice. Mindfulness involves an awareness of our internal feelings, while also taking note of what is going on around us and how that impacts on our immediate well-being. It is a form of self-therapy which is believed to be beneficial to our mental health and can help us identify when our bodies are acting adversely to stress or anxiety.

The next time you are out with your camera looking for inspiring photographs, try to become more aware of how you are feeling emotionally as you search your environment. You could try naming emotions you are experiencing aloud, or acknowledge how a captured image makes you feel inside. By doing this, you are becoming aware of your internal and external worlds – you are practising mindfulness.

When invited to view another person's photographs you are gaining an insight into their lives and it can be an inclusive experience. They control the information they tell you, but by viewing an image you also have the ability to ask questions and this forms a relationship between the viewer and the photographer. Control also arises at several points in the process for the photographer – when they decide what they want to capture, when they press the shutter, when they display the image, and what they choose to say about the image. The fact that the photograph is an object also provides safety in that the content is objectified and externalised, and can therefore be easier to speak about.

Harnessing these advantages to get the most from therapeutic photography involves more than simply playing to these benefits. To truly use photography to explore situations there needs to be a consideration of how to structure its use.

Structure

One of the primary fields of professional practice which has utilised photography is that of research. Griebling *et al.* (2013) explain that "photography, with its ability to render details, has an aura of authenticity that gives it a unique power and fascination" (p.17) and therefore it lends itself perfectly to gathering information about a person's lived experience. They go on to suggest that this form of authentic research works on many levels, and to summarise the ways in which photography can be used for this purpose:

- *Auto-photography* – this is the practice of working with individuals and encouraging them to photograph elements of their immediate environment in order to capture aspects of personal experiences. The methodology assumes that the participant will be able to identify significant parts of their cultural and social environment which are important to them, and by producing a visual image of a subject or issue it becomes easier to talk about. Auto-photography is typically accompanied by an interview so that the participant can explain why they took certain images and it is closely tied to identity formation and understanding the self (Combs & Ziller, 1977; Ziller, 1990; Noland, 2006).

- *Documentary photography* – viewed as a research tool, this is the practice of studying the social impact of a phenomenon, with the intention of asserting marginalised voices within society. With hindsight, documentary photography can be a powerful tool to capture the changing tides of history, but can also be used for small-scale projects too. The assumption is that the photographer will have a skillset that enables them to utilise a camera to produce quality images with impact, and that any viewer of the image will understand the meaning being conveyed within the photograph without need for an explanation.

- *Photo journalism* – this is similar to the practice of documentary photography but more short term in nature as the focus tends to be on one unique event rather than the longer-term impact of a social phenomenon. Understanding an image used within photo journalism tends to be easier as the photograph usually has mass appeal and is aimed at a wide audience. Again, the assumption here is that the photographer using this approach knows how to use their own camera and usually analyses a situation that is not familiar to them. This leaves both photo journalism and documentary photography open to the criticism that the images reflect an outsider's perspective, and not the perspective of those who are directly impacted.

- *Photo ethnography* – ethnographic research is the close and detailed study of a small element of society and the culture it exists in. The addition of photography into the practice is thought to increase researcher objectivity, although bias can never be eliminated because the researcher has to decide which images are relevant, and which are not. Often, an ethnographic researcher will immerse themselves in the culture they are studying and may even become an active participant. By doing this, they attempt to live the experience for themselves and aim to reflect a truer picture through their findings than a documentary photographer might do. The photographs are also typically used when research participants are being interviewed as a catalyst to enhance and deepen conversations about the culture they live in.

- *Photo language* – this technique views the photograph as a means of communication, one which facilitates the creative exploration and expression of ideas within small groups. Griebling *et al.* (2013) describe this method as one which can be particularly effective when evaluating something, be it a programme or course, or progress through a service. The method employed usually consists of pre-selected images being used to initiate discussion with a small group of participants. The facilitator has to consider this pre-selection carefully to ensure that the images offer aesthetics, as well as stimulating participants to explore memories, views and emotions. The logic behind this approach is that it facilitates the free flow of information within the selected group of participants who, in turn, learn from one another and gain more self-awareness.

- *Photo elicitation* – building on from photo language, photo elicitation recognises the benefits of using photographs to facilitate communication with individuals who might not be linguistically confident and attempts to empower research participants by giving them the camera and asking them to document relevant issues. Once the participant has produced images, a discussion can be had to discover why certain content has been chosen, and what the image represents. Where photo language typically works with pre-selected images, photo elicitation places the power of capturing the image firmly in the hands of the participant. Within research, this approach attempts to uncover strengths and weaknesses within the participant, and within the community they live in. Harper (2002) explains that this methodological approach gives insight into sociological and anthropological elements of a person's lived experience.

- *Photovoice* – this particular approach aims to give a "voice" to minority communities so that they can teach others about what is important to them (and will be explored in more detail in Chapter 9). Deemed to be an empowering approach, photovoice gives participants cameras and asks them to work individually to gather photographs on a particular theme that may impact on their lives. The idea is that participants work alone to explore the positive and negative qualities of the theme, and then come together with other participants to share images and explore the commonality within them. The shared dialogue should focus on both personal and group/community issues and the facilitators should be prepared to learn from the participants. Consideration also needs to be given as to what might be done with the images the group produces as there exists the potential to display these to inform wider audiences, and to influence the future direction of policy (Wang, 1999).

Clearly, there are similarities across these approaches, and each method recognises the value of incorporating a visual element into the methodology to enhance the communication, to evoke memories and emotions, and to have a lasting representation of the research. These approaches attempt to gain understanding of life, but from different angles – some look at the personal feelings and emotions, others look at the cultural impact, while others take a broader approach and try to understand the sociological factors that arise from the experience. Therefore, there is an appreciation that photography assists exploration, and if we recognise that this can be achieved on many levels, then by adding structure to the approach of therapeutic photography we can facilitate the examination of issues on a number of levels. To do this, we need to adopt a systems approach.

A systems approach

An individual does not (nor cannot) function in isolation. Human beings are social creatures and we need to be nurtured to survive; we learn from others around us, and we form attitudes and beliefs from the culture and society we live in. In short, we are affected by the system we exist in, and a problem in that system can result in a problem for the individual at the centre of the system.

Ecological systems theory

Urie Bronfenbrenner recognised the large number of societal and environmental factors that influenced the life of an individual and he developed the ecological systems theory to explain child development and the forces that affect it. He modelled his theory in a nested system, which he called the socio-ecological model, and it is this model that can assist in the structure and delivery of therapeutic photographic interventions.

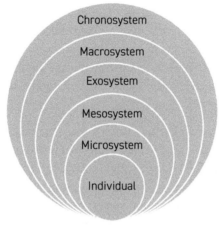

Figure 3.1: Bronfenbrenner's (1986, 1992, 2009) ecological systems theory model

Bronfenbrenner (1986, 1992, 2009) recognised the impact families had on individual human development. He also recognised that the family did not function in isolation, therefore other factors had to be incorporated into our understanding of human development. He proposed that every individual functions within a microsystem which, in turn, is nested within a mesosystem, exosystem, macrosystem and chronosystem.

Microsystem

The *microsystem* involves membership of various groups such as family, school, work, peers and neighbourhood. Obviously, for a child, there is very little choice in the "membership" of a group, but clearly these interactions with significant people in the microsystem can have long and lasting influences on the behaviour of a developing child. The most immediate influence will be that of family and how a child forms their ideas of relationships based on what they experience from their primary carers. When a child begins school their microsystem gets wider and they interact with peers and teachers, and this widens again as development continues through senior school and further education. Entering the workplace widens the circle again and involvement with intimate partners might ultimately lead to the formation of a new family unit which influences behaviour. Therefore, we can recognise that the microsystem and indeed all of Bronfenbrenner's levels are not static phenomena and continue to change as we continue to mature.

◼ CRITICAL THINKING

Looking at photographs you have, can you identify significant people from your own microsystem? Are you able to describe bonds you have with the people in your images? They might be older images from family photograph albums, or new images from a recent night out, but you should be able to say something about what the person (or people) in the image means to you. It is also worth recognising that the images may also include animals (or pets) that are significant.

Tommy was participating in a group for people recovering from substance use issues and he was asked to find images on his camera phone of a significant person in his life. He had a large number of images of his chihuahua and he explained that his dog was like therapy to him and she helped with his mental health issues. He went on to say that without his dog he would not know what to do and called her "my inspiration". Tommy was isolated and did not have much of a support network, and this became clearer as he explored images of his microsystem.

Mesosystem

The *mesosystem* is the environment where various groups from the microsystem come into contact with each other, directly or indirectly, and impact on how the individual functions within the microsystem. This extends the focus on one-to-one relationships which the microsystem tends to recognise and looks at how interactions take place between various players within the microsystem, and the consequences of this on the individual. The impact on the individual is that they learn how to adjust behaviours and values based on observing these interactions; for example, they may see a parent interact with their school teacher and, following this conversation, may have to readjust behaviours and perceptions based on the outcome of this transaction within the mesosystem.

■ CRITICAL THINKING

This is often harder to recognise in pictorial form as it looks at the issues arising from relationships out of the control of the individual, but which clearly impact on them. It is worth considering when you are working with photographs looking at the microsystem to explore interactions between the people who are a major influence on the life of the individual.

There have been occasions where participants have explored the interaction between estranged parents, and the differing beliefs and values each one holds. It may also be an opportunity for a participant to look at which relationships make them feel safer than others – some younger participants like to talk about important relationships they have with teachers at school, and how this relates to the relationship they experience with their parents.

In Chapter 5, we look at exploring relationships, and some of the exercises outlined in this book involve abstract expression of emotions that might well give insight into the quality of these bonds and the issues that lie underneath.

Exosystem

The *exosystem* encompasses the micro- and mesosystems and elements within this domain are normally outside the direct control of the individual at the centre. These factors might relate to the cultures and attitudes which prevail, and which may contribute towards oppression and stigma or negative attitudes which impact on the individual at the centre. To give an example, the environment an individual works in might be one where output and pay are performance driven, and this might mean working long hours in stressful situations. A parent who works in this environment may come home at the end of a long day and feel exhausted and worried, which, in turn, might manifest in the family environment as being short tempered and angry, thus impacting on the children – in this scenario the parental workplace in the exosystem is impacting on the life of the child at the centre.

This level is often dominated by larger institutions such as mass media, social services and local politics – institutions that clearly impact on the lives of those functioning at the microsystem level.

■ CRITICAL THINKING

Exploration of the exosystem can involve looking at the lived environment as well. It encourages participants to look around them at their immediate environment and evaluate what is good and what is not so good.

In a group for young adults living with autism, one participant explored her journey to school and took the following image.

This photograph shows the view from the school taxi as she journeys to classes. She lives in the countryside, but the taxi that takes her to school also picks up two other students, both with learning disabilities. She explained that she sits in silence on her journey to school and feels as though she has been categorised as someone with a learning disability because of the "special" taxi that takes her to her destination. The attitude of the education system and the support structures are giving her a label that she feels she has to bear.

Again, have a look at your own images and see if you can identify factors that depict the exosystem you experience. Are there significant cultural elements to your picture that you feel you conform to in order to fit in? They do not need to be negative – some cultural factors can be positive – but will still shape your values and attitudes.

Macrosystem

The *macrosystem* is found towards the outer edge of Bronfenbrenner's model and he describes this as the overarching culture which impacts on the functioning of the inner systems. Ethnicity, religion, social status, values and attitudes all impact on the macrosystem, as do the effects of legislation and policy, which impact on everyone living within society. Again, values and beliefs that stem from elements within the macrosystem have a resulting impact on the individual at the centre of the model.

CRITICAL THINKING

In a group for women within the criminal justice system, the participants were asked to explore their environment and to decide what was good, and what was not so good, about the city they lived in. A large number of images were produced, and the group discussed the positives of the city, but also highlighted issues such as poverty, neglect of certain areas, and stigmatisation by the police. One participant produced the following image:

She had photographed wrappers for novel psychoactive substances, also known as "legal highs". These products had become a problem in the city, and she explained that there were real dangers in taking these synthetic substances because there was no guidance as to how to use them, and no quality control in terms of what was in them. She argued that it was actually "safer" to use street-bought illegal drugs than these synthetic alternatives. The group went on to talk about the ways in which the government was attempting to address the issue through creating new legislation, but also spoke about how there was an assumption from their peers that, because they had previous drug offences, they would automatically be drawn to using these products.

This image allowed the group to explore attitudes, stigma and government actions. In your own images, are there elements you can identify that define your social class, religion, gender, nationality and race?

Chronosystem

The *chronosystem* encompasses all of the other systems and takes into consideration life transitions which can impact on an individual. These include the natural course of events such as birth, childhood, puberty, school, work and marriage, but can also include unexpected life transitions such as divorce, illness and death. Bronfenbrenner recognised that these life transitions could impact on the individual and their functioning within the family depending on how natural or unnatural the transitions were. Throughout our lives we experience these transitions, and with the increasing availability of cameras on mobile devices, capturing images of these moments has become commonplace.

▓ CRITICAL THINKING

Perhaps this is the easiest of Bronfenbrenner's systems to recognise in your photographs. Looking at your images, what kind of life transitions do you see? Some of your images might capture memories of a significant event, such as the birth of a child, or celebrations at a birthday or wedding. Some might be of a social gathering which brings old friends together and provides a chance to reminisce.

In these images, you should also be able to think about age as well. Is the activity depicted age appropriate? Can you chart the passage of time in your images?

Photography and the ecological system

Bronfenbrenner (2009) believed that his ecological perspective helped provide an understanding of the development of a growing human, their interactions with the family, their perception of the wider world, and the way society shapes these relationships. Therapeutic photography also aims to understand human development, family structures, narrative construction and societal influences.

In recognising that photography can help to form identity through exploration of self-identity and family roles, Newbury (1996) highlighted the impact of photographic images at the exosystem and macrosystem levels, particularly in advertising, media, and popular culture. He explained that photographic images were bound to our knowledge of modern society and how an individual aligned themselves to this. Where this can become problematic is when the images presented at the exosystem and macrosystem levels stigmatise the individual within the microsystem. Newbury (1996) used photography with disabled students to explore how they were portrayed by charities and adverts, and family photographs, and then encouraged them to explore how they viewed themselves and how photography could assist in *reclaiming* identity. The advantage of using photography for this exercise was that the students could illustrate how they felt they were viewed by others, and how they viewed themselves, and this resulted in the students developing a critical awareness of the social environment and how they were viewed within this. The experience facilitated the students to become involved in a discourse to challenge and change their representations and was described as an empowering exercise.

Sharland (2006) believes that professional disciplines such as social work have become burdened by contradiction in that the traditional roles which aimed to support and empower service users have become more regulatory and disciplinary because of an emphasis on policy, procedure and legislation. She highlights research by Cohen and Ainley (2000) which acknowledges the importance of an ecological approach to help understand how identity is formed as it is impacted through learning in differing situations including the family, peer groups and community groups, all of which are locally and structurally situated. Therefore, to truly do quality social work with service users, a professional must understand how individuals feel about themselves, interact with their family, are influenced by their peers, are viewed by the community, are treated by society and are controlled by the political environment.

Strack *et al.* (2010) suggest that the photo-based interventions, or "photoventions", all have the potential to bring about change in, and for, participants, and that specific interventions such as photovoice can be directly aligned to a social ecological model to highlight benefits. They believe that a change occurs on several levels: on an individual level, as it brings about self-efficacy and knowledge; on an interpersonal level, there can be positive changes in social interactions and group empowerment; on an organisational level, information can bring about policy change; and on a community level, there can be changes in social norms, community participation and action.

Yohani (2008) also uses Bronfenbrenner's ecological framework to support using photography with younger children. She stresses the importance of Bronfenbrenner's *proximal processes*, which refer to the way a developing individual interacts with people, objects and places within the external environment that ultimately generates knowledge and skills (an extension of Vygotsky's (1980) writings on the zone of proximal development). She explains that by giving children cameras to photograph their environment, and then reviewing the photographs with the children, proximal process is enhanced, which impacts on coping strategies and development. This approach to understanding proximal processes by using photography has also been used to explore issues faced by young refugees (McBrien & Day, 2012).

Applying structure to therapeutic photography

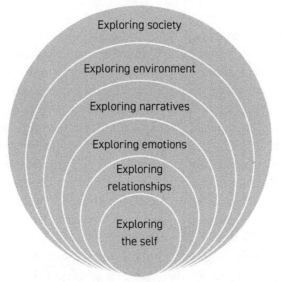

Exploring society

Exploring environment

Exploring narratives

Exploring emotions

Exploring relationships

Exploring the self

Figure 3.2: Structuring therapeutic photography – Gibson's model

The areas that can be explored through therapeutic photography straddle all of the levels on Bronfenbrenner's model, and as such can be structured in a similar fashion. Each of these levels encompasses a wide range of theories which can be used in conjunction with the photographic image by professionals to help understand some of the underlying issues being explored. When exploring the self, psychodynamic and psychosocial theories come into play and the question "Who am I?" is asked, and self-acceptance is sought. The exploration of relationships within photographs extends the importance of psychosocial theories and incorporates family systems theories. Moving into the realms of exploring emotions and narratives, this practice also has roots in psychodynamic approaches but looks at the way in which we view the world and has links to narrative therapy, resilience and how we tell our story. Exploring society then looks at how we interact with our environment and draws on empowerment, power alignments and societal norms. The end result is a nested system that draws parallels with Bronfenbrenner's ecological systems theory model (see Figure 3.2). Each of these stages is further explored in the following chapters, which will explain theoretical concepts which can be used at each level and will give examples of exercises to use for exploring issues.

Challenges

As well as the advantages of using therapeutic photography, it is also important to highlight the limitations and challenges involved. Like every intervention, the professional must be sure that they are choosing the most beneficial approach for their client, and this should be done in discussion with the client. It is important to explain what the purpose of therapeutic photography is and what will be expected from the participant. Aspects of control must also be addressed as it can often be reassuring for clients to hear that they will not be expected to photograph or discuss anything they do not want to, or may not be ready to. It is often useful to think about the choice that people have to participate as well; this intervention aims to address self-esteem, self-efficacy and empowerment, which can really only be done if participants opt into the intervention, rather than are ordered to participate. To that end, it is good practice to highlight that participants can withdraw at any time if they do not feel the intervention is meeting their needs.

■ GROUP RULES

When I am involved in therapeutic photography group work I draw up a participant contract so that individuals can read about the exercises they will be participating in and the outcomes the group will be working towards. I ask the participants to sign this contract as it also emphasises their right to withdraw at any time. What I do not do is set group rules as this automatically creates a barrier in terms of power dynamics. The intervention of therapeutic photography aims to empower, and part of this comes from the therapeutic alliance between the facilitator and the participants. If the facilitator exercises too much power over the group through the enforcement of group rules, this can inhibit the sense of control the participants have, so it is worth considering whether this is a comfortable fit with the types of groups you may be working with. If group rules are necessary, then try to address this from the outset so that the participants are still as free as possible to explore and narrate their images.

To give an example, I worked with a group of clients who were recovering from substance use and the agency had a rule that participants were not allowed to speak about drugs. Clearly that was going to inhibit free exploration so I worked with the agency to suspend this rule during our therapeutic photography sessions.

Taking photographs may require an element of physical dexterity. Using a camera to analyse the environment can actually be an advantage to many as it almost gives permission to put yourself into strange positions to capture the image you want – imagine staring intently at an object and moving your head from side to side without having a camera in front of you! Therefore, some consideration should be given as to the ability of the person or group you are going to be using therapeutic photography with. However, any disability or impairment should also not be viewed as a barrier to using this approach as many valuable studies have been produced using visual means to gather views from people with disabilities (Newman, 2010; Mitchell *et al.*, 2016; Agarwal *et al.*, 2015). The provision of an assistant for the person capturing the image might also need to be considered so that the participant can direct the assistant in getting a pictorial representation of what they require. This technique has been used when working with clients with visual impairments, but it is also worth seeking out technology that could also assist in the image-capturing process – software has been developed which can describe what is on the image-capture screen to assist visually impaired clients who are interested in photography. Ultimately, inclusion should always be aimed for.

The term "therapeutic photography" can be a barrier in itself, in two different respects. First, for participants to opt into a programme or project they have to understand what they are choosing to participate in. The word "therapeutic" may suggest that someone who participates requires therapy, and many people may view this as a sign of weakness, or may feel that they do not need therapy. Yet the intervention does not offer therapy in a traditional sense; it offers a milieu which is conducive to exploration and growth. This message has to be communicated to potential participants to encourage them to overcome a perception that they are doing this as a form of therapy. Second, the word "photography" may conjure up perceptions of complex single lens reflex cameras with elaborate lighting settings and expensive lenses, and potential participants may think that there is a high expectation of technical skills involved. This may encourage some, thinking that they are going to be taught how to take photographs, but for others with low self-efficacy, this may be off-putting from the start. Both these views should be challenged in the recruitment process as it is not right for people to sign up for "lessons" if that is not what is being offered, nor do you want to deter those with low self-efficacy as one of the aims of the intervention is to enhance self-efficacy. The means of taking the photograph is almost incidental as the therapeutic aspect comes from talking about the image, so the image can actually be captured using any device the participant is happy with. Many participants opt to use their own mobile phones or tablet devices, while some will use a digital camera, but the technical device used to capture the image should not be a barrier to participation. As long as the participant is comfortable with their device, that's the most important thing.

Although the practice of therapeutic photography is underpinned by the intention to encourage self-disclosure and control, there still needs to be some consideration as to what constitutes confidentiality. When working with photographs there is the added challenge of ensuring that nobody's rights are breached by the project you are conducting. Under the Human Rights Act 1998 there is a right to the respect of family and private life, and participants of therapeutic photography have to recognise this; therefore, if participants want to photograph another person they should seek permission from them to do this. However, most of the exercises in this book encourage creative expression and there are ways of capturing images which *represent* other things, including people.

CONFIDENTIALITY

During one group project, one participant wanted to photograph something to represent the emotion of "joy" and he spotted three female university students sitting in a park chatting to one another. He explained that he felt joy when he saw this scene as it appeared to be friendly and inclusive, and he wanted to capture this in his photograph. He was, however, very shy and wandered round the park several times before plucking up the courage to go and speak to them. He explained that he was involved in a photography project, and then went on to explain why he would like to take their photograph. They happily gave him permission to do so.

Later, he explained, that if he had not had the camera in his hands he would never have been able to approach this group to talk to them. He found the experience to be a confidence booster.

Some areas are private, such as shopping centres and stately homes, and in these environments permission to photograph should be sought. Normally there will not be a problem in doing this as the photographs are not going to be used for commercial purposes, but it is always better to ask as you do not want clients getting into trouble while you try to encourage the enhancement of self-esteem and self-efficacy. Fortunately, in the main, it is legal to photograph in public spaces so there are ample spaces to choose from when conducting an exercise utilising therapeutic photography. Certain countries have more restrictive laws when it comes to photographing, so ensure you are aware of your own country's legislation and the information your participants need to know before they begin a task; for example, it is illegal to photograph a member of the police force when in Spain.

As well as considering the legality of taking photographs, you need to consider the safety element too. You do not want any participants to place themselves in danger in the pursuit of an image, yet sometimes there will be issues that someone wants to capture in a photograph that might jeopardise their safety. Looking across the stages Bronfenbrenner identified, there are potentially dangerous issues which might arise such as domestic violence in the microsystem, bullying in the meso- and exosystem, and drug use and other criminal behaviour in the macrosystem to name but a few. Clearly, it would be unwise for a participant to attempt to capture criminal behaviour in an image so that it can be discussed in sessions, but, like issues pertaining to confidentiality, the encouragement to capture an image to *represent* the issue would always be a safer alternative. For facilitators, the other way to deal with this risk is to ask participants if there was anything they wanted to photograph but could not. This will allow any issues to come out in the discussion by recognising things that were actually absent from the image, yet still using photography as an inroad to these conversations.

Once photographs have been produced and the participant or group is engaging with them and narrating content, a decision has to be made about what is going to happen to these images and who owns them. If a participant is taking the photographs then it stands to reason that they own the copyright for the image, but at the end of the programme or project, if a participant wants to exhibit any of the images, or share them with an agency for promotion, some consideration needs to be given to the ongoing copyright of the photographs. As a facilitator, you have prompted the production of the image and have viewed it with the participant, but there might be other people within your agency who wish to view photographs from your project and you need to consider if it is acceptable for images to be shared with a wider audience, and if you need to seek permission from the photographer to do that. As Weiser (1986) points out, some agencies could argue that anything produced by an employee during working hours automatically belongs to the agency, and that could mean that a therapeutic photography project conducted within a certain setting would have to recognise that the photographs belonged to the agency and not the participants. Again, you do not want issues like this acting as a barrier to participation, or exploration, as this might see participants self-censoring if they do not hold the copyright for their own images. This is an issue that could be addressed in the initial participant information sheet which explains the project to interested parties, and clarifies, from the outset, who owns the images produced.

■ COPYRIGHT

In all of the groups I have conducted I have always insisted that the participants owned the copyright for their images, and had the final say over whether they shared their images or not. However, all of the images used in this book are from various groups I have been involved in. I asked participants to volunteer their images for sharing, and asked them to sign a consent form which allowed me to use their photographs, waiving rights under the Copyright, Designs and Patents Act 1988. This was always done at the end of the programme so that there was no pressure at the outset and to alleviate any concern that participants might feel that they might be "penalised" for not agreeing to submit images. All of the participants who chose to volunteer images went through their selection and edited out ones they did not want to share prior to submission.

The final issue to consider when conducting a therapeutic photography intervention is what to do if a participant discloses information that causes concern. Every agency will have their own policies and procedures which will inform your response to serious disclosures, but they do vary from profession to profession and it is worth making it clear from the outset which information can remain "private", and which information would need to be passed on to appropriate agencies. Within a social work setting in the UK, any disclosure of harm to a child or vulnerable adult would automatically need to be shared with appropriate authorities, but other types of disclosures can result in a variety of reactions from various settings. Substance use is a good example, wherein a statutory service dealing with court orders may well have to share information with the police if a client talks about continued illegal activity, yet if the same client were to receive a service from a voluntary agency, the duty to share information about illegal activity may not be quite as rigid. Medical professionals are bound by different codes of conduct from those of social workers, and the general advice would be to seek permission to share information whenever this is practical, but information can also be shared without consent if a doctor is legally required to do so, or if it is in the public interest to share. Counsellors and therapists are also bound by different ethical frameworks, and these also aim for confidentiality unless a disclosure is deemed to suggest imminent harm to the client, or someone else as a result of the client's actions.

Within ethical guidelines and codes of practice, the terminology used in defining when disclosures need to be shared can be ambiguous and open to interpretation so it is a good idea to think about how you may broach this issue before setting out to utilise this intervention. Again, using a participant information sheet to address these general issues at the outset is good practice, and when proposing how disclosures will be dealt with, it may be advantageous to spell out exactly what kind of information would need to be passed on so that clients are aware from the very beginning.

Summary

This chapter has outlined some of the major points to consider when setting up a therapeutic photography group and has demonstrated that the advantages of the approach far outweigh the challenges, yet challenges do need to be carefully considered and addressed before any work commences. Adding structure to any therapeutic photography intervention helps provide clarity for the facilitator and the participant so that exercises can be used to explore issues within the lives of clients. The following chapters go on to explore these different structural levels and suggest exercises and theories to help maximise the impact of therapeutic photography.

◼ Chapter 4 ◼

USING PHOTOGRAPHY TO EXPLORE SELF-IMAGE

In this chapter, the focus of using therapeutic photography turns to the exploration of the self-image and outlines specific approaches and techniques. Practitioners and writers who have studied this approach will be introduced, before we explore some of the key theorists underpinning work in this area. Within the chapter, some consideration will be given to the different approaches to working with the self-image, including the phenomenon of taking "selfies", but the purpose of the chapter is to highlight the therapeutic approaches that assist in working with individuals who may have a negative self-image, and how approaches can be adjusted to address this issue. Throughout the chapter, examples of how these exercises have been used in practice will be included, alongside a discussion of some images produced by previous group members.

◼ SELF-PORTRAIT TASK

When using photographs to explore self-image, I usually set participants the task of doing a self-portrait, but with one specific instruction – the self-portrait must capture a positive quality of the person, something the person likes about themselves. I encourage participants to think creatively and tell them they can be as abstract as they like. I also instruct them that there is no "correct" way to do a self-portrait, and no photograph will be "wrong" if it captures a positive quality of the self. This might result in participants doing a full self-portrait, a head and shoulders self-portrait, a more personal image of a tattoo, a piece of jewellery or something completely abstract to represent a positive quality. The important thing to remember is that the client has to be in control of what they photograph, and feel encouraged to share the narrative.

Photographs to understand "the self"

Taking photographs of the self, or self-portraits, can be used therapeutically to explore issues pertaining to the self, mainly with regards to esteem, knowledge and confidence (Weiser, 2001). It is a technique that encourages introspection with an aim to highlight positive aspects of identity to facilitate self-acceptance (Glover-Graf & Miller, 2006; Weiser, 2004).

There is no set format for doing self-portraiture. Clearly, the primary remit is that the photograph must be of the client, preferably taken by the client. The photograph is then used in some way to analyse how the client is perceived, which will involve analysis of how they see themselves, before looking at how others see them. In many professions, the reasons clients seek intervention are wide and varied, but the way people feel about themselves underlies the majority of contacts, including self-esteem issues, self-worth issues, feeling disempowered and feeling undervalued. Any therapeutic intervention should begin by looking at how the client feels about themselves and work towards trusting self-acceptance before the client can trust others to accept them. Working with self-portraits helps this process by encouraging the client to work with the question, "Who am I?" (Weiser, 1999; Berman, 1993).

To address this question, there is an element of communication with the self through the image, and this may involve an exploration of self-concept, along with self-disclosure, to be able to address issues (Barbee, 2002; Ziller, 1990). Burns (1984) explains that self-concept is a key factor in "the integration of personality, in motivating behaviour and in achieving mental health" (p.2). Ziller (1990) believed this was a factor that was worth exploring through self-portraiture. He explained that perceptions of self-concept link into confidence and will impact on situations an individual is willing to place themselves into, which in turn impacts on the behaviour of the individual. Through exploring self-portraits, Ziller assisted the process of finding meaning, which he believed had a direct impact on enhancing self-concept. He also recognised that internal thoughts and feelings about the self had to be set in a societal context and consideration given to how individuals are expected to behave in the given culture in which they exist. He recognised the value of theorists such as Mead (1934), Stryker (1980) and Cooley (1902), who all highlight the social concept of the self, and was drawn to Cooley's "looking-glass self" (1902, p.152), which describes how the view of the self, and the beliefs an individual holds about how others perceive them, can be different and are tempered by the emotions of pride and shame. Mead (1934) explored societal roles in identity formation and described the process as the impulsive, unique driving force behind behaviour (which he termed the "I") being tamed and shaped by interactions with society until a social being emerges (which he termed the "me"). In their study of photographic self-representations produced by university students, Combs and Ziller (1977) stated that "the photographs become the 'me' that can be experienced by the 'I'" (p.454), and although never mentioning Mead (1934) in the research, they appeared to recognise his influence.

Mirroring

From a very early age children are fascinated by their own image; a photograph can confirm a child's identity and place within the family; "from very early in life, the need to have oneself reflected is crucial to the development of the self" (Berman, 1993, p.3). From birth, a baby needs confirmation of its own identity and will look to its primary carer for this; cries initiate a reaction from the carer, and a response brings confirmation that the child exists and can command attention in order to have needs met. Later it will look into the face of the carer, test out a facial expression such as a smile, and look for a reaction from the carer, a process Winnicott (1971) calls *mirroring*. When the mother mirrors the baby's action, the baby recognises that it has been seen and therefore exists. As we grow, our identity formation is informed by how our interactions with our community and society are mirrored to us. Self-portraiture through photography allows us to see how others see us, and allow us time to reflect on how we project ourselves. In a formal therapeutic setting, the therapist will provide the therapeutic gaze which echoes that of Winnicott's "*good enough mother*", allowing clients to explore their full range of emotions (Martin, 2009). However, because therapeutic photography does not necessarily involve a trained professional, this protective milieu may be absent.

Berman (1993) explains that, for some, being photographed is not always a positive experience. As children, they may have been forced to pose; low self-esteem might make being photographed feel unpleasant, which ultimately may create a fear of seeing and being seen in ways that are deeply uncomfortable. This might result in a participant disengaging from the process, but it is also something that could be managed by a professional facilitator if they are aware these emotions may occur. Berman argues that the photographs that appeal to us most are the ones that we have taken, or the ones that include us in the image, and this is because, if taken by ourselves, there is an element of control over what is included and what is said about the image, or, if they include us, they conjure up memories, emotions and feelings we attach to the image.

Nunez (2009) believes that a fear of the camera stems from problematic relationships with our own self-image. She explains that we are dominated by two ways of seeing – how we think about ourselves internally, and what we think about ourselves when we view ourselves in a mirror, externally. She uses self-portraits as therapeutic photography for three reasons: first, as self-portraiture forces the individual to become the subject of the photograph this can expose vulnerabilities; second, once the person is confronted by the self-portrait, a process begins that is akin to a formal therapy session wherein an inner dialogue looks at self-perception, begins to question, forms judgements, and moves into acceptance; and finally, the multiple meanings taken from the analysis of the self-portrait can help to unify differing aspects of the personality.

Nunez (in Loewenthal, 2013) underpinned her work with self-portraits with experiential knowledge, helping the subject broaden self-perception. She has since gone on to develop a programme for clients who are interested in using self-portrait as a means of self-exploration. The programme involves clients photographing three different areas of their lives – photographs of the self where participants are encouraged to consider emotions, identities, and the physical body; photographs of the self with others exploring one-to-one relationships; and photographs of the self interacting with the wider world (www.cristinanunez.com). She believes the process should culminate in the intimate sharing of the produced images so that clients can free themselves from the confines of the ego. Nunez is a professional artist and has personal experience of psychotherapy, but no formal training in photography, and in her own words, "through self-portraiture I had found a way to re-create the loving gaze of my mother" (in Loewenthal, 2013, p.95).

■ IS A "SELFIE" SELF-PORTRAITURE?

The "selfie" phenomenon has grown with the rise of the smartphone camera, and in essence, could be classed as a "self-portrait", yet many have criticised the practice as narcissistic (Sorokowski *et al.*, 2015; Weiser (E.B.), 2015; Warfield, 2014). There is no denying that the end result is a self-portrait, but the intention behind capturing the image can define how selfies are regarded. If the intention is simply to represent yourself in the best way possible, and then to display yourself to others to illustrate how good your image is, then they could probably fall into the realms of narcissism, but in this sense, any self-portrait could be classified as narcissistic.

This can often act as a barrier when working with self-portraits. Often, participants will state they don't like their own image, or they don't like looking at themselves, and part of this may well be that society views this as being self-absorbed, and self-obsessed. Therefore, it is important to focus on qualities beyond the image, and that is why it is good to set participants the challenge of capturing a *positive aspect* of their self. This gives a reason to do a self-portrait, gives permission to be self-analytical, but in a way which moves beyond capturing a simple "selfie".

Phillips (1986) highlights the value in using photography to address the loss of ego boundaries and states that a photographic image can help the client take one step back from reality and view the self-image from a safe distance. Phillips talks about the importance of the therapeutic alliance which suggests that the programmes developed are intended to be delivered by a "professional" and not a programme to work through on one's own. The programme devised by Nunez also appears to have underpinnings in art therapy and the belief that creative interventions can help service users realign their self-images when the gap between how they define their identity and how society interprets their identity is large enough to cause self-esteem issues.

Milford *et al.* (1984) recognise the value of using self-portraiture in group settings, a process they refer to as *visual self-confrontation*, and explain that the process can provide the client with previously unknown information – a simple example they use is when someone's opinion of themselves is challenged by group feedback, albeit they assume this feedback to be positive. However, using this approach to address self-esteem issues comes with a warning. Being confronted by one's own self-image will result in a state of objective self-awareness, which can lead to a comparison with one's internalised standard, and if this comparison results in a negative discrepancy between the two states then aversive arousal takes place and a fight or flight response is often initiated. If a therapist is involved in this process, their job is to keep the service user in a state of objective self-awareness; however, this underpins the argument that therapeutic photography requires a professional to guide it (Duval & Wicklund, 1972). Again, this is linked to a psychodynamic approach wherein the anxiety produced when viewing oneself may result in adaptive ego functions, but it could also be argued that an aroused state makes the service user more accepting of further therapeutic intervention (Milford *et al.*, 1984).

■ SELF-ESTEEM AND SELF-PORTRAITS

During a group for clients of a mental health support charity the participants were set the task of taking a self-portrait, but with one specific remit – the portrait had to capture something the client liked about themselves. This suggestion seemed to fill the room with fear, but, as the facilitator, I wanted to see how the group would help each other with the task, and reduce the feelings of anxiety that were evident.

One particular participant, Julie, reported that she went home on the bus after the group session and spoke about the self-portrait task with two other participants. They all discussed the challenge of capturing something they liked about themselves, and they all began to share comments about what they liked about each other. From this, they were not only reflecting on their own positive qualities, they were receiving affirmation from others, thus boosting self-esteem.

During this conversation, Julie was told that she had beautiful hands, so she decided to incorporate them into her self-portrait. She set her camera up in the house and, because she also wanted to get her face in the shot, she partially hid her features to represent her shy side, but captured the quality she most liked about herself – her hands.

In the UK, Jo Spence (1986) was one of the dominant voices behind the use of self-portraits for therapeutic gains. Spence died in 1992 but prior to this she had worked to highlight the therapeutic benefits of using self-portraits to deal with her health issues. Like Nunez, Spence had no formal training as a therapist but was a photographer by trade. When she was diagnosed with breast cancer she found the experience of dealing with medical professionals disempowering and alienating, and ultimately she felt infantilised by the experience. She decided to use her photography to try to gain some control and to help her understand what was happening to her body and created a series of visual illness diaries. These diaries helped Spence come to terms with her struggle between her real appearance and society's impression of what an ideal woman should be and, consequently, after a successful lumpectomy, her work went on to inform women's rights groups as well as disability movements in their campaigns for rights (Dennett, 2009).

Spence went on to formalise some of her techniques with other interested parties such as Terry Dennett (2009) and Rosy Martin (2009), who were also interested in identifying the therapeutic benefits of using photography for self-study. Therapeutic staging was one technique developed wherein participants are encouraged to express internal feelings by thinking about how they want to be photographed and staging the scene. This was heavily influenced by Spence's love of cinema and her appreciation of Sergei Eisenstein as a director who believed in guiding the viewer through a series of "shocks" (Dennett, 2009). With Martin, Spence developed collaborative phototherapy, which is a form of co-counselling conducted in partnership with another person, but again, unlike traditional counselling, no involvement of a trained professional is necessary. The technique involves revisiting images stored in memory which may be problematic to the client, then reconstructing them and capturing them in a photograph, thus challenging the mythologies of others who have attached stories to old images, and therefore defined identity (Spence, 1986). This technique assumes that the images to be recreated in photographs are readily available to the participant, thus suggesting that conscious memories, as opposed to unconscious memories, are the focus of collaborative phototherapy. The work of Spence and Martin allowed them to challenge social and psychic construction, but they believed it was the process of engaging rather than the production of a finished image that provided therapeutic value. In their own experience, their traumas were not the same but each could identify with the other and once the work was shared, others too found recognition (Spence, 1986).

The idea of challenging social construction is continued in other forms of therapeutic photography. In terms of using self-portraiture to do this, Newbury (1996) found that incorporating self-portraiture into a programme which looked at how disability was constructed within society helped students to integrate different levels of understanding of how images were used to define disability, but also revealed ways that they could reclaim their own identity through self-portraiture. This technique has also found its way into research practices where it is termed *auto photography* and asks research participants to capture data through self-portraits and environmental photography. It is believed that this practice empowers participants and gives them the ability to select what is important to them (including people and environmental factors) by asking them to capture this in a photograph, thus avoiding the constraints of verbal communication with which some people might struggle. However, the practice is not without criticism, as some believe that a photograph will potentially distort the objective image it aims to capture because the photographer is subjective in the means they use to portray the image (Noland, 2006; Sontag, 1977). The viewer of the image can also distort the information, but Noland (2006) argues that by visualising the distortion, it still brings it to the attention of the facilitator and it can then be discussed, and what is said about the image may be more important than the image itself.

Overview

A key theme to emerge from the therapeutic use of photography to look at the self is the ability to explore self-concept in terms of how the participant views themselves, and how they believe others view them. In using a visual approach, issues can be objectified in an image and held at a distance, and a dialogue begins where the individual looks at their relationship with the self. There are risks that the participant will find this uncomfortable or upsetting, and this suggests that a facilitator with professional skills to identify discomfort and work with it would be advantageous. Accepting the fact that people have a relationship with themselves is important, and this means appreciating that people can be accepting of their own image, but equally can be critical, punitive and obstructive if a negative self-image is present (Sudbery, 2002). With visual images such as photographs, the therapeutic relationship can be enhanced by listening to what an individual says about their photograph, rather than the professional attaching their own meaning to the image (Weiser, 1999).

■ POSTCARD EXERCISE

When working with self-portraits, it is good to introduce the general concept of working with images before asking participants to produce their own self-portrait. I use two specific exercises before doing the self-portrait task.

The first exercise is an ice-breaker where I use a variety of images and spread them out on a table, asking the participant/s to select two images that they really like, and then explain why they chose the images. It is based on the use of spectro-cards (developed by Halkola, in Loewenthal, 2013) which are postcard-sized abstract images traditionally used in phototherapy with a trained counsellor where a participant is encouraged to pick a number of images from a selection laid out in front of them and talk about why they chose the ones they did. The spectro-cards have been used in research by Loewenthal (2013) and Saita et al. (2014), but instead of spectro-cards, I use a selection of postcards for the ice-breaker. When this exercise is conducted in a group, the participants learn that there is no "correct" meaning for an image, and everyone interprets images differently.

The second exercise asks the participant/s to find a meaningful image on their camera (or whatever device they are using) that they would not wish to be deleted or lost. I also encourage people to use photographs they may carry with them in their purses/wallets too. Again, they are then encouraged to say a bit about the image they have chosen. This makes participants aware of the importance of our emotional attachment to photographs.

After these two exercises, participants are generally more relaxed about the concept of working with photographs and, importantly, talking about photographs.

Theory to consider when working with exploration of "the self"

The exploration of photographic self-portraiture reveals the dominant theoretical approach is psychodynamic theory (Nunez, in Loewenthal, 2013; Berman, 1993; Ziller, 1990; Phillips, 1986). Psychodynamic theories stem from the work of Freud and have been built on by other theorists to facilitate workers in their practice to help understand behaviour based on relationships, motivation and emotions (Brearley, in Lishman, 2015; Payne, 2014). Payne (2014) explains that working with vulnerable clients should involve the consideration of internal psychological pressures experienced by the client, alongside how they are affected by external social factors. The difference in these two factors may cause disequilibrium between the client and their environment, and it is the job of professionals to help the client address attitudes and reactions caused by internal psychological pressures, as opposed to directly trying to change the external social factors, which may require resources beyond the means of professionals.

The work of Sigmund Freud is a good starting point to understand the implications of psychodynamic theory when working with therapeutic photography. At this stage, it is important to note that an in-depth knowledge of psychodynamic theories is not essential within therapeutic photography as the work of phototherapy (as discussed in Chapter 1) will tend to use this approach, but an awareness is very useful.

Freud believed that every human has an instinctive biological drive but that they long to maintain homoeostasis which is affected by a three-way struggle between the id, the ego, and the superego.

The id relates to the unconscious component of an individual's mental life where primitive instincts drive actions, but where unpleasant memories and repressed emotions are also stored which continue to influence behaviour. The superego relates to how an individual has been nurtured, which contributes to how the wants of the id are met and will impact on how moral values are developed. The ego manages the relation between the id and the superego and will work to protect the id if the superego is unable to provide what the id wants.

Central to Freud's driving forces is the concept of anxiety, which is an emotion created when homoeostasis is not achieved. The ego then has to create defence mechanisms to cope with this (Brearley, in Lishman, 2015; Payne, 2014; Borden, 2000).

Repression is one of the more common defence mechanisms employed by the ego and leads to memories that are painful, threatening or highly emotionally charged, being seemingly *forgotten* by the conscious part of the mind. These memories take root in the unconscious and resurface at a later date in coded forms such as behaviours and emotions, often directed towards people who had nothing to do with the original memory (Brearley, in Lishman, 2015). Splitting often arises when an individual has had to deal with contradictory emotions in their relationship with others, which leads to the individual viewing others as all good, or all bad, and stems from an inability to view other people in their lives as holistic beings capable of both good and bad actions. This leads to the mental compartmentalising of other people in their lives – if needs are being met then the person is good, but when needs are not being met, the person is bad. This can often be accompanied by the defence mechanism known as projection, which sees characteristics of the self being externalised and attached to another person. The purpose of this defence mechanism is to remove unwanted qualities of the self from the unconscious and place them on others (Brearley, in Lishman, 2015; Payne, 2014). Brearley (in Lishman, 2015) notes that not only are negative qualities ascribed to other people, but also positive aspects can be attributed, resulting in the idolisation of others.

▓ CRITICAL THINKING

Other ego defence mechanisms include:

- *Sublimation* – where impulses from the id are satisfied by a substitute object in a socially acceptable way; for example, redirecting aggressive impulses into sporting activity.

- *Displacement* – when emotions are redirected at a substitute object.

- *Rationalisation* – when the real reasons behind activities are repressed and explained by other, more acceptable reasons.

- *Denial* – where the truth is too painful to handle and the mind refuses to acknowledge reality.

- *Regression* – where the mind reverts to an earlier phase of development where it felt more comfortable and behaviours at this stage can manifest (Brearley, in Lishman, 2015; Payne, 2014).

Thinking about your own experiences, do you recognise any of these defence mechanisms in your behaviour?
Do you recognise them in other people's behaviour?

Midway through the 20th century, psychodynamic theorists began to challenge Freud's view and moved towards a relational perspective which recognised the importance of conscious decision-making and motives, but also viewed the quality of relationships and interaction with the social environment as important for personality development (Borden, 2000). These theorists included Adler, Jung, Klein, Winnicott, Bowlby and Erikson, all of whom contributed to the professional knowledge base by recognising that human beings are social creatures and are influenced in their development through their interactions with others. Borden (2000) explains that it was the work of Suttie (1999) which drove the relational perspective; he believed that problems stemmed from the dynamics of the family, social and cultural circumstances, as opposed to purely biological influences.

Nunez (in Loewenthal, 2013) and Martin (2009) refer to the work of Winnicott in their approach to self-portraiture with photography. Winnicott (1971) wrote about mirroring and recognised that developing children have to rely on others to meet their needs. In a caring relationship, when a child exhibits a need, that need is met, which demonstrates to the child that they exist and that their actions will result in corresponding reactions, much like looking in a mirror and learning from the reflection. This mirroring relationship contributes to the development of the identity of the child, a process Winnicott referred to as the formation of a *true self* (Beckett & Taylor, 2010). However, a *false self* can also develop when a child is inadequately mirrored and the needs of the child are ignored or unmet. This false self is a defence mechanism which sees the feelings and needs pushed into the unconscious while the child becomes preoccupied with trying to second guess how significant caregivers are going to act. Winnicott recognised that caregivers can never meet all of a child's needs constantly, but parenting had to be *good enough*. He also recognised the importance of the transitional object in helping a person mature from a protective relationship into a new relationship with the wider world, or a stage of relative safety into a more unpredictable stage. For children, this can often be an old toy or blanket which they will eventually emotionally outgrow, but the importance of photographs as transitional objects has also been suggested by others (Prins, 2013; Hills de Zárate, 2012; Weiser, 2004). Borden (2000) believes that Winnicott's work in psychoanalysis has made him one of the seminal figures within therapeutic practice, and along with the other relational theorists he drove forward the object relations movement.

▨ HUMOUR IN SELF PORTRAITS

Mary was asked to produce a self-portrait that captured a positive aspect of her self, so she produced the following image.

She said she rarely saw the back of her head, so she worked out how to photograph this through the positioning of bathroom mirrors, and capturing her sense of humour. As she delved deeper into the meaning behind the image she revealed that she would never dream of taking a "selfie" as she did not like to see herself in pictures, stating that all she saw was an old woman staring back at her, but photographing the back of her head was acceptable.

Throughout the experience of engaging with the therapeutic photography exercises, Mary explored her changing identity, her role as an ex-carer since her husband had died, and her move towards a new identity where she could live life just meeting her own needs and not the needs of another vulnerable adult. She appeared to use the photographic exercises to help her come to terms with her new identity, exploring feelings of guilt and sadness, but also feelings of relief and hope. It seemed that by mirroring her image, she was able to begin the process of finding her true self.

Another significant theorist for practitioners to consider is Erik Erikson (1963) and his eight stages of psychosocial development, which took Freud's theory of psychosexual development and applied the cultural and social impacts on these. Freud believed that children begin life by seeking gratification for needs:

- The first is oral, where needs are met by taking food in through the mouth.

- The second is anal, where a child learns that they have parts of their bodies that they cannot always see and that excretion needs to be managed.

- The third is phallic, where the same sex parent is identified with and the child learns about appropriate family relationships.

- The fourth is the Oedipal stage, when the child is attracted to the opposite sex parent, ending in latency when social learning redirects attraction towards people outside the family (Payne, 2014).

Erikson (1963) believed that these factors influenced development, but his approach to ego development differed from that of Freud in that Erikson did not believe that individuals are solely driven by internal factors and that development takes place across the life stages. He proposed eight stages of development across the lifespan at each stage of which an individual must deal with a psychosocial crisis; for favourable outcomes to be achieved, an individual must resolve each one with a larger share of experiences, which fosters learning towards the positive polarity of each crisis. If favourable outcomes are achieved at each stage, the developing adult ends up with positive basic virtues (see Table 4.1). Much like Winnicott's recognition that parenting needed to be *good enough*, Erikson did not advocate an entirely positive outcome at each stage (indeed, he argued that this was not possible), but that the ratio only needed to be favourable for healthy development (Gibson & Gibson, 2016).

Table 4.1: The eight stages of development by Erikson (1963)

STAGE	Psychosocial crisis	Positive outcome	Age
1	Basic trust vs basic mistrust	Hope	Infancy
2	Autonomy vs shame and doubt	Will	Early childhood
3	Initiative vs guilt	Purpose	Pre-school
4	Industry vs inferiority	Competence	School age
5	Ego identity vs role confusion	Fidelity	Adolescence
6	Intimacy vs isolation	Love	Young adulthood
7	Generativity vs stagnation	Care	Midlife
8	Ego integrity vs despair	Wisdom	Maturity

Self-portraiture provides a means to explore identity, and Erikson recognised the importance of identity. His fifth stage concerns itself specifically with ego identity, which was the starting point for his definition of the eight stages as he worked backwards and forwards from this one stage, recognising the crucial importance of identity formation and how it impacted on everything else. He believed that the combination of the ego's ability to adapt to all previous stages that incorporated Freud's psychosexual development, the skills learned as a person moves from childhood through puberty and into adulthood, and the opportunities offered by society should all culminate in a positive identity for the individual (Gibson & Gibson, 2016; Erikson, 1963). However, if outcomes from previous stages have been negative, and opportunities within the environment and society are not positive enough, Erikson believed that the individual may experience a loss of identity because they can over-identify with others and try to project their diffused ego image onto others to see if they can gain clarification through reflection.

The impact of each stage can be considered when working with images. The first stage of basic trust versus basic mistrust can underpin the initial engagement between client and facilitator. If a person experiences many negative experiences which culminate in a suspicion of the world around them, then it may be that they find it very difficult to trust other people and open up to them. The advantage of therapeutic photography, in this respect, is that it does recognise issues of control and endeavours to place the power with the client. However, the challenge may be to continually engage a client who has trust issues long enough for them to realise the positive power dynamics. Similarly, stage two can also impact on initial engagement as it recognises the impact of experiences when a toddler begins to explore their environment and the feelings of safety and encouragement they receive from their caregivers. If encouragement is consistent and reliable, then the toddler learns to be determined and understands their influence on the world around them, but if they are constantly chastised or berated for exploration, then they develop shame within themselves and doubt about the environment. If these feelings are carried into later life then a person may become suspicious about trying new things.

In many cultures, stage three coincides with the start of primary school education where a child is thrust into a new environment and learning becomes a strong focus of development. Encouragement is important at this stage for a child to develop initiative in order to develop purpose, and responsibility, and develop new skills. If the child experiences too much criticism or punishment for not achieving, then the risk is that they internalise the guilt they feel and the more inhibited they may become. Again, this might mean that a person will not readily try new things for fear of failing at the outset. Therapeutic photography has no "right or wrong" way of producing images, so this should free participants from feeling that they have to "achieve" when taking part.

Industry versus inferiority addresses the later years of primary education and hypothesises that children begin to rein in their creative play and learn the rules of society in order to conform to expectations. This can seem quite a bleak and stark observation, but what Erikson recognised was that the developing child now has a much wider social circle and they learn social skills from everyone around them. They should be encouraged for their endeavours, but at the same time, not pushed to be over-achievers as this could result in someone having a narrow virtuosity.

As explained above, stage five was the one that fascinated Erikson and initiated his studies in the field of identity development. Peer learning and peer support become vital components in the lives of teenagers, where people try to find out where they fit in with certain social groupings. Stigma and labelling become much more evident and can shape actions and reactions. This can be a significant point to consider when thinking about delivering a therapeutic photography group. If potential participants have struggled to fit in with peers in the past, then there might be suspicion and mistrust, yet if isolated participants can work together they can discover that they have similarities and can learn support strategies from one another. The main crux of this stage, Erikson believed, was answering the question "Who am I?" which, in essence, is what working with self-portraits aims to answer.

Erikson wrote that stage six begins at around 18 years old, but it should be noted that he primarily wrote about American cultures in the latter part of the 20th century. It could be argued that society has significantly changed, resulting in children living at home longer, and thus the age at which stages start and end should be viewed as moveable. In stage six, the importance of forming and maintaining relationships outside the family becomes the focus. The purpose of experiences at this stage is to learn about love for another person, for community and for society. If learning is negative, the risk is that a person will simply isolate themselves from all relational experiences.

Middle adulthood extends the concept of love from stage six and views the raising of a "new" family, the development of a career, and contributing to the betterment of society as vital components. There is a risk at this stage of over-exertion, where someone tries to be too productive in all walks of their life, and the end result may be a physical and emotional burnout. Sometimes we hear the term "midlife crisis" and this might relate to a person trying to acquire new skills or talents in order to be seen to be productive and generating output. On the other side of this, Erikson highlighted that stagnation could occur, where a person becomes rejecting of the world around them and gives up caring about the society they live in. An important component of therapeutic photography which has not really been highlighted yet is that it is fun. It is easy and creative, and allows a person to stop and think about what is important to them, thus giving them important rest and relaxation which, at the stage of generativity versus stagnation, might be required.

The final stage, ego integrity versus despair, is an opportunity for a person to reflect on their life, their achievements and their future course of actions. The challenge at this final stage is to not become preoccupied with the past where "things were better", and to develop wisdom about the life lived. Within therapeutic photography there are often many opportunities to use images from the past, and explore feelings, memories and emotions from bygone times, but the purpose must always be to look at the future, and what can be learned from these images.

■ APPLYING ERIKSON'S THEORY

To illustrate how Erikson's theory can be utilised in therapeutic photography I want to give an example from a group of carers I worked with. Brian was a young man in his 20s and he presented the following image when asked to find a photograph with significant meaning.

He explained that this was his dog standing on the golf course where he worked. It was a frosty morning so the flag was frozen mid flutter. He had inherited the dog from a friend who had an emotional breakdown, but he felt he could care for the dog as he had time in between his part-time job, his role as a befriender to a young man with learning disabilities, and caring for his grandmother.

Brian shared a lot of information about his childhood with the group and portrayed a loving family who travelled because of his father's work. He also explained that he had had an emotional breakdown himself. According to the writings of Erikson (1963), Brian was now in the stage of intimacy versus isolation, where he should begin to explore adult relationships alongside a strong sense of his own identity. However, from his narratives there was a sense that he wanted to portray purpose in his everyday activities – his caring responsibilities, his befriending and his employment – but all left little time for his own needs and all suggested a heavy leaning towards "industry" from stage four of Erikson's writings. From the information Brian offered to the group, he explored a childhood that involved a number of moves from location to location because of parental employment, something Bronfenbrenner (1986, 1992, 2009) also recognised as being a significant impactor on an individual from events that occur in his "exosystem". Brian's schooling may have led to him becoming an over-achiever, or alternatively, he may have withdrawn from education because of repeated experiences of change. The revelation of mental health issues and, in his own words, a "breakdown" in early adulthood, suggested a culture of striving for achievement, which had had a negative impact on his well-being and self-esteem.

Through sharing his images with the group Brian received positive feedback and appraisals of his images, and he also allowed himself time to indulge in photography, an interest that was purely for himself. At the same time, he was spending time with other individuals doing the same and learning from them that it is okay to have time for yourself. Using Erikson's stages, the hope was that redressing the balance in previous stages would impact on the current stage, so helping Brian to recognise issues from the past would allow him to revisit stage five of ego integrity versus role confusion. This might assist him to come to terms with his upbringing, gain a sense of how he now fitted into society and develop a stronger sense of self.

Borden (2000) believes the importance of psychodynamic theories in professional practice lies in the fact that they help to enhance understanding of intrapsychic processes so that the client can look for other ways to manage experiences that cause conflict. Key to this is the therapeutic alliance wherein the professional will show empathy and can explore experiences, narratives and learning to help modify the client's self-perception and representation, as well as address emotional issues (Ogden, 2009; Borden, 2000). Borden (2000) also highlights the fact that a therapeutic alliance does involve mutuality in that the client and professional should both be involved in the process. The power should be shared and the professional should be a co-participant, willing to learn from the client and empower them to explore solutions.

> In the broadest sense, relational perspectives seek to encompass biological, psychological, and social domains of experience and to link concepts of person and environment in process-orientated models of human functioning. (Borden, 2000, p.366)

Summary

When working closely with clients to address issues of self-worth, self-esteem and identity it is important to consider working from a relational standpoint, both in forming therapeutic relationships to enable change, and in understanding relationships and the complexities within these (Borden, 2000; Suttee, 1999). These complex relationships begin with the individual and how they feel about themselves. As Weiser (1999) identified, any therapeutic intervention needs to begin with an exploration of self-perception as it is important to accept who you are before looking for acceptance from others.

Psychodynamic theory has developed from a belief that all behaviour is driven by the motivation of inner drives to an encompassing view that external influences play an equal role in defining identity. The by-product of any problems this may cause is *anxiety* (Ruch, 2005; Howe, 1998), and the ego may work to protect the inner self by engaging defence mechanisms. A knowledge of these can help practitioners address them when they arise and, as Erikson (1963) explained, assist clients to reflect on issues in order to seek clarification of the self.

Using the technique of therapeutic photography may help to bypass defence mechanisms through the *objectification* of an issue; the photographer makes an issue tangible by giving it form, and it can then be discussed in its externalised form. However, the relationship with the self is only one of many relationships that the application of photography can creatively explore, as Chapter 5 will go on to explain.

USING PHOTOGRAPHY TO EXPLORE RELATIONSHIPS

Being human is a social activity and we are all exposed to a multitude of relationships throughout our lifespan, perhaps the most relevant experiences being the ones that relate to our own family members. This chapter explores these formative relationships and suggests how photographs can be utilised to open up dialogue about relationships. To do this, some of the key authors will be introduced and the reader will also be guided through theories which attempt to shape our understanding of relationships within families. Throughout the chapter, exercises will be explored and examples will be given of the type of information elicited.

■ VISUALLY EXPLORING RELATIONSHIPS

Working with photographs in a therapeutic manner involves creativity and exploration, and occasionally it also offers up the opportunity to work with pre-existing images when clients bring in older photographs of their family. These insights should be explored when presented, but exercises can also be used to explore relational issues.

One such exercise asks the client to produce two photographs – one to represent how they see themselves, and another to represent how others see them. This should be left deliberately vague as it is up to the client to choose who "others" are. It might be a family member, friends, or society at large; the choice is up to the client and creates further opportunity to explore why the "other" has been chosen.

Another exercise you could try is to ask the client to take an abstract photograph to represent a person in their life. Again, the content of the image invites exploration and interpretation using some of the theories outlined in this chapter.

Photographs to understand relationships

Family photographs are a link to the past; images can display unity, cohesion, rituals and chronicles of the development of family life. The concept of "family" is not an easy one to define as every family will be affected and shaped by history, sociology, psychology, culture, institution and relationships. Using family photographs can be a useful starting point for exploring relationships in general by looking at the boundaries of the family and how they have impacted on an individual (Hirsch, 1997). Family albums can be a rich source of autobiographical storytelling, and images also contain non-verbal communication such as facial expressions and body language, as well as historical and cultural references. Traditionally within western culture, family photograph albums document success: birthdays and weddings, celebrations and holidays. The ways in which photographs are presented can also be telling, for example gaps in chronology might suggest the family was facing particularly challenging times, which were obviously not photographed. There are also cultural variations to the family album as it is not uncommon for some societies to photograph the dead so that they have a complete record of a person's life from cradle to grave. Ultimately, the traditional family photograph album acts as a public relations document for the family (Martin, 2009; Weiser, 2004; Berman, 1993).

Ulkuniemi (2007) believes there are four different ways in which family photographs are commonly used:

1. In relation to the traditional family album, photographs *document* historic events and preserve memories.

2. Photographs are used as iconic symbols – on walls, in wallets, and on mobile phones – to bring *unity* to the family and are even used to provide a visual reminder of a relative who has passed away.

3. Photographs provide opportunity for *interaction*, an area which is showing growing popularity on social networking sites such as Facebook, Flickr and other photo-sharing sites. Showing photographs can be inclusive and adds another dimension to a person's life when they can enhance their stories using visual examples.

4. Photographs aid in *building the identity*. Looking back at a photo collection can reaffirm your life journey so far and gives opportunity to relive experiences at a later date.

These four areas do not require the need of a formal therapist or counsellor to facilitate the use of photographs and Ulkuniemi (2009) highlights the benefit of exploring family photographs in peer groups, as social patterns that impact on identity formation can emerge through the conversations.

Family photographs are closely tied to memories. Research into the construction of memory suggests that one of the main contributors to how they are formed is the way in which autobiographical narratives are retained by an individual (Brookfield *et al.*, 2008). These autobiographical narratives are formed through storytelling and this includes stories told within families to bind and strengthen identity. Many of these stories are formed around visual prompts and materials that we have within the family unit, therefore these visual records can provide useful tools to help remember and access these family narratives (Spence & Holland, 1991). Photographs will contribute to these visual prompts, but they can also include a multitude of other items, and narratives may differ greatly as each person will have their own interpretation of the memory. Weiser (2004) explains that within a story, a narrative is constructed using linguistics to verbalise memories, and family photograph albums are constructed using a sequence of images, but like any story, the family album is not an objective historical document but rather a subjective construction by the album's maker, which is open to interpretation by every family member who can incorporate their differing viewpoints into their unique personal narratives.

Within formal family therapy, photographs are often used to look at times of change within the family unit. This might include using the images to look at power alignments within the family and to look at complexities of the different relationships between various members (Phillips, 1986). The theoretical underpinning builds on the Freudian approach, but also incorporates theories that aim to define and understand the quality of the relationship being discussed, such as Fairbairn's (1952) theory of object relations, as well as Bowlby's (1979, 1969) attachment theory, which recognises that the quality of the relationships experienced in childhood will impact on relationships formed in later life. Fairbairn (1952) looked at how an infant will internalise aspects of positive (pleasurable) and negative (painful) experiences and then carry these through to adult life in a process known as "transference" which unconsciously informs relationship formation. Freud (in Yerushalmi & Yedidya, 1997) hypothesised that the unconscious brings memories to the fore via visual means such as dreams and fantasies, yet he favoured verbal techniques to elicit information from his clients. Others argue that because many childhood memories are in the unconscious, photographs can help to access these and bypass the censorship of the conscious. As most therapeutic relationships rely on verbal information, using a visual component as an added sense can aid the communication of meaning and message (Yerushalmi & Yedidya, 1997; Feder & Feder, 1981).

The main argument for using family photographs to understand the dynamics within the family unit is that they provide a window which gives insight into how internal relations interact with the external world. Again, this is tied up in non-verbal cues, what Stern *et al.* (1998) term "implicit relational knowing" (p.302), which is largely unconscious but not in the Freudian way of being repressed or removed. This implicit relational knowing is gathered through our interactions as we go through life – we naturally gather conscious material but at the same time will be adapting ourselves so that we can connect with people we like, and avoid people we do not like. This unconscious material is stored as implicit memory, which Stern believes can be accessed through our non-verbal behaviour and body language (Rodolfo de Bernart, in Loewenthal, 2013). Hence, using photographs to look at non-verbal behaviour and body language is a useful starting point for accessing the implicit relational knowing.

Working with family photographs assists in identity formation and clarification but the taking of family photographs is not a static phenomenon and over the past 100 years has seen some considerable changes. At the beginning of the 20th century, photographs recorded the dignity of life, rites of passage, and the formal recording of the developing generations; at the beginning of the 21st century, photographs record fun aspects of life, the family playing together, and the emphasis on leisure time. It used to be the case that exploration of body image and open displays of feelings and emotions were taboo, but nowadays these are common images in our family albums or on social networking sites, and modern-day taboos may consist of illness, the monotony of everyday life and work, failures and hard times (Ulkuniemi, 2009).

Identity is also not a static phenomenon, but Slater (1995, in Ulkuniemi, 2009) warns that identity is becoming tied into the consumerist way of thinking and that presenting our image is becoming more important than being represented by our image, an aspect of self-presentation which Goffman (1959) referred to as *impression management*. Images are becoming more and more public and social networking sites are being used to tell others about the experiences we are having, the events we have been to and the active lives we engage in; the danger here lies in how we decide which photographs make up our true identities, and which make up our *digital* identities (Martin, 2009; Van Dijck, 2008).

Van Dijck (2008) believes that photography now plays a major role in identity formation, and with the ever-increasing use of social networking sites, photo blogging and camera phones, the role of the photograph as a means to capture memory is now secondary to photography's function as a tool for communicating one's identity. He recognises the importance of the camera within family life and notes the writing of Sontag (1977), wherein the taking, organising and presentation of images helped the family understand their connections while documenting ritualised moments of development, but points to the work of Harrison (2002), whose research has suggested that self-presentation has become the main function of photography. This shift is attributed to a change in culture, alongside developing technology, which has allowed a younger generation to use photography to facilitate peer bonding and conversation.

> Individuals articulate their identity as social beings not only by taking and storing photographs to document their lives, but by participating in communal photographic exchanges that mark their identity as interactive producers and consumers of culture. (Van Dijck, 2008, p.63)

The consequence of this is that generational perceptions of identity through photography may differ depending on the participant's experience with photography. Where people once took photographs on film and had them printed onto photographic paper so that the image became a tangible object, the digital photograph has become a means to share experiences which can become transient in nature

(Kindberg *et al.*, 2005). Kegan (1982, 1994, in Modlin, 2015) states that we perpetually interpret meaning from our surroundings across the lifespan, and in adulthood the two main systems are *socialised* and *self-authoring*. The socialised adult has the capacity to identify with others, share beliefs and values and empathise, whereas the self-authoring adult becomes more autonomous and does not rely on the validation of others as much. This might suggest that the photographic experiences described by Harrison (2002) and Van Dijck (2008) are activities for enhancing the socialised meaning system, but deeper analysis of the image is an activity for the self-authoring meaning system.

Using photography within family work can also have practical applications. Genograms are often used in a wide number of settings, including social work, counselling, psychology and medicine, and aim to provide a pictorial overview of family generations and relationships within. Often, symbols are used to represent family members but by including photographs this can provide a visual layer of communication that can be read to elicit non-verbal communication and body language. When using photographs in genograms there are three parameters used to read the pictures:

1. An interactive parameter aims to understand how people within the image relate to one another through their interactions.

2. A relational parameter looks at the generations and the narrative of the family to try to identify specific patterns that may repeat over time.

3. A symbolic metaphoric parameter is used to establish whether there are underlying meanings or messages attached to the images selected for the genogram; for example, the image might provoke a memory which may not be immediately apparent from the image, but for the person who selected the photograph the memory can be very vivid (Rodolfo de Bernart, in Loewenthal, 2013).

Brookfield *et al.* (2008) point to the importance of using photographs when engaging in life story work with adopted children. Again, this work involves looking at the narrative and should construct an accurate history so that the adopted child can have some coherence in their journey through care; it should aim to strengthen the child's resilience and build on attachment by recognising positive experiences with people in their past. However, the tendency is that challenging experiences will be omitted and this can result in an incomplete narrative which may hinder the child in the future when they try to locate difficult events from their past.

As well as assisting the exploration of relationships, attachment theory also underpins the use of photography in bereavement. Within family therapy, photographs of the deceased are used to evoke associations and to investigate unresolved grief. Research suggests that the older we get the more important photographs become as they can provide repositories for memories, so much so that it has been suggested that photographs of people who have passed away can provide a "tenuous immortality" (Csikzentmihalyi & Halton, 1981, in Johnson, 1999, p.232).

Photographs that include significant others create opportunities to explore the relationships and bonds between the object and the photographer. These opportunities arise from using pre-existing family images and new photographs to open up a dialogue which allows for the exploration of family issues and can reveal a multitude of memories but also values, culture and beliefs. Sudbery (2002) also highlights that any work that attempts to explore relationships invites issues that may arise into the professional relationship between worker and service user. It may be that some of the difficulties experienced by the service user are transferred into the working relationship, projected onto the worker, or cause emotional disturbance; therefore, it would be advantageous if a professional working to explore relationships has a good theoretical understanding of how these are formed and how they impact on behaviour.

■ THEORY TO ASSIST IN THE EXPLORATION OF RELATIONSHIPS

Jane was asked to photograph how she sees herself, and how others see her. She thought about this for a week and then returned with two images. In the first was a Care Bear, a soft toy from the 1980s, and she described this as how other people saw her. She said she is perceived as being "soft and cuddly". As she was showing this photograph within a group, the other members agreed with this and gave her positive feedback about her image.

However, she went on to say that this image is not who she is, and produced another image of an iconic toy from the 1980s, a Rubiks Cube.

She had deliberately posed this image so that the cube is not sitting in its perfect form. The colours are not in order, and the angles are not aligned, and there is a strong shadow being cast. She explained that this is how she sees herself, a complex character with a dark side. Being a child of the 1980s, she had used icons from this time in her exploration.

The purpose of this task was to explore discrepancies between the two images, and in Jane's images there was a clear difference. Yet, she was able to verbalise to a group of people she had only known for a few hours that she felt like this. They explored her Rubiks Cube image in more depth, asking her to elaborate on how she felt and to talk about her depression (represented by the shadow). This was an opportunity to explore her real self with an interested group of peers.

Gerhardt (2006) explains that the human being is a social animal and because of this our physical and emotional development is shaped by social interactions. Howe and Campling (1995) also believe that humans are defined by the quality of social relationships, and experiences of previous relationships will shape how individuals handle new relationships. Howe goes on to explain that because workers in caring professions often deal with clients who are in distress, or cause distress, they are dealing with people's emotions that are likely to be in a heightened state and it is therefore important that effective working has to be underpinned with a good knowledge of the human condition, including why certain reactions might be provoked by stress and anxiety.

The family life cycle

Arguably, the first experience individuals have of relationship formation occurs within the family unit. A good introduction to working with participant photographs which may address family issues is to consider the family life cycle. The family life cycle encompasses a number of different theories and, much like Erikson's eight stages, proposes that a family moves through a number of sequential stages in its lifespan. It also recognises that many of these changes can cause anxiety, so Freud's recognition of adaptation to reduce these emotions is present, along with psychological transitions occurring around losses and changes experienced. Carter and McGoldrick (1988) adapted the family life cycle from the work of a sociologist (Duvall, 1977), who recognised that the transitions families experience are also impacted by socio-logical pressures and expectations, which drew similarities to the work of Bronfenbrenner and his ecological systems theory model. Their work, along with the work of Alan Carr (2003), offers practitioners eight generalisable steps that families will transition through.

1 The origin family

This is the core of the family unit and is applicable to young children and how they may view their home environment. Ideally, the family should be viewed as a safe place to explore from and return to. It is a place of security, warmth and understanding and offers routine and predictability where needs can be met. At this time, a child learns about their role within the family, and this will often be defined by the overall identity of the family. Sometimes a family can carry a reputation, be it as a family of achievers, or a family of trouble makers. This label can define how individual members view themselves and how they might conform to, or rebel against, these ideals. As the child grows it enters the world of nurseries and schools, but still returns to the familiarity of the family unit at the end of the day.

2 Leaving home

In the late teens to early 20s, a child parts company with the parental home and moves off to start an independent life. They carry with them their identity from experiences throughout their childhood and teenage years, but now have to continue building on that identity and testing it in the wider world. This will involve becoming involved in new relationships, possibly even experimenting with new behaviours with an unfamiliar peer group. Independence brings autonomy, and to enable this, income must be sourced to fund this new freedom. The relationships with parental figures are adjusted to reflect these new, mature responsibilities, and it is a time to explore sexual relationships and find equilibrium in adult-to-adult relationships.

■ CRITICAL THINKING

This is clearly a period of significant transition and can bring about a number of emotions for an individual. In Chapter 6, we will look at exploring emotions, but this is an area that invites exploration through photography. You could encourage participants to look back and pictorially represent lessons learned that will be important in the future, or you could set tasks to look at hopes for the future.

Try to remember the emotions you experienced at this time in your life – it may have been going to university, starting a new job, or going travelling for a significant period of time. Could you represent these feelings and emotions in an abstract manner?

3 Pre-marriage

At this stage, Carter and McGoldrick (1988, 1999) recognised that there should be stability within the romantic relationship, where monogamy with one partner should prevail. It is a period where an individual's identity finds compatibility with another person, and this process will naturally involve trial, error and adjustment. Ideally, the identity of an individual should be enhanced by this relationship, and the future is considered in light of these experiences.

4 Married (pre-children)
Commitments have been made and a new partnership is legally formed. Traditionally, this would have been viewed as a period of significant learning and readjustment because the couple would have moved in together for the very first time, but nowadays it is commonplace for couples to have been cohabiting for years before this stage, so those lessons would now be more applicable to stage 3. Regardless of how the couple adjust, there is also recognition that marriage brings a new set of extended family members into the lives of the newlyweds, and new relationships to explore for each one.

5 Family with young children
The arrival of children brings with it new roles and responsibilities, and the identity changes again to take on these new labels – those of mother or father. These changes will also have an impact on finances, lifestyle and relationships, as other new parents are introduced into their lives. It might invite a period of reflection to consider how styles of parenting influenced current experiences of being a new parent, and this might invite an adjustment in relationship styles with older generations within the family. Of course, new roles are introduced to the older generations as well, and parents become grandparents. After many years, the education system is also re-entered, but this time as an interested observer, rather than a direct participant. A different appreciation may arise as individuals realise that there are many societal issues that they cannot protect their children from.

■ CRITICAL THINKING
If you are at this stage yourself, or have been through this stage, it is worth reflecting on how you felt back in stage 1, when you were within the folds of the "origin family", and how parents feel now, at stage 5, when they are trying to provide the safety and security within the "origin family", but have to buffer societal issues and pressures. This is also an interesting exercise to explore through photography,

looking at hopes and fears, or strengths and weaknesses, in a visual form.

In one group, Jenny was exploring her own upbringing in a rough area of the city where she felt isolated and scared. She later moved to a small village by the sea to raise her own family and took the following image:

She called this image "blown away" and explained that this was her daughter. Together, along with two other children, they had faced adversity, but had grown as a unit. Now that her daughter was getting older, Jenny realised she couldn't protect her from everything life threw at them. Therefore, she was able to express through her image the feelings associated with having a teenage daughter and the process a mother goes through when independence and autonomy are sought by the child.

6 Family with adolescents

Within the family unit, further readjustment becomes inevitable as young children develop into teenagers and seek autonomy. They seek their own identity among new peer groups and this can cause friction and concern to parents. Alongside this, the older generation may become frailer and require care, particularly parents from the "origin family". It is a time to be aware that roles may subsume identity.

▊ FAMILY ROLES

The issue of roles came to light in an exercise with a group of carers. The group were asked to take two photographs – one to represent how they saw themselves, and another to represent how others saw them. Jeff took the following image to represent how others saw him.

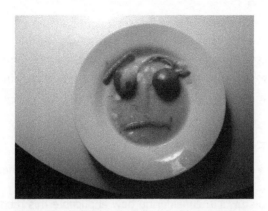

He explained that the plate of food represented "providing nutrition" and he believed that other people saw him as a provider. Because he cared for his wife, she viewed him as a carer; because he had teenage children, they viewed him as a "taxi service"; and, generally, he provided financial security and shelter for the whole family. He then went on to explore his identity beyond these roles and spoke about the image only offering a partial truth about who you are, because knowledge only comes from interaction, and from this knowledge comes a deeper understanding. He then finished his explanation by adding humour and stated that the face in the plate looked a bit odd, much like himself!

7 Family with children leaving/just left home

The time comes for children to move away from the family home, and this loss of children from the home environment is a major transition to deal with which brings with it many emotions. When considering the emotions at stage 2, we now see the situation reversed as the parents have to deal with what they put their own parents through so many years ago. As the children explore their own social circles, new relationships enter the family – children may marry and bring a new set of in-laws into the fold, and the birth of more children might see an additional role for parents, as they become grandparents. Meanwhile, the ailing health of parents from the "origin family" may result in death, which requires significant psychological adjustment.

8 Later life

The final stage acknowledges the significant decline of physical health and well-being and the impact that has on the family. At this stage, the carer often becomes the cared for. The reliance on one's children becomes greater as they become the focus for meeting ailing needs. Loss increases as independence declines, loved ones die, and eventually, you die. However, throughout all of this loss, it is also a time to reflect and relish the wisdom gained throughout a lifetime.

▓ YOUR FAMILY LIFE CYCLE

How does this family life cycle apply to your life? What stage are you at?

It is also worth considering how applicable this model is to the lives of people you know. I am assuming that there will not be many people who fit neatly into this model as it assumes a progression of a "perfect" nuclear family, and, as we know, in society these are few and far between (Carr (A.), 2003). There is no consideration of factors such as homosexuality, childless couples, divorce, long-term unemployment, education in later life, or criminality, yet this model does outline a perceived norm, and if we cannot live up to these perceived norms and expectations, that too may cause anxiety. This means we should not dismiss the model as it does highlight times in the life of a family where anxiety and pressure can occur. These are natural "pinch points" in the life cycle, and do not mean that a family should be defined as "bad". It is useful information for professionals to be able to consider these pressures with clients and help them identify and process these issues.

Family systems

Traditionally the word "family" conjured up images of a heterosexual couple with children who lived in the same household, but Walker (in Lishman, 2015) warns that this assumption is outdated and that professionals need to recognise the wide diversity of family units within today's multicultural society. Consideration needs to be given to issues such as ethnic diversity, extended families, lone parent families, same sex partnerships, unmarried parents, divorces, stepfamilies, as well as adoption and fostering. Working with families, from a professional perspective, may take a systemic approach which views an individual as functioning within a number of systems and subsystems, and defining their identity from these interactions (Minuchin, 1974; Burnham, 1968). Genograms are often used with clients to build a picture of the family unit and can be useful at both the assessment and intervention stage. They can be drawn with symbols or pictures to represent family members, but Rodolfo de Bernart (in Loewenthal, 2013) argues that using photographs is a more effective method of building up a genogram and allows exploration of systems outwith the immediate family that images from the photographs offer up. Berman (1993) also argues that the potential for using photographs to explore family systems, and dynamics within, is a rich source of information.

■ APPLYING BOWEN'S THEORY

When working with photographs and listening to the narratives of clients, Bowen (1993) offers up interlocking concepts which are worth considering:

- Has the client got a good sense of self? If not, and if self-esteem is low, there is a greater risk of peer (and family) conformity. Bowen (1993) termed this *low differentiation* and suggested that this leads to a client viewing their identity as part of a collective or group. To be accepted by a group, there needs to be conformity and acceptance of roles and values, and this is also true of a family. If the family is entrenched and interdependent, then any change affecting one family member will impact on all family members, leading to greater stress and anxiety.

- As stress and anxiety increase, how are family members managing this? The risk is that anxieties are externalised onto other family members, particularly the marital partner, and a battle for control may ensue. Sometimes anxieties can be projected onto another family member and they become the focus of the problems within the family and are scapegoated for all the issues. Or, another alternative is that all family members withdraw from one another and emotionally shut down to protect themselves.

- Is scapegoating leading to problems? If a family member is being scapegoated, they may "act out" behaviours that they are being accused of, thus creating a self-fulfilling prophecy – if they are being accused of the behaviour, why not do it anyway?

- Are issues multigenerational? Bowen (1993) recognised that history within families has a tendency to repeat itself. If a family is entrenched and preoccupied with each other's problems, they cannot differentiate and see themselves as an individual, free of the confines of the family, and will likely seek a partner who is also equally entrenched in their own families. When they have children, the pattern repeats.

Much of the theory used in family therapy stems from the work of Minuchin (1974), who believed that the structure of a family needed to be analysed to find the source of any issues or problematic behaviour (Walker, in Lishman, 2015). Minuchin (1974) states that repeated transactions within the family unit will establish family norms and structure. This structure is then maintained by two systems: a *generic* system, which governs how families are organised and delineate lines of power, and an *idiosyncratic* system, which sets forth mutual expectations of family members. This system should be adaptable and there should be clear boundaries for every member of the unit. In turn, analysis of these boundaries can determine whether the family has become disengaged (where certain members become peripheral and separate), or enmeshed (where family members have a heightened sense of belonging and a loss of autonomy) (Burnham, 1968).

An analysis of boundaries can also help understand the subsystems. There will be a number of naturally occurring subsystems within each family unit, for example parental subsystems, sibling subsystems, and parent–child subsystems (Janzen & Harris, 1986). If the boundaries of a subsystem become confused and affect a person's role within a family, they can become problematic (Minuchin, 1974). To give an example, a mother might begin to use her daughter as a form of support if she is having problems with her husband, a situation which may result in the daughter becoming a confidante and "friend" for her mother, leading to isolation of the father, and ultimately leading to role confusion for the daughter.

Triangulation is also an issue to consider when working with families and it occurs when a two-person system experiences anxiety and brings a third element into the relationship in the hope of providing stability (Janzen & Harris, 1986). This third element can be another family member, a child, or even an issue, such as alcohol use. Sometimes, the triangulation of the relationship can provide homoeostasis, but it also has the potential to become perverse and pathological (Haley, 1967). It is important to note that homoeostasis could also be problematic if the effort to maintain this is not always serving the interests of all the family (Janzen & Harris, 1986). Through discussing family issues and structures, a professional also has the opportunity to explore whether there are explicit and established family rules that govern the behaviour of family members, and also whether family myths exist that define expectations of the family members and their relationships with others (Janzen & Harris, 1986; Minuchin, 1974; Burnham, 1968).

The work of Klein (in Mitchell, 1986) and Fairbairn (1952) developed object relations theory which proposes that human beings are driven by the need to form and maintain relationships with significant others. Klein surmised that young babies see the world from a paranoid schizoid position where the main carer is viewed as either all good or all bad, depending on how needs are met. However, this viewpoint soon moves into a depressive position and the baby realises that the main carer is not split into *good carer* or *bad carer* but is actually a whole person who is capable of being both good and bad. This is the beginning of the integration of the ego and the beginning of synthesis between internal and external situations. At times of difficulty and stress, an individual may revert to a paranoid schizoid position and be unable to see another person for both their good and bad aspects, simply viewing them as all good or all bad, but healthy relationships should be able to move back into the depressive position (Beckett & Taylor, 2010; Klein, in Mitchell, 1986).

Fairbairn (1952) further developed Klein's theory and took the standpoint that healthy relationships involve the capacity to invest the self into a relationship, while accepting something back from the other person, thus making the relationship reciprocal. However, when needs are unmet or punished in childhood, splitting occurs and unpleasant experiences are buried in the unconscious within two clear domains – the libidinal and the anti-libidinal. The libidinal part of the unconscious contains the feelings associated with having needs that were not met by the primary carer such as the carer being unavailable, or love being withheld. In contrast, the anti-libidinal part houses emotions associated with being shamed or punished. Fairbairn (1952) proposed that every human being will have elements of a libidinal and anti-libidinal ego, but where childhood experiences have resulted in strong, dominant libidinal or anti-libidinal egos, they can adversely affect relationships in adulthood. This might mean that a dominant libidinal ego might seek out partners to meet unmet needs from their childhood and exhibit behaviour often described as clingy and needy, whereas a dominant anti-libidinal ego might isolate themselves for fear of being hurt in adult relationships, and to hide their own emotions. As a result, an individual is not seeing their partner as a whole person if the partner is only satisfying a certain part of the whole ego. Again, this is an unconscious defence mechanism and is not a conscious decision that a person makes (Gibson & Gibson, 2016; Gibson, in Lishman, 2015; Borden, 2000).

■ CRITICAL THINKING

With therapeutic photography, it is what is said about the photograph that carries significance, and, when exploring relationships, it is often worth applying object relations theory to see if it can assist in understanding dynamics.

The best way to do this is to consider the theory in two separate parts – how the client has internalised previous experiences, and how this shapes their view of relationships.

If we begin with the client's view of themselves, we need to recognise that we are dealing with three components:

1. The central ego, which is the part of the self that is conscious and aware.

2. The libidinal ego, which is the part of the unconscious self that supresses emotions related to not having all of our needs met when we wanted them met, resulting in frustration and questioning about how loveable we are, and neediness and clinginess at times of stress and anxiety.

3. The anti-libidinal ego, which is, again, part of the unconscious self where emotions relating to feelings of rejection and punishment are suppressed – this results in punitive behaviour towards others at times of stress and anxiety.

Central ego

Libidinal ego

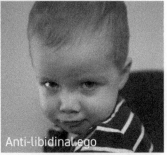

Anti-libidinal ego

If we have experienced a lot of uncertainty and unreliability when growing up, we may have a dominant libidinal ego. If we have experienced a lot of punishment and rejection when growing up, we may have a dominant anti-libidinal ego. This will define our behaviour when our central ego is no longer able to function normally. These may not be behaviours we "wish" to display, but at times when we lose control, they will be our default behaviours due to our experiences growing up. Our behaviours in adulthood are defined by our unmet childhood needs and emotions.

Now we must consider how this defines behaviours towards other people, and the impact this might have on our choice of relationships. Again, there are three components to how the ego relates to another person. Ideally, in an adult relationship where we accept that everybody has strengths and weaknesses, the client's central ego relates to the ideal object of another person, the real person with all of their good and bad points. The ideal object also excites, and sometimes rejects, and that is why, unconsciously, the libidinal and anti-libidinal ego relate to the exciting object and the rejecting object. This can become problematic if a client has a dominant libidinal ego, making them needy and clingy, as they will be attracted to the exciting object (rather than the ideal object) and expect the person to meet their needs. This is unattainable within a long-term relationship because someone cannot remain an exciting object forever. Similarly, an anti-libidinal ego within a client can quickly decide that they are relating to the rejecting object in another person, concluding that they are bad and cannot be trusted or relied on, thus immediately shutting down any emotional connection to them. Again, they are not relating to the ideal object, only the rejecting object, but the dominant anti-libidinal ego does not want to experience childhood emotions and moves to protect.

Ideal object

Exciting object

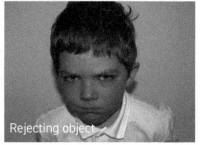

Rejecting object

OBJECT RELATIONS IN PHOTOGRAPHS

As the actions of the libidinal and anti-libidinal ego are unconscious, the practitioner has to watch and listen for signs of these in how the client narrates the content of images with regards to relationships. However, you could ask the client to take three photographs to represent how they feel about themselves – one to represent how they believe they are viewed, another to represent their strengths, and a third to represent their weaknesses. Or, you could ask them to pictorially represent another person, again using three images – one to represent how they generally perceive that person, one to capture their strengths, and a third to capture their weaknesses. These will give useful insight into how the client relates to others.

Early and GlenMaye (2000) warn against solely looking for problems and issues within relationships and suggest that professionals need to take a strengths approach when practising with families in order to allow clients to define and attribute meaning to their situations. They believe that the homoeostasis that keeps families together, including traditions and myths, and the systems in which they are embedded, means that they are already drawing strengths from these resources. If working to empower clients, professionals needs to highlight existing coping strategies and build on these. To do this, Early and GlenMaye (2000) explain that a professional needs to form a collaborative relationship with the client and be guided by them in all areas, from initial assessment, right through to evaluating the intervention, and they also highlight the importance of considering resilience.

Gilligan (2004) states that the more resilient a person is, the better they are at avoiding the impact of adversity when faced with challenges. He explains that resilience is built up when an individual experiences repeated interactions with favourable elements of their environment. Daniel and Wassell (2002) highlight six areas where these favourable elements can be built up:

1. Experiencing a secure base which a person feels safe to explore from, and safe to return to.

2. Engaging in education.

3. Establishing friendships based on patterns of secure attachment (which will be discussed in Chapter 6).

4. Developing talents and interests.

5. Having positive values and feeling able to contribute to society.

6. Having good social competencies to facilitate communication and engagement with society as a whole.

Gilligan (2004) points out that resilience may well occur in only one or two of these domains, rather than all six, but where domains of resilience occur, these can be viewed as protective factors. In considering resilience, a professional is considering relationships with the wider world, which mirrors Bronfenbrenner's ecological systems theory model. Gilligan (2004) states that professionals must try to understand clients in their own social contexts and attempt to identify their whole needs. In doing so, there is more opportunity for a therapeutic alliance to develop, and it is this trusting relationship that is often the most productive element of professional, therapeutic contact (Gilligan, 2004). Folke (2006) also believes that considering resilience factors alongside socio-ecological systems is not only useful for identifying where strengths lie, but also for identifying where there is capacity for development.

Summary

People form relationships based on their own experience of being in a relationship, and for the large majority of people, the first relationship experienced is the parental one. Here, the foundations are laid and an individual builds up beliefs in the world around them based on feelings of safety and trust in their carer and in the environment. Good experiences result in a strong sense of self and a positive internal working model, but negative experiences during formative years may result in a poor internal working model and suspicion of the world around us (Gibson & Gibson, 2016; Bowlby, 1969).

Knowledge of family relationships can provide the professional with an insight into the internal working model through the expression of beliefs, values and attitudes, and this insight can be used to create interventions that give the client control or structure which can be useful in addressing anxiety within problematic areas.

Psychodynamic and relational approaches encourage introspection and an examination of past experiences to see how they have shaped lives, but these experiences also need to be viewed in situ with the environment, culture and society to consider external factors that may be problematic (Folke, 2006; Gilligan, 2004).

■ Chapter 6 ■

USING PHOTOGRAPHY TO EXPRESS EMOTIONS AND ATTACHMENTS

In Chapter 5, the concept of using photography to explore relationships was introduced, and in this chapter, the idea will be furthered by looking at using photographs to represent, in an abstract way, emotions linked to feelings that may be difficult to verbally explore. To do this, focus will be placed on attachment theory, and the work of John Bowlby (1969, 1979, 2008) and Mary Ainsworth (1989) will be applied. Sue Gerhardt's (2006) work on brain development has also been linked to attachment and will be brought in here, before looking at "normal" emotions people experience and how these can be captured in an image with the purpose of exploring the accessibility of these to an individual. Problems in conceptualising images at this stage can indicate underlying issues which can be explored through the photographs.

Introduction to attachment

Knowledge of attachment theory is one way for practitioners to assess the quality of relationships the client has with others. In the 1950s, Bowlby (2008) introduced the concept of attachment theory for understanding the quality of the caregiving relationship between mother and child. Since then, his theories have been developed by a number of other authors, including Ainsworth (*et al.*, 2014), who worked to classify the insecure attachment styles through an experiment known as the "strange situation", and Howe (1995), who recognised that the importance of attachment goes beyond childhood as it continues to impact on relationships throughout all stages of the life cycle. This chapter will explain the concept of attachment theory across the lifespan and highlight areas where therapeutic photography can be beneficial when attachment theory is being considered. In order to do this, we must consider when attachments become significant, and how they impact on behaviours.

Bonding

When we form emotional connections with another person, we are *bonding* with them. This general term describes an inbuilt human need to connect with other people. For many, the first bonding experience a human will have is in utero; from the moment a pregnancy is discovered, a bond forms between the parents and the developing foetus – the bump is stroked, calming voices soothe, and often a name is given to the developing foetus to give it character. Of course, this may not always be the case, and there are a number of things that can affect bonding at this stage, such as mental and physical health, the movements within the womb, the development of the foetus, and the level of excitement surrounding the pregnancy (particularly if it was not expected or wanted). All of these issues feed into the early process of attachment.

Once the baby is born then bonding serves more of a purpose. The baby is not bothered about emotional connections at this early stage, they are concerned with survival, and bonding serves to meet needs. To do this, babies have an inbuilt ability to seek out the face of the person who is holding them by turning their head towards them (Christiano, 2008). As the infant develops, feelings of safety and security should accompany the visual sights of the face of their carer, and so begin the early stages of mirroring.

The concept of Winnicott's (1971) mirroring was introduced in Chapter 4 and describes the process of learning through reading other people's facial expressions. If a baby smiles, it has no concept of what its face is actually doing, but the reaction it gets from the carer is warm and friendly, so the baby associates that action with pleasure, warmth and security, thus is more inclined to repeat that action. Beckett and Taylor (2010) state that when mirroring is positive, the "true self" will flourish and a strong sense of identity will prevail, but if mirroring is inconsistent or unresponsive, the infant pushes these unpleasant feelings into the unconscious and spends time trying to guess how it should act to have needs met by the carer, and a "false self" emerges.

It is here, in the emergence of the "true self" and "false self", where the early seeds of attachment are sown.

It is also worth noting that mirroring also refers to the holding environment a child is raised in, one where needs should be appropriately responded to so that a child can learn how to self-regulate – realign their emotions at times of distress, sorrow or excitement. One vital component of this is learning about their emotions. If a child is upset, ideally the carer should be saying to the child, "It's okay, you're feeling sad", and this statement should be adjusted for all emotions experienced as a child explores the world around them – happiness, joy, fear, surprise. These are all valid emotions and all there to be experienced, yet if we are not taught that these emotions are "normal", then they can feel scary and overwhelming.

SIX EMOTIONS

It is from this acknowledgement that emotions are experienced by us all, and should be a normal part of our development, that our next exercise is derived. This task is called the six emotions exercise and asks clients to take one photograph to represent each of the emotions of fear, sadness, anger, surprise, joy and love.

The client should then end up with six images, one for each emotion. The idea behind this is twofold: it encourages abstract thought which should lead to creative expression, and it gives "permission" to connect with our emotions and think about what each one means to us and how we express it.

Throughout this chapter, I have presented some of the images produced during this exercise – some have been revealing and offer alarming insight into thought patterns, while others are stark in their simplicity, which invites questioning into whether that emotion has ever been properly explored and experienced by the client.

Attachment

If bonding is concerned with the emotional connection between two people, attachment focuses on the quality of the connection. Bowlby (2008) recognised that the quality of the affectional bond between a child and the primary caregiver had an impact on coping strategies and skills. The safer a child feels in their connection with the caregiver, the more likely they are to explore their surroundings, thus learning and developing in an appropriate manner. Bowlby (2008) believed that developing children form a view of the world around them in three stages:

1. Through observation, a child learns about the physical world around them.

2. They then observe their primary carer to see how they behave in this physical world.

3. They then ascertain how they are expected to behave.

The interaction of these three components, Bowlby believed, forms the *internal working model* for the child and allows them to predict what is going to happen in their environment – their behaviour has an impact on the physical world, and on their carer. In an ideal situation, their needs will be unconditionally met, but if the primary carer struggles to cope in the physical world, resulting in unpredictable behaviour, the infant spends time adjusting their behaviour in an attempt to make everything okay – this might involve hiding their own emotions so they avoid upsetting the carer, or it might mean that they have to overtly express emotion to get attention in order to have their needs met. This is the basis of attachment theory, which Bowlby suggested provided a blueprint for how to deal with future relationships.

When we talk about attachments, there is no such thing as "no attachment". Humans are social animals and we need relationships to survive, therefore, as young children, we are predisposed to form relationships with people who interact with us, no matter how good or bad the interaction is. Ainsworth *et al.* (2014) developed an experiment known as the "strange situation" to look at behaviours and attachments and created a scenario where a parent and child were interacting together in a room, a stranger entered the room and the parent left. The reaction of the child was then gauged, and, importantly, the parent re-entered the room and the reaction of the child was again noted. Three distinct patterns were noted throughout the experiment:

1. Some children got distressed when the parent left, but were consoled when the parent returned and soon calmed down.

2. Some children got distressed when the parent left, and remained distressed when the parent returned and appeared inconsolable.

3. Some children did not get upset when the parent left, and did not give much regard to the parent when they re-entered.

These three styles were named secure, anxious ambivalent, and avoidant respectively. A fourth style was later identified by Main and Solomon (1986), which was termed "disorganised".

Secure attachment

This is the ideal when looking at attachment styles. It denotes a relationship a child feels safe to explore from, and safe to return to. The child is able to express themselves without fear of reprimand, and without having to suppress their own emotions so as not to upset their main carers. It signifies that there is age-appropriate autonomy within the relationship, and the child has built up trust in the world around them. This arises from experiencing care where the child feels they are listened to, they can express feelings and emotions without being punished, and are able to reach emotional stability from this relationship, which later contributes to learning about self-regulation. These elements are important for professionals to recognise because they are all factors of effective therapeutic working with clients. In essence, the therapeutic milieu replicates that of the feelings associated with a secure attachment – supportive communication, warmth and empathy, trust and autonomy.

■ THE JOY OF SEARCHING

One of the advantages of using photography as an intervention is that it allows the client to enjoy the process of exploration. As the client has a camera in front of their face, it becomes socially acceptable to stand in strange positions and stare at things for an inordinate amount of time! As a result, many participants report that they have noticed things around them that they had never noticed before.

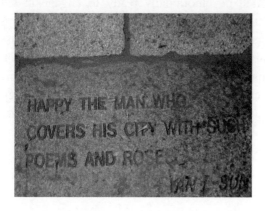

One such example happened during the emotions exercise when a participant returned with the image above to represent joy. She said that she had walked around the city for over 30 years, and it was only because she had a camera in her hand and was looking for "joy" that she noticed the writing on the pavement. The words – "Happy the man who covers his city with such poems and roses" – made her smile, and she was surprised that she had never noticed this before. When she showed this image, the other participants also expressed joy at the words, and confessed that they had never seen this either, so she walked over to the inscription and pointed it out to everyone.

Anxious ambivalent attachment

Within Ainsworth *et al.*'s (2014) "strange situation", the child displaying an anxious ambivalent attachment style was upset when the parent left the room, and remained upset when they returned. The experiment continued by repeating the process again, and what they observed was that the child did not really want to play with the toys in the room; instead, they just watched the parent to make sure they were always present and were not going to go away again. Emotions towards the parent from the child tended to be anger and frustration, followed by anxiety, and this can denote inconsistencies in parental attention when needs have to be met. The child has learned that there is no predictability in how they achieve their carer's attention – sometimes crying and laughing works, other times they get no response – and this results in confusion for them when trying to ascertain an internal working model of the world around them and how to behave.

The result of these inconsistencies is that the child may become clingy as they are anxious that the parent/carer will leave them and not return (Fonagy, 2003). Gerhardt (2006) also highlights that the child will often be emotionally ready to engage in behaviours to attract attention from the carer at short notice, resulting in a child who may seem volatile and "attention seeking", but this is simply a survival strategy they have developed in order to react to situations quickly to have their needs met. What this means for the anxious ambivalent child is that they rely on others to regulate their emotional outbursts because they have never really learned how to self-regulate effectively.

▨ EXPLORING ATTACHMENT

Danny wanted to find an image to represent *joy* and was walking around a small seaside town. He happened across an old-fashioned sweet shop selling jar upon jar of confectionary and chocolate. He explained that he was immediately transferred back to his childhood and remembered being taken to shops like this with his pocket money and being allowed to fill a small paper bag with a selection of treats of his choosing.

This allowed him to reminisce further about his childhood and about living abroad and moving from location to location because of his father's work. This meant that he never really settled in one place and had to make new friends wherever he went. His father was often absent for long periods, and was tired when he was at home.

When Danny took this photograph the shopkeeper asked him what he was doing in an accusing manner. He apologised and quickly left the shop, but after a few minutes he returned to the shop and apologised for taking the photograph without first asking permission. The shopkeeper was understanding and they continued to chat about his project.

Through conversations with Danny it was clear he had an anxious ambivalent attachment style – he freely admitted he tried to meet everyone's needs, to the detriment of his own, and did not like people thinking negatively about him.

Avoidant attachment

Where the anxious ambivalent style denotes unpredictability in the relationship between parent/carer and child, the child displaying an avoidant style has a much more predictable environment in which they grow and develop, but this predictability has taught them that they must become self-sufficient as their needs may not be met when they arise.

Within Ainsworth *et al.*'s (2014) experiment, the avoidant child did not get distressed when the parent/carer left the room, and did not appear to be that interested when they re-entered the room. This may appear as if the child is emotionally absent, but in reality, the child has learned to suppress these emotions into the unconscious because they have realised that emotional displays do not result in needs being met.

Avoidant children have learned that it is not a good idea to express emotions. This may be because there have been adverse reactions to doing this in the past, or simply that their cries go unaided, so they give up. As a result, avoidant children can appear to be very independent, but this comes at a cost because their internal working models also learn that they cannot trust others to meet their needs and will carry this belief into future relationships. Because they may feel they are not worthy of their carer's attention, they may develop low self-esteem and self-worth.

■ SUMMARY OF ATTACHMENT

There is nothing inherently *wrong* with these three attachment styles; they are all simply survival strategies for coping with the world around you, and specifically coping with relationships. They help a developing child form some kind of predictability of their environment and give them a blueprint to base future relationships on. Admittedly, there can be consequences in later life with regards to anxious ambivalent and avoidant styles as they do tend to produce considerable anxiety for the individual, which may lead to behavioural problems and mental health issues in adulthood.

When using therapeutic photography with children it is very useful to keep these styles in mind because of the element of control within the technique:

- An avoidant child has low trust in others, but good trust in themselves, which means that practitioners should allow the child to feel that they are master of the task they are doing, and that the child is educating the practitioner.

- An anxious ambivalent child has low trust in themselves, but a high sense of trust in others. Practitioners need to foster the therapeutic relationship with this knowledge, reassuring the child that the task in hand is being achieved, and that they are interested in what is being explored – remember, there is no "right" way to take a photograph, therefore it is an achievable task.

Disorganised attachment

Of all the attachment styles, a disorganised attachment causes the most concern. Identified by Main and Solomon (1986), it describes extreme and adverse reactions to situations caused by experience of relationships. Anxious ambivalence recognises unpredictability in relationships, but the disorganised attachment style magnifies unpredictability to distressing extremes. This might manifest in violent outbursts, or moments where a child appears to be frozen in fear, but the concerning thing is that it is difficult to predict reactions.

A disorganised attachment may signify abuse or neglect within the relationship. As a result, the child cannot form any predictable reactions to situations – any reaction they engage may result in adverse reactions from the parent/carer, and they live in perpetual fear, constantly on guard, a situation Hesse and Main (2006) term *fright without solution*.

Identification of this attachment style poses issues for the professional as it may require more complex interventions to address and rectify the situation. However, it is entirely plausible that working with a client may trigger old memories, and exhibited behaviours may be a product of these experiences. The body is trying to deal with immense and oppressive feelings of anxiety, and defence mechanisms simply want to make those feelings go away, so behaviours will be engaged to make that happen.

Any child experiencing a disorganised attachment will have low trust in themselves, and low trust in others, so in any intervention, the skills lie in building trust initially so that the client can feel safe to explore through their images. Again, the fact that therapeutic photography places control in the hands of the client should assist, but bear in mind that control might also be frightening for a client experiencing disorganised attachment, so be prepared to slowly explore feelings and emotions, alongside trust.

VISUAL EXPRESSION

The visual representation of emotions invites creative and adaptive interpretations which can often give deep insight into a lived experience. In this image, the emotion of *anger* has been captured. This was taken by a carer and he explained that he had been drawn to the rope which, for him, represented tension. However, another carer in the group said that she also saw the emotion of anger in the image, but for her it was about restraints.

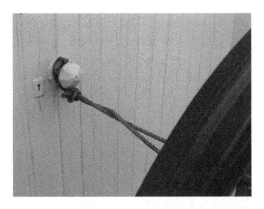

For both carers, there was recognition that their personal situations resulted in restricted freedom. They were bound by duty, as well as lack of formal care provision, and this resulted in feelings of frustration and anger. This image created further opportunities to explore these emotions in a peer setting, and when linked to identity formation there was learning in terms of social identity and the roles people have to adopt, and adapt to.

Links to brain development

The implications of childhood attachment have also been linked to neurology and the development of the brain in young children. Gaskill and Perry (2011) have identified neurosequential development of the brain which is linked to the experiences we have as we grow up. This means that as we are exposed to new situations and environments we are also exposed to new emotions and feelings which contribute to how our brains develop.

The limbic area of the brain is found at the top of the brain stem and this is the section which is responsible for emotions and arousal within the body, particularly our basic instincts, including our fight or flight responses. This area of the brain is regulated by two different systems known as the sympathetic and parasympathetic nervous systems that work to help manage brain and body functioning by releasing cortisol to facilitate the increase or decrease of our heart rates and our breathing. This, in turn, helps manage stress, anxiety, muscle tension and the health of our internal organs. The sympathetic system helps us at times of arousal or stress and gives us the ability to react quickly to alleviate any risks. Conversely, the parasympathetic system aids us when we are at rest and helps us to relax. Babies and young children do not have full control over these systems so must learn how to manage them through observing responses from their carer and mirroring or reacting to these. When we link this information into what we know about attachment theory we can see that if a baby is left in a state of high arousal (crying, anxious, stressed etc.) then the sympathetic system keeps producing cortisol and the baby is unable to relax (or self-soothe); however, in times of extreme anxiety the parasympathetic system automatically takes over and floods the brain with a chemical mix to immediately relax the system. As a result, the body freezes and we can see the unusual response in a child where they appear to be unable to react to a situation. If this continues, then the natural equilibrium of cortisol production is jeopardised and the neurosequential development of the brain is impacted (Bernard & Dozier, 2010).

The other important aspect of brain development occurs in the cortex, specifically the pre-frontal cortex and the orbito-frontal cortex, which are located behind the forehead. The orbito-frontal cortex links to the visual aspects of the right-hand side of the brain which is largely responsible for managing emotional responses. This aspect of brain development relies as much on nurture as nature for appropriate development, and the role of others to facilitate learning is essential. Without caring, consistent feedback, the brain will miss out vital learning about higher social functioning such as empathy, reasoning, and problem-solving skills (Schore, 2000, 2001; Gerhardt, 2006; Gibson & Gibson, 2016).

Therefore, without good attachments, the development of the brain can be compromised through lack of appropriate learning, and a risk of chemical imbalance. This, in turn, risks missing out on learning about appropriate emotional responses and, as a result, may expose a person to subsequent mental health issues later in life.

■ WHAT IS LOVE (PART 1)?

The six emotions exercise is a chance to explore understanding and interpretation of emotions. Often it is a chance to normalise these emotions, but at other times it can give you an insight into areas of emotional deficit. In a number of occasions, overly simplistic representations of an emotion can be photographed and this invites an opportunity to explore why this is. In the photograph above, the client photographed the emotion of *love*. It is a simple representation. Through further discussion, the client was able to express issues within her relationships. She had been raised in residential care because her parents did not want her, she had developed mental health issues in later life, and because of this she became isolated and mistrusting of relationships. Starkly, she revealed that she had never experienced love. Therefore, if you have not experienced something, it can be very difficult to represent that emotion in an abstract way.

Attachment in adulthood

Through adolescence, our own experience of attachments help us form relationships with peers, and when we reach adulthood, most of us will be seeking appropriate relationships with a partner. Yet the need for safety and security never appears to wane and our experiences of attachment in childhood go on to influence how we select partners in adulthood. Bowlby (1979) identified the importance of *affectional bonds* when forming significant relationships with another person and described this as the need to seek closeness, comfort and proximity. Ainsworth (1989) also recognised the significance of affectional bonds when adults seek life partners and identified that these bonds feel exclusive and create emotional closeness between two individuals which drives them to a desire to be mentally and physically together.

When this is not possible, distress and emotional turmoil are experienced.

Within adult relationships, there should be a didactic element to these wherein both parties benefit from the union. A sexual element does not necessarily denote an affectional bond within adult relationships; instead, there should be obvious signs of support for the individuals involved, namely psychological, emotional and physical. However, the types of relationships we seek out are influenced by our internal working models because they define our expectations (Hazan & Shaver, 1987). Bartholomew and Horowitz (1991) researched attachment in young adults and concluded that the internal working model shapes expectations of the self, and of others, and has significant influence on self-esteem, an area which the practice of therapeutic photography aims to address. They concluded that:

- secure attachment = good self-esteem and good perception of other people

- avoidant attachment = good self-esteem but poor perception of other people

- anxious ambivalent attachment = poor self-esteem but good perception of other people

- disorganised attachment = poor self-esteem and poor perception of other people.

This suggests that our own attachment style may drive us towards a particular type of relationship so that we can gain certain things from the relationship, based on unmet needs.

Bartholomew and Horowitz (1991) suggest that the attachment styles from childhood develop into adult attachment styles based on observations of trust, and opinions of relationships. For children who experience a secure attachment, this should continue into adulthood with the attachment style remaining secure. This means that the adult should be relatively autonomous, trusting, have a good self-image and feelings of self-worth, and be able to commit themselves to the intimacy of a close relationship.

The attachment style of anxious ambivalence continues into adulthood as a *preoccupied* attachment, which means that the adult becomes entrenched in other people's lives and other people's stories. Much like the clingy nature that is evident in childhood, the adult style of preoccupied attachment also exhibits clingy and needy behaviour where relationships are sought in order for the adult to feel needed and wanted. Self-esteem and self-image are low, so the adult finds it difficult to believe that anyone actually wants to be with them and often becomes suspicious of their partners, leading to behaviour that can be overbearing because they constantly seek reassurance from their partner. In order to maintain relationships, the preoccupied adult will often place the needs of their partner before their own. Sometimes this results in the adult seeking out relationships with a partner who has significant problems so that they can be seen as rescuing them.

■ WHAT IS LOVE (PART 2)?

Simone, by her own admission, was isolated and wanted to have a relationship with another adult. She had children and recognised that caring for them was underpinned by *love*, and she loved them unconditionally, hence this image of the pandas to represent the emotion. Simone also exhibited a preoccupied attachment style as she often spoke about putting the needs of others before her own, and the way in which she described episodes in her life meant that she could often become entrenched in the lives of other people. She described being fond of the community she lived in, and was an active participant in many events. In another picture, she had photographed her son at a carol concert at Christmas time, but he was not in the centre of the picture as she had also tried to include her neighbour's children in the image as they did not have a camera.

Using photographs to help Simone explore her own issues actually helped her to contain her narratives and restricted opportunities to go off on tangents to involve other, less important, characters.

If a child advances into adulthood with an avoidant attachment style, this becomes a *dismissive* attachment. A dismissive attachment style denotes an isolated individual who chooses to avoid many relationships for fear of being hurt. This is a protective strategy that means a person becomes very self-reliant and can have a strong sense of self-identity, but this comes at the cost of intimacy. Often, a dismissive adult can reinvest energies into other areas of their lives and aim to achieve in other domains, such as their career. Achievements become important to them and these may not always be positive – becoming notorious in your community might be viewed as an achievement to some. Dismissive adults also like to be in control and view emotional expressions as a sign of weakness, believing strength comes from self-sufficiency.

◼ CONTROL

The aspect of control is an important consideration when using therapeutic photography with a person who may have a dismissive attachment style. Because the participant chooses what to photograph, who to show the photograph to and what to say about the photograph, there are several stages of "choice" in the process. This allows a high degree of control within the technique and, for a dismissive adult, this is attractive as they have the power within the dynamic.

In one group, I worked with Roger, who was very suspicious of forming relationships and preferred his own company to that of others. His comments were aimed at alienating himself from other people around him and he tried to be deliberately provocative so that people would stay away from him. However, as we progressed through some photographic exercises it became clear that he enjoyed taking pictures, and other people were interested to hear what he was saying about each image. This encouraged him, and gradually he opened up.

When he explored his upbringing with the group it was evident that he had grown up with a mother who did not want him around, and with no father, he had emotionally isolated himself to become an avoidant child, and a dismissive adult. However, through the photographs he found the control and power to acknowledge this.

The final adult attachment style to be aware of is the *fearful* attachment, and this stems from the disorganised childhood attachment style. Similar to the style in childhood, unpredictability underpins the fearful attachment style. The adult wants to be intimate with partners, but at the same time constantly fears loss or rejection, which creates high levels of anxiety. This may result in isolation, much like the dismissive attachment style, or can drive someone to be clingy and emotionally needy, much like the preoccupied style. Fortunately, it is difficult to maintain this attachment style and many adults will mature into one of the other two insecure styles of dismissive or preoccupied.

■ MENTAL HEALTH IN PHOTOGRAPHS

One of the consequences of an insecure attachment style may be poor mental health. The styles of preoccupied, dismissive and, particularly, fearful mean that an individual has to live with high levels of anxiety, which can be a contributor to poor mental health.

During an exploration of a local botanical garden centre, one participant, Julie, photographed a bridge over a small stream which was filled with rocks and fish. She explained that the image represented the emotion of *fear*. This surprised the other participants because the picture looked so tranquil and lush. Julie began to explain that she cannot walk across a bridge without thinking about jumping from it – she had constant suicidal thoughts. She went on to talk about bridges that she had to walk across in the centre of the city, some high ones crossing motorways, and some crossing rivers, and one, in particular, that was notorious in the city for suicide attempts. She spoke about the feelings she experienced when she was on any of these bridges, and the voices that spoke to her when she was there.

Julie used this photograph to explore a deep-rooted issue for her, suicidal ideation, which her peer group was able to identify with and to empathise with her emotions. Because the session was facilitated by a professional with a social care background, she was also able to get advice on how to seek support for the issue she had disclosed.

Establishing the style

George *et al.* (1985) devised a set of questions known as the "adult attachment interview", which sets out to help practitioners define what kind of adult attachment a client has. The questions ask about the upbringing of the client, and about their experiences of being parented in comparison to their experiences of parenting (if they have children). The questions themselves are designed to elicit information from the answers given and explore areas where loss and change have been experienced and where trauma and stress may have been prevalent, and look at patterns of attachment throughout development. However, the way in which the questions are answered can also give an indication of attachment style too. The person asking the questions needs to consider how coherently the answers are given, how concise the narrative is, how logical the explanations are, and how the answers appear to impact on identity. There is no exact script for asking the questions, but the basic structure of the adult attachment interview is as follows:

1. Can you tell me about your family? Where were you born, and where did you grow up?

2. How would you describe the relationship that you had with your parents?

3. Which five adjectives would you use to describe your relationship with your mother?

4. Which five adjectives would you use to describe the relationship you had with your father?

5. Were you closer to one parent? If so, who and why?

6. When you were upset as a child, can you remember how you acted and what you did?

7. What is your earliest memory of being separated from your parents?

8. Can you describe memories of ever feeling rejected when you were a child?

9. As a child, did you ever feel threatened by your parents?

10. Now you are an adult and looking back at your relationships with your parents, how do you think this has affected you?

11. Why do you think your parents behaved as they did when you were a child?

12. Besides your parents, were there any other significant adults involved in your life as you grew up?

13. Are you able to describe any memories of the loss of a loved one when you were a child? And as an adult?

14. Have you experienced any traumatic incidents within your life?

15. During your teenage years, how would you describe your relationship with your parents?

16. And now, in adulthood, how would you describe your relationship with your parents?

17. If you have children, how do you think you cope when you are separated from them?

18. If you have children, where do you see their lives leading them in 20 years' time?

19. Have you learned anything about yourself from answering these questions?

20. How do you think your own children would describe your parenting skills?

(Adapted from George *et al.*, 1985)

The way the questions are answered should fall into one of the following four categories:

1. *Secure* – answers are logical and coherent and there is a clear flow in the narrative. The client has a good sense of who they are, and their role within the family and the wider environment. They are reflective and have processed previous

losses and changes in a satisfactory manner. There should not be any defence mechanisms evident.

2. *Dismissing* (avoidant attachment) – answers given will be very short and to the point. There will be little detail offered and virtually no emotional engagement with the answers. Answers will probably be superficial in manner as the client does not want to explore issues in any depth. Unpleasant periods will be glossed over, or may even appear to be forgotten as there is an attempt to minimise past experiences. There will probably be a strong sense of independence within presentation, and often an emphasis on the normality of their upbringing (using phrases such as "but that's just the way it was").

3. *Preoccupied* (anxious ambivalent attachment) – answers tend to be long and rambling, often going off on a tangent and involving a number of other characters in the narrative. There can often be considerable emotional entanglement in the lives of other people and it can be difficult to keep the client focused on the original question. Emotions can fluctuate between appearing to be very angry one moment, to quite passive and ambivalent the next.

4. *Fearful* (disorganised attachment) – answers are very disjointed and there is no clear, coherent narrative at all. Sometimes, unpredictable behaviour can be witnessed as the levels of anxiety experienced by the client when they are asked to explore significantly emotive periods of their lives become so overwhelming that defence mechanisms are engaged and they try to make the questioning stop.

The adult attachment interview is a tool to assist in the identification of attachment styles, and the practitioner does not need to be too directed by the 20 questions. Opportunities to use photographs will arise where discussions around the questions can be initiated; if a client is showing a family photograph album, then these questions could be introduced; and if a client finds one-to-one interviews intimidating, then introducing photographic exercises to explore these questions changes the dynamic of the interaction and focuses attention on images, rather than direct eye contact (Halkola, in Loewenthal, 2013).

Discussing attachment styles with clients raises awareness of patterns within relationships. It can give insight into how they were parented, and how they have incorporated many of their own experiences into their own parenting, and wider formation of relationships. By naming the styles and exploring the implications, clients can learn and identify common traits in their relationships, and may even be able to challenge themselves on some of their problematic behaviours. When working with attachment, the ideal goal is to help someone move towards a secure attachment, and part of that involves having a coherent narrative which can help in the exploration of upbringing and development. Using photographs uses the visual portions of our brains which have been working since birth. Mikulincer and Shaver (2008) highlight research which suggests that exploring narratives and learning about attachment aid the re-education of the brain to assist in becoming more emotionally attuned, resulting in behaviour that is compassionate, empathetic and altruistic.

▨ REFLECTING ON RESILIENCE

This image represents two emotions, *sadness* and *anger*. It was taken by a young carer who explained that when he feels either of these emotions he will go down to the water and throw stones into the waves to get a release. As he told this he went on to reveal that "emotions are easy", and explained that he had recently had a breakdown because of the pressures that were around him. Since then, he has found it much easier to recognise his emotional state, and deal with any build-up that could be detrimental. In his narrative, there was recognition that he was moving from a preoccupied attachment style towards a secure attachment.

Summary

Within practice, the four attachment styles are now recognised as i) a secure attachment, which is defined by a constant, positive and available relationship between carer and child; ii) ambivalent attachment, where the quality of the relationship is inconsistent and the child has to demand attention in various ways and therefore feels undervalued; iii) avoidant attachment, where the care is constantly unavailable and rejecting, and the child develops self-reliance very quickly; and iv) disorganised attachment, which is defined by unpredictable and frightening responses that are often accompanied by violence and abuse (Gibson & Gibson, 2016; Aldgate & Gibson, in Lishman, 2015). These attachment styles are mirrored in adulthood wherein those service users who formed secure attachments in childhood may be autonomous, secure individuals; those who experienced ambivalent attachments may be preoccupied, entangled individuals; avoidant styles may be demonstrated in dismissing, detached individuals; and disorganised attachment styles may be repeated in fearful, avoidant personalities (Gibson & Gibson, 2016; Howe & Campling, 1995; Bretherton, 1991). These styles are discernible from responses given in an interview known as the *adult attachment interview* (George *et al.*, 1985) where the ways in which questions are answered can direct practitioners to certain attachment styles. The 20-question format elicits direct responses to the answers, but by listening to the way in which the narrative is communicated (such as the amount of detail offered, focus on the subject matter, levels of anxiety displayed), insight can also be gleaned into certain adult attachment styles.

Attachment is adaptable and it does not automatically follow that an attachment style from childhood will define adult attachment styles; human beings will learn from different circumstances and relationships and will adjust internal working models to adapt, and professionals should be aware of this ability to change (Iwaniec & Sneddon, 2001). Aldgate and Gibson (in Lishman, 2015) believe that attachment theory can inform specific techniques such as genograms, eco-maps and life story work, interventions that some believe can be enhanced through the use of photography (Rodolfo de Bernart, in Loewenthal, 2013; Brookfield *et al.*, 2008). The value of considering attachment theory in practice also relates to the therapeutic relationship between worker and client. If the worker can provide a milieu that lets the client explore issues in a non-judgemental manner, where emotions and feelings can be considered, and where empathy informs communication, then the client can experience what a secure attachment should feel like and the relationship between the worker and client can be described as *earned secure* (Gibson & Gibson, 2016).

Chapter 7

USING PHOTOGRAPHY TO EXPLORE CHANGE

One of the certainties of life is that we will all experience change. Change can be positive and negative, planned or unexpected, but whenever it occurs it sets in us coping strategies to deal with the emotional upheaval we experience. The ways in which we deal with this psychological process are largely shaped by our history of dealing with change, and the skills we learn from those who raise us and befriend us.

Given that the practice of therapeutic photography is effective for people who are looking to address issues within their lives, enhance self-esteem, self-efficacy and empowerment, it is an intervention that benefits from an understanding of the change process. This chapter will outline the main components of loss and change and will give examples from groups as to how photographs can assist clients to work through these issues.

What is loss?

Loss can occur at any time. It may be completely unexpected, it may be planned for, or it may happen progressively over a long time period, but however and whenever it happens it can have a profound impact on a person. For professionals working with clients, it is an area that can often be overlooked, but should be dominant in our approaches:

> It is seen that many of the troubles we are called upon to treat in our patient are to be traced, at least in part, to a separation or a loss that occurred either recently or at some earlier period in life. (Bowlby, 1979, p.81)

Therapeutic relationships often form to help someone who is dealing with a situation or circumstance where change has occurred, and this change is usually as a direct consequence of a loss of some kind. One of the most obvious losses professionals come into contact with is a person dealing with bereavement, but there are many other types of losses which impact on a person's ability to cope, including a loss due to illness, loss of an identity or role (perhaps due to loss of a job), loss of power, or loss due to the process of ageing. The impact of loss depends on what has been lost, and this chapter will go on to look at the varying scale of loss and the process of dealing with the loss. It is also important to note that loss and change are situational experiences, but the psychological readjustment that arises from loss and change is known as the *transition*, and this will be discussed at the end of this chapter.

▧ EXPLORING LOSS

Consideration of loss, change and transitions when working with therapeutic photography is an important tool for understanding how a person is adapting to recent events. Anxiety is often experienced and this will increase depending on the scale of the loss.

Being able to objectify an issue and explore it at arm's length provides a degree of safety for the client, and this is why practitioners should have an understanding of these concepts and how a person may be transitioning through periods of change. Exploration of loss, change and transitions can occur during any exercise, but you may want to structure a particular photographic exercise to assist in the exploration of a recent event.

One such example asks a participant to think about a loss they have experienced that has impacted on their life. Ask them to take two photographs – one to represent how they felt about the loss at the time it happened, and another to represent how they feel about the loss now. The resulting images create an opportunity to explore how someone has adapted to the change they have experienced.

Freudian view of loss

Freud's writings on bereavement were influential on the psychodyna- mic movement and underpin how theorists attempted to understand the process of loss and change. At the turn of the 20th century, Freud (1957) wrote about "mourning and melancholia" where he attempted to differentiate between the two states. His view was that the process of mourning a lost person involves experiencing a multitude of emotions, which includes demotivation, painful dejection, disconnect from relationships and surroundings and an inability to express love. He noted that this is very similar to the state of melancholia, but that melancholia includes feeling a sense of worthlessness, and an expectation that punishment is deserved.

Freud went on to explain that the ego (which works to provide equilibrium for the id and the superego) becomes completely preoccupied by the loss that has been experienced and works to find a status quo again. It has to redress the balance between the energy that has previously been invested in the relationship which has gone, and the void that prevails. He termed the emotional energy invested into relationships "cathexis", and resulting withdrawal of this energy following the loss "decathexis", but recognised that there follows a period of reflection on the memories of the person, which he termed "hypercathexis". The end result, Freud wrote, is a detachment from the old relationship. This inevitably involves the ego accepting the loss and coming to terms with the new situation. This does not involve *forgetting* the lost person, but emotionally relocating them and allowing the ego to seek out new relationships, not in order to replace the lost person, but to meet the inner needs and desires of the id. In fact, Freud believed a continuing connection could still be had if someone moves through this process in a healthy manner (Mallon, 2008), but problems can arise when a person cannot move from cathexis to decathexis because they become fixated on what has been lost – then there is a risk that mourning becomes melancholia.

What Freud had identified was the importance of relationships, and the quality of attachment people have within these partnerships. He recognised that grieving is a natural process and that it can become problematic if there have been issues within the relationship. These ideas were expanded and explored by psychodynamic theorists throughout the latter half of the 20th century. Worden (2008) focused on the process of moving from cathexis, through decathexis, and into hypercathexis and viewed the journey as one that involved a series of tasks using four distinct steps:

1. The first step is to accept the loss, recognising that a reunion with the lost person (or object) will never happen and that readjustment is required.

2. Once this has been accepted, the next step involves experiencing the emotions that accompany the loss. This may be a prolonged period where grief, pain and anger are felt in varying degrees of severity.

3. Following this comes a lengthy period of readjustment which was recognised in the first step. This involves coming to terms with a world wherein the lost person (or object) no longer resides. There will be environmental adjustment where spaces occupied by whatever has been lost have to be revisited and accepted; there will be emotional adjustments where coping strategies have to be explored; and there will be psychological adjustments where the person who has been left behind has to readjust themselves to the new experience. There may well be associated losses, such as loss of finances, loss of status, and loss of security, and each of these will need to be negotiated and readjusted in turn.

4. The end stage is similar to Freud's observation, in that there will be an emotional relocation of the lost person (or object), and the person living with the loss will be able to move on with their life.

Worden (2008) offers a simplistic view of moving through the stages of grief, but what is evident is the end result wherein a person has to deal with significant events which impact on their identity. This underlines one of the primary aims and functions of working with therapeutic photography, which can act as a tool where an exploration of identity can take place, roles can be explored, and a sense of self-concept can be arrived at.

■ THE LOSS OF A ROLE

While exploring his typical day, Graham took a photograph of his wife's lunch. He is her carer but he was previously married to a woman from Scandinavia and he said this has influenced how he prepares food, preferring to make open sandwiches. The cultural implications of his image were interesting, but the reaction from another participant was even more telling.

Betty sat quietly listening to Graham talk, and once he had finished she began to speak. She said that she had noticed the block of butter in the butter dish at the far left of the image. Specifically, she noted the way the butter had been cut from the block and left an indent. She explained that she used constantly to argue with her own husband while he had been alive about the butter dish that they had. He would take big scoops of butter from the block with his knife, leaving big gouges in the block, whereas she would delicately and neatly slice butter from the end of the block. She said she used to get angry that the butter block was left in such a mess after he had used it, but now he had gone she was always presented with a nice, neat block of butter in the fridge every time she went to use it. Every time she opened the fridge she was presented with a reminder of him.

Through using an image that was not her own, she was able to use the contents of the image to explore her own loss of identity as a carer for her, now deceased, husband. This highlighted the polysemic nature of images, and it was a vehicle for her to continue this narrative and explore the emotions associated with the block of butter. She explained that she had felt guilty for feeling relieved when her husband finally passed away because of the length of time he had been ill, and she explored her search for a new identity now that he had gone.

Stages of grief

Wortman and Silver (2001) identified four grieving patterns – normal, chronic, delayed and avoided. Worden's (2008) task of grieving may well define a "normal" course of coping with loss, but if we are to understand why some people find dealing with loss and change so difficult then we must revisit attachment theory and consider how it shapes reactions, particularly those where chronic, delayed and avoided patterns are observed.

Bowlby (1980) was instrumental in defining attachment styles through the observation of reactions of children during times of separation, and went on to define a pattern of behaviour which moves from initial feelings of sadness, through to anxiety and protest, then grief, and, if the separation becomes permanent, mourning is experienced. Parkes and Prigerson (2010) believe there is also a social side to mourning and that acceptable ways to mourn are defined by the cultures and societies we exist in. They explain that grieving is a psychosocial transition and at times of mourning, people *learn* what is acceptable and what is not acceptable – for example, it would not be acceptable to become so angry and enraged that you violently attack random strangers, nor would it be acceptable to act as if nothing has happened. A socially acceptable balance must be found where the mourner can work through emotions while society recognises their pain.

Parkes (1988) identified that loss brings about change within the assumptive world that we form which helps us make sense of the world around us and the pattern and order of events; our assumption that the person (or object) that is lost will return is challenged, assumptions with regards to identity gained from the relationship will also be challenged, and assumptions about the reliability and predictability of the world around us will most certainly be challenged. All these elements bring further losses to be experienced. Bowlby (1979, 1980, 2008) also identified that the safe haven and secure base that have been relied on may also be lost, which he linked to the breaking of an affectional bond between the individual and the thing which has been lost. As soon as the affectional bond is broken, the grieving process begins. The combined works of Bowlby and Parkes (1970) arrived at a proposal of a four-stage process of grief:

1. *Shock and numbness* – the immediate impact of the loss has to be comprehended, but the assumptive world struggles to accept

what has happened. The brain is rationally trying to make sense of the situation, yet the feelings and emotions are causing the body to experience anxiety unlike anything it might have had to deal with before. Fight or flight responses are considered, and defence mechanisms may well be engaged in an attempt to deny what is happening. Physical distress is evident, and emotional outpourings are common, yet this is a cathartic process as they assist in the processing of the information, and the transition into a state where inner feelings can be explored and communicated in a clearer manner. If the relationship that has been lost was a complex one, or one where there was considerable distance between the two people, problems may arise at this stage wherein a person may find it difficult to emotionally process the loss and move to the next stage, or perhaps supresses emotions for fear of exposing themselves to unpleasant memories.

2. *Yearning, separation and pain* – the reality of the loss has dawned and the void has to be dealt with. At this stage, it is common to find reminders of the deceased in many places. Often the lost person is idolised and they are viewed as an exciting object (see Chapter 5), but waves of grief are experienced that compound the anxiety, which exists from the previous stage. Feelings of guilt are not uncommon and "what if?" thinking can occur. For some, becoming entrenched at this stage is an easy thing to do where reminders are deliberately sought and a sense of punishment may prevail – "I'm responsible for the loss, therefore I deserve to hurt!" If there were relationship problems, and high instances of guilt and shame between the couple, then these familiar emotions become magnified at this stage.

3. *Despair* – reality moves into acceptance and a person begins to come to terms with the fact that things are never going to be the same again. Similar to the previous stages, emotional fluctuation is common, including anger, frustration and questioning. Low mood, lethargy and depleted energy levels may be experienced and there is a risk that this leads to someone becoming entrenched in anger and depression. There is also a sense that control has been lost and this has resulted in disorganisation, which may compound existing reserves that

may be fuelling coping strategies. Withdrawal and isolation are also prevalent risks at this stage.

4. *Acceptance and reorganisation* – at the end of the process there should be hope, and the recovery process can begin. This may entail considering future plans and goals, restoring faith in the important things around you, and readjusting the attachment once experienced with the deceased. This does not necessarily involve letting go or forgetting about the attachment, more allowing the loss to recede in the mind and permitting trust and positivity to return (Bowlby, 1980, 2008). Life, it is hoped, can now move on.

There are, of course, many other factors that can compound the experience of loss such as whether the loss was expected, whether the loss was timely, and the nature of the loss (Parkes & Prigerson, 2010; Gibson & Gibson, 2016). It is also important to remember that loss is a natural occurrence in life and, as practitioners, we should not just apply it when we are dealing with bereavement – other types of loss must also be considered.

▨ CRITICAL THINKING

Think of a time when you lost something (not a person). Now try to recall the feelings you experienced when this happened and relate them to the four stages described by Bowlby and Parkes (1970). An example might go as follows:

I once worked for a TV company making documentaries. It was a great job and I enjoyed doing it, but one day I got a phone call to tell me that I was no longer on the project, in fact, they no longer wanted me to work for them. *Shock and numbness* set in and I thanked the person on the other end of the phone, hung up, and tried to put the conversation to one side and continue with what I was doing. I couldn't. I thought there had been a mistake, but the conversation had been real.

Yearning, separation and pain soon followed. So much of my identity was tied into my job and I felt like a failure. Without that job who was I? I was anxious about my future, worried about what friends and family would think, and felt guilt for any actions that may have led to losing the job. I rejected sympathy and tried to act as if it was no big deal, but inside I was screaming.

Despair followed and I realised that the loss was real and I had to deal with it properly. I was angry at the company, I wanted to get back at them, but I did not know what to do next. Fortunately, because I was young and I had a supportive network around me I soon realised that people did not reject me because of the loss of the job – I was still the same person they knew before I had the job (only slightly cockier!).

Acceptance and reorganisation soon followed and I was able to reconsider my career path. I thought about things I had enjoyed about the job, and things I hadn't, and was able to search for an appropriate alternative.

The loss of the job still lives with me, but I now view it as an important part of my formative years – a necessary step to where I am now.

Preparing for loss

Not all loss is unexpected. Loss can be a gradual process and one that can be planned for. Loss of abilities due to old age creeps up over a long period of time, while the loss of certain identities, such as a school pupil or university student, can be momentous events to be celebrated. However, not all expected losses are cause for celebration.

Kubler-Ross (1970) worked with terminally ill patients and recognised a pattern in many of her patients who were preparing to die. She recognised the stages defined by Parkes and Bowlby (1970) but observed that a similar process could also precede loss. Although she argued that these stages were not necessarily linear, and that patients could become entrenched at certain stages, or randomly move around others, she did describe five distinct ones:

1. *Denial* – at the point where an initial diagnosis is received there is an air of suspended belief and a need to reject what has been stated. Similar to Bowlby and Parkes's initial stage, the ego wants to protect the fragile id from having to deal with unpleasant emotions, and this is one of the most unpleasant to process, so denial is often the safest option.

2. *Anger* – denial is no longer an option, and emotions are extraordinarily fragile. The mind attempts to make sense of the news but struggles to do so. Somebody, or something, must take the blame for the emotional pain experienced and this

often emerges as anger. The anger can be directed inwards to the self, but more often than not it is directed at those closest to the person. Family members might receive the brunt of anger for being overly sympathetic; medical staff might receive it because they did not pick up on the symptoms quickly enough. Whoever is on the receiving end, it should be viewed as a natural response to the norms being challenged.

3. *Bargaining* – for some, there may be spiritual needs to be addressed, and this may involve asking for a cure, or some extra time. Hope is something to be held and there are no shortages of media stories to support miracle cures and unbelievable recoveries. Many faiths also herald tales of sick people travelling to places of worship to partake in transformational pilgrimages. Others may find solace in existing faith.

4. *Depression* – dealing with one of the most shocking diagnoses will often affect mental health. Kubler-Ross recognised that there is always a lowest point in the whole process and this is encapsulated by feelings of depression and a loss of hope.

5. *Acceptance* – the outcome, Kubler-Ross hoped, is that a person arrives at this final stage having moved through the self-grieving process. Acceptance results in time to reflect and contemplate life before the end comes. Regardless of age, the whole process is akin to being accelerated into Erikson's (1963) eighth stage of ego integrity versus despair.

THE LOSS OF BEAUTY

Loss can be a gradual process. Betty used the image above to explore her past. Now in her late 70s, she is coming to terms with a number of losses. She recently lost her husband, she is losing her mobility, and because of this she is also losing some of her freedom. However, during an exercise which asked the participants to capture photographs to represent emotions, she photographed a plaque on a park bench to illustrate the emotion of sadness. The plaque was weathered and difficult to read, but the name "John G. Boyd" could be made out, as well as a birth year of 1940, and a year of death being 2001. Betty explained that John Boyd was a local artist whom she had known when she was younger. She explained that she had been asked to pose for paintings and drawings by him on many occasions and had fond memories of her encounters with him. There was some joking among the participants that she may have done nude modelling and she laughed it off, but John G. Boyd did paint a wide variety of subjects, including nudes, so her laughter may have been hiding the truth.

In Betty's revelation, she was telling the group that she had been worthy of an artist's attention at one time in her life. She described herself now as "an old, ugly woman". Of course, she wasn't ugly, but age had taken its toll and she knew this; however, the memories of her encounter with an artist still lived on and her beauty has been immortalised on a canvas somewhere.

Dimensions of grief

So far, this chapter has looked at linear models of grief that explore specific stages people might move through as they experience loss. Payne *et al.* (1999) introduced seven dimensions of change that professionals should consider when working with loss and change. The seven areas were identified by Susan Le Poidevin who worked with Colin Murray Parkes (who defined the four stages of grief with John Bowlby in 1970) in an effort to highlight how grief affects a person, and how professionals can make sense of actions and reactions. Again, these seven elements should be considered alongside *any* loss, not just grief specifically.

1. *The emotional response* – strong emotional responses are normal. The loss of something provokes anxiety within the body and reactions can be unpredictable. Depending on the quality of the attachment, emotional responses may be delayed, or they

may be extreme and overwhelming. In an ideal situation, the person dealing with the loss will find the right balance between the level of emotional expression and the control of these expressions. Again, there is a societal exertion on this as every culture will have a perception with regards to acceptable levels of emotional expression.

2. *The impact on the social network* – the loss may have an effect on other people around the person dealing with this. It may be that the person who has experienced a loss also finds that their social status is affected, such as the loss of money, or the loss of a job. In this situation, work colleagues cease to be a part of life, and this may lead to periods of loneliness and isolation.

3. *Associated physical symptoms* – because the risk of increased stress and anxiety accompanies any loss, this can put a strain on the body and mind. Stress and anxiety upset the equilibrium and often manifest in painful physical symptoms such as stomach pain, headaches and poor mental health. Often these can be overlooked, but it is important to consider the impact of loss on overall health.

4. *Changes in lifestyle* – loss may impact on social standing and finance (as point 2 highlighted), and this will also have an impact on feelings of security. Depending on the scale of the loss, there may well be implications resulting in the sale of property, which creates additional losses that need to be dealt with. Reduced finances mean that lifestyle choices need to be reassessed which, in turn, may impact on the social network again (reiterating point 2).

5. *Practical issues* – for some, the loss of a person may have profound implications on their ability to cope. Given that many societies rely on informal, unpaid carers to fill the gaps in care provision, the loss of a person within a relationship may jeopardise the safety of the person who is left behind. It may be that there was a reliance on personal care, medicinal care, or basic provision of food and shopping.

6. *Spiritual issues* – Kubler-Ross (1970) identified a spiritual aspect to her stages, and Le Poidevin recognised that spirituality

may go in one of two directions. It may be that an existing belief system becomes challenged and undermined by the experience of loss, or it may drive a person towards a belief system to cope with the loss. It is also fair to recognise that it may have absolutely no impact on the person at all; however, professionals need to be aware of spirituality and the importance of religion in the lives of some clients. As many of us live in secular societies, it can become all too easy to dismiss this aspect of life and assume that because it is not important to one person, then it is not important to anyone.

7. *Identity* – finally, and perhaps most importantly when working with therapeutic photography, is the impact loss has on the overall identity of a person. The previous six factors will individually, or cumulatively, reshape a person's identity. Self-esteem, self-worth and self-efficacy will all be impacted and there is no accurate clinical tool to assess these nebulous concepts, but therapeutic work needs to consider these important concepts and work to address them. Enhancing these aspects of a person's characteristics is one of the primary aims of using photographs in a therapeutic manner.

Change

When we encounter loss, change will inevitably follow. Marris (1986) recognised the inseparability of loss and change and went on to explain that the intensity of the experience is often dictated by the nature of the loss. He outlined three categories which defined change:

1. *Substitution* – this is often viewed as a positive change, where the old is replaced by the new and life continues as was, or is even an improved version of what was.

2. *Evolution* – here, change is a natural product of the life course, where change may take place over a long period of time and force a gradual reassessment of attachments within relationships.

3. *Deep loss* – with this aspect of change, a person has to deal with the loss of love.

Whatever the nature of loss, Marris (1986) identified that humans can often struggle with change because we like equilibrium, familiarity and predictability – change threatens this and forces us into unfamiliar territory. This is akin to Bowlby's (2008) writings on the importance of the secure base and safe haven where secure attachments can be fostered because there is a sense of routine in a world that can seem chaotic and scary. Marris believed that humans have an innate need for safety and security (much as Maslow (1943) identified in his hierarchy of needs) and one way humans achieve this is by looking for predictability and order. If this goes, then we feel endangered and we try to cling to what we know. Anything that disrupts this order can trigger feelings of futility and bewilderment. Marris (in Parkes *et al.*, 2006) believed that this is compounded when existing attachments are threatened and affected. Any sudden change in relationship status adds to disruption and can have a negative impact on self-esteem and self-identity.

Change in our environments and society also causes disequilibrium and can increase anxiety. Acts of terrorism can leave civilised societies wondering at the barbarity and capabilities of fellow human beings, pushing values and ethics into new, unfamiliar territories. The norms of everyday life are no longer as secure as they once were. Our comprehension of events can also unseat us and force us into dealing with a change in our beliefs, such as trying to fathom why babies and young children can become terminally ill when our expectation of disease is that it targets the elderly and infirm.

The speed at which events unfold can force us into sudden change. If change is both sudden and unexpected it can bring on an immediate juxtaposition within our world. Fortunately, Marris also highlighted the importance of protective factors to assist in coping strategies when change is unleashed. He believed that supportive relationships with open communication and feelings of mutuality are a major protective factor. In analysing these support structures, he returned to the importance of trust, an element Erikson (1963) focused on in his first of eight stages, and wrote that without this, attachments become threatened and important future support structures to assist in guiding through change may be lost:

> The motives for living are confused by anxious impulses to test, conciliate or defend oneself against attachment figures…this underlying mistrust is likely to inhibit the relationships which could provide support in misfortune. (Marris, in Parkes *et al.*, 2006, p.83)

This may be an important starting point for any therapeutic relationship where someone is dealing with change. Trust is a building block to successful communication between a professional and their client. What therapeutic photography does is put the control into the hands of the client and asks them to capture and document issues that are important to them. All the professional has to do then is listen, empathise and learn from the client.

In an attempt to explore the challenges that change can bring about, Holmes and Rahe (1967) constructed a social readjustment scale to capture major life events, and then categorised them in terms of their severity. In total, they included 43 "events" which impacted the life of an individual. At the top of the scale they included major life events such as the death of a spouse, divorce and marital separation; then elements such as injury, illness and loss of a job were noted below these. Potentially positive changes such as retirement, pregnancy and a new job were included further down their list, acknowledging that the impact of change did not always have to be linked to negative life events. At the bottom of their list they included change which could be linked to social status, activities, family events and even Christmas! The purpose of the scale was to provide a tool where the cumulative effects of a variety of changes could be added up and considered if the impact of the resulting stress could pose a threat to an individual experiencing these.

■ SUDDEN CHANGE

Simone had experienced significant change over the past six months and she chose to share this information with her peers through her self-portrait. In the image (above) she was asked to capture a positive characteristic of her self, so she wanted to portray her creative side. When she was explaining this image, she reported to the group that she had had a stroke a few months ago and it impacted her mobility and speech quite significantly. She said that she still has problems with some words and letters, and she is adapting to the sudden change in her lifestyle. It was clear that Simone had experienced personal illness, a change in finances, a change in living conditions, and a change in social activities, but there may well have been other significant changes to Simone's life that are not captured within her image and the resulting explanation.

Despite the impact of her stroke, Simone was positive and recognised that she had made improvements since the incident. The reason that she captured her creative side, making Christmas tree decorations, was that she was relieved that the stroke had not taken that element of her identity from her as this was an aspect of her personality which she felt defined her the most.

Holmes and Rahe (1967) recognised the impact of change, and what their work did was align change with stress, even with change that can be viewed as positive. This means that our internal working model, as described by Bowlby (2008), is constantly challenged when facing change, and this is something that professionals need to work with and recognise in practice. Ordinarily, if therapeutic work is required, the client will have either recently experienced change which has been difficult to cope with, or is currently experiencing change (or about to) and needs to find strengths to work through it. This is where knowledge of psychodynamic theories can help professionals understand how change has been dealt with, or how it might be dealt with in the future. For example, if attachment theory is used alongside work with loss and change, it can be assumed that someone with a secure attachment may be able to draw strength from relationships and find resilience within themselves. Someone with an anxious ambivalent attachment style (or a preoccupied adult attachment style) may well become entrenched in the process of loss and change and may experience heightened anxiety, while becoming overly needy towards support structures. Someone with an avoidant attachment style (or a dismissive adult attachment style) may well try to delay dealing with the emotional impact of loss and change, attempting to control exposure to the experience but risking psychosomatic reactions due to an inability to externalise emotions. Similarly, someone with a disorganised attachment style (or a fearful adult attachment style) may experience a variety of unpredictable and volatile reactions throughout the process.

Transitions

Bridges (2004, 2009) recognised the inevitability of change and regarded the state of change as a situational experience that humans need to deal with, but did not see this as necessarily problematic. He expanded on this idea and identified that problems tend to arise from the process of *adapting* to the change, the psychological process of moving through change and coming to terms with it – a process he termed "transition".

Bridges (2004, 2009) believed that there are three ways to deal with the psychological process of change. First, there is familiarity and comfort in what you know, so the temptation to reminisce and pine for the past can be strong. Striving for what once was in an effort to find a lost routine can be emotionally draining, particularly if what is searched for is no longer there, and the risk of inhibiting forward progression and growth is high. Second, there is hope and excitement in the future, so some might see opportunities within change and aim to implement them. This approach to change does require an individual to be optimistic about their future and this may not be immediately apparent in clients who are seeking therapeutic interventions; however, it is worth acknowledging that this would be the goal when considering transitions. Third, there exists a zone between living in the past and striving for the future, and Bridges (2004, 2009) termed this the neutral zone. Within this neutral zone, the psychological ambiguity of adapting to change can be tested out and new situations can be considered. If the prospect of change becomes too much in the neutral zone, the temptation to revert to the past presents itself, so Bridges (2004, 2009) highlighted the importance for professionals to work with ambiguity to explore the positives within situations.

Often equated to the seasonal elements, the process of transition takes an individual from the endings associated with autumn, through the void of winter, and into the season of spring where rebirth and regrowth are experienced.

Autumn

Changes begin with endings. There is a process of shedding the old to bring about the new, and an end has to occur. Take, for example, the process of change brought about by losing employment. The psychological process involves disengaging from an identity of an employee, departing from established colleagues and clients, and mentally preparing for the final day. If this was a change in employment which was self-initiated, leaving to go and work elsewhere, there may well be a formal ending where workmates have a party to mark the occasion. This is often shaped by cultural approaches to endings, celebrations to symbolise the termination of the old and the opportunity of the new – graduation balls and ceremonies, leaving parties, New Year's parties, and even funerals; formalising the occasion marks an obvious ending. However, if the ending is not punctuated by an obvious event, an individual must recognise that they have been through an ending before transitioning to the next stage, and this might prove problematic for some.

Winter

Continuing the analogy of leaving employment, the season of winter represents the neutral zone where ambiguity is experienced and the psychological aspects of change can be considered. There may be feelings of regret, frustration, impatience and uncertainty, but mixed in with this there may also be feelings of excitement and opportunity.

For some, it may feel as if they are between two safety zones, one being the familiarity of the past, and the other being the hoped for certainty of the future, but, like a trapeze artist in mid-flight, these two points are just out of reach. For clients, the terminology often used is "being in limbo" and the opportunity for professionals is to explore the two safety zones with the client, striving for reasons why movement towards the future goals should be pursued.

Spring

Following on from the previous two stages, positive signs of the change should be evident and the person can try out their new identity as they emerge from the neutral zone. This is often an exciting and creative time, but it also brings challenges and risks of more loss and change, particularly if people close to the person feel threatened by the changes they see and are forced to consider change within themselves.

This may lead to resistance and retreat into the neutral zone for the person who has the new identity.

Bridges (2004, 2009) suggests the use of the four P's in this final stage:

- Be clear about the **P**urpose of the change.

- Visualise the end goal in a **P**icture.

- Decide what you need to do to achieve the outcomes by forming a **P**lan that is achievable and realistic.

- Consider the support you will need from people around you, and what **P**art they will play in the process.

■ MEMORIES OF SAFETY

From the outset of her involvement with a therapeutic photography group, Wilma was quiet and private. However, over the course of six weeks she opened up about her losses and told the group about the death of her father and the loss of her husband, and was also able to show a visual documentation of who the important people in her life were (above). She admitted that she found comfort and solace in old images as they allowed her to experience "happy memories", and her narrative suggested that she had come to terms with the bereavements and losses she had experienced and found acceptance and reorganisation (Bowlby & Parkes, 1970). Wilma found reminders of her losses in many of her images and presented an ideal picture of the past, often romanticising her childhood (e.g. bathing in tin baths), but there was no suggestion in her narrative that this was "problematic". Instead, she had found a way to find solace in her acceptance and reorganisation of the deceased.

The writings of Bridges (2004, 2009) on transition suggest that the psychological process of change involves coming to terms with future possibilities. This often involves optimism and hope and, if this is absent, the temptation for individuals dealing with change is to revert to the familiarity of the past, thus preventing forward progression. With change comes ambiguity and uncertainty, and Wilma's narratives suggest comfort and familiarity within her memories of the past. However, within her narratives she acknowledged to herself that she had been building a wall around her, denying what had been happening, and she was ready to take this down and find her voice. By using images, she acknowledged the importance of family, history and memories for her identity and felt she could use this to move forward and test out her new identity.

Summary

Recognising the process of loss and change within therapeutic work is an important aspect of any relationship. Helping a client understand the "normal" and "natural" processes that people move through can assist them in understanding some of the emotional and behavioural responses they might experience while going through major changes. Using photographs to facilitate this exploration provides an opportunity to focus in on any life event and highlight strategies employed to cope with adverse situations.

Chapter 8

USING PHOTOGRAPHY TO EXPLORE NARRATIVES AND PERSPECTIVES

The focus of the previous chapters has been on internal factors within the exercises and the theoretical explorations. The following chapters move to look at external factors and explore the use of photographs to look at personal narratives and life stories. In order to do this, the work of theorists will be highlighted so that the impact of societal factors can be underpinned in any work with photographs. The implication of stigma and labelling is identified, alongside identification of the value of routines and patterns in everyday life. Again, exercises are used to capture "a typical day" in images, then look at the photographs in more detail to analyse important or problematic areas.

Photography to elicit narratives

Photo elicitation stems from research practice wherein photographs are used with research participants to elicit a response which is thought to be deeper than using linguistic means alone. Harper (2002) relates the value of using photo elicitation to the evolution of the brain. Because the part of the brain that processes visual information is responsible for learning long before the part that processes linguistic information, Harper argues that using images can access a deeper level of consciousness than using words alone. Certainly, research into brain development would support the fact that the right side of the brain is responsible for documenting visual reality and this is the portion of the brain that develops initially from birth to around two years of age, until the left side begins to develop in equal measure with the arrival of linguistic ability (Gerhardt, 2006; Weiser, 1988). However, McGilchrist (2009) warns that viewing the right and left side of the brain as being responsible for visual and verbal development respectively is too simplistic and that neuroscience suggests the left side is actually responsible for structuring, ordering and defining detail in the world around us, whereas the right side is used to make sense of visual cues, consider alternative options, and remain vigilant when structure is absent. He continues to state that modern society is becoming too reliant on the left-hand side of the brain, seeking rationale and order in everything, and that approaches to exercise the right-hand side of the brain should be favoured. The influence of the image continues to permeate human life and the value of working with images extends beyond the early years of childhood; images become "part of how we experience, learn and know as well as how we communicate and represent knowledge" (Pink, 2013, p.1).

Using photo elicitation in a therapeutic sense can be viewed as a means of accessing the unconscious (Loewenthal, 2013; Trainin Blank, 2009). This is built on the Freudian belief that unpleasant memories, thoughts and desires are removed from the conscious and buried in the unconscious, a process which Freud (2001) termed *repression*. Using photographs to access the unconscious assumes that clients will attach meanings to the image through projection as a result of previous repression. There are three main approaches to using photo elicitation:

1. *Auto-driving* – interviewees discuss photographs they have been presented with. The interviewees have no personal connection to the photographs used and may be asked to select a particular image that they are drawn to. This technique is often used in the practice of phototherapy where trained counsellors or therapists will use photos printed onto postcards (also known as *spectro-cards*) to elicit a response in connection to the image (Saita *et al.*, 2014; Loewenthal, 2013; Halkola, in Loewenthal, 2013).

2. *Reflexive photography* – interviewees are asked to create their own photographs and then bring them to an interviewer where they will explore the deeper meanings of the photographs produced.

3. *Photo novella* – participants document their daily routines and perhaps explore challenges within these. Noland (2006) highlights that photographs can capture the mundane aspects of life, but by exploring the image and drawing attention to certain elements, issues and experiences can be brought into the conscious realm. Photo novella is similar to the practice of photovoice (discussed further in Chapter 9), which aims to challenge injustice or inequality and to highlight areas where change could benefit the participant (Loewenthal, 2013; Parker, 2009).

John Collier (Collier & Collier, 1986) is credited as being the founding father of photo elicitation when, in 1957, he developed the technique to research environmental factors affecting service users with mental health problems. His team later used photographs to help define environmental factors when they were having problems trying to categorise themes using words alone. They found that by using photographs to assist in the interviews, the respondents demonstrated better recall from memory as well as reduced misunderstandings between the researchers and participants (Harper, 2002).

A DAY IN THE LIFE OF...

An interesting exercise to engage participants in is to ask them to document a typical day in their life. It is a good idea to discuss and agree a set number of images to use for this so that the participant can think about what constitutes a "typical day" and which images they might use to represent this.

In reality, every day is different and there may not be a typical day, but participants should be able to recognise elements within their day that give them routine, security and pride. Many images will be related to their social identity and the roles they have, while others may focus on support structures within their lives.

Where participants can struggle with this exercise is when they lack routine in their lives, an example being someone who is a substance user and whose lifestyle could be described as chaotic. Yet, if this exercise is conducted with a group of participants, it is good for those who find this exercise difficult to hear from those who managed to produce a set number of images as they can learn from them the importance of structure, order, routine and security.

Thinking about this task, try to replicate your own typical day using only eight images.

In an approach informed by auto-driving, Schwartz (1989) used a variety of images that were taken by photographers and asked participants to determine meanings and messages behind each picture. He found that all participants used their own personal narratives and social experiences to draw meaning from each image, and that the messages that the photographers had intended were not apparent. He concluded that photographs were a useful medium for eliciting perception, social constructions and memories. The photograph itself has been described as a "neutral third party" (Parker, 2009, p.1119) within the relational dynamic between the interviewer and the interviewee in that the discussion can be focused on the image rather than the interviewer focusing attention on the interviewee which, in turn, reduces the power imbalance within that relationship. It also empowers the interviewee, as ultimately they are the experts of their own situation and will hold the knowledge behind the images they have produced (Parker, 2009). Photo elicitation can also be conducted in a group scenario and is particularly good for identifying common themes or common issues among minority communities, as well as the polysemic nature of a photograph, that is, the multiple meanings people can attribute to one image (Clark-Ibanez, 2004). However, as with all group situations, there may be participants who feel inhibited in the presence of other people, therefore caution should be used when selecting appropriate group members, especially at the expense of one-to-one work (Collier & Collier, 1986).

Within society, images form a major role in communication; the average person is exposed to an enormous amount of visual information every day through sources including films, TV, advertising, internet use and print media. Children learn to recognise visual images long before they develop linguistic skills and as a result photo elicitation has proved to be a successful tool to use when trying to get views from young children and adolescents. Photo elicitation has been used in pedagogical environments to seek information from young children on what they find is important within a classroom setting (Popa & Stan, 2013; Cappello, 2005). In their study on the importance of play for children, Alexander *et al.* (2014) opted to gather data through photographs produced by the children, as the visual element appeared to give the children confidence and the power to voice and express feelings. Their data was backed up by interviewing the children, using the images to guide and explore what the children were aiming to express, and concluded that this approach was more inclusive than using interviews alone.

The success of this method has been attributed to the focus on visual information rather than lexical information, and also the manner in which information is sought deviates from the average adult–child relationships where the balance of power typically lies with the adult. Power dynamics were also a major consideration in research conducted into bullying by Walton and Niblett (2013), who recognised that children who had been bullied may be wary of power, control and authority. The visual aspect of the questioning allowed the discussion to develop in a different manner, which elicited new information when compared with previous studies that had relied on questionnaires and interviews alone. Goffman (2009) highlights denigration and social marginalisation as factors contributing to stigmatisation that should be considered when thinking about power dynamics within an interview situation. As photo elicitation addresses some power dynamics, this suggests it could be a particularly suitable intervention to use when working with stigmatised clients.

▩ CLEAN?

Charlie was exploring his typical day. He lived alone and experienced fluctuating mental health problems and took a series of images to represent what he does on a daily basis. In one image, he photographed a bottle of cleaning liquid.

The group he was presenting his images to assumed that he liked to clean his house, and they were correct, but he went on to offer further insight. He explained that if his house was clean, then he felt clean on the inside, but if his house was dirty, then this negatively affected his inner feelings. He said it was also about putting on a front, so that if he could present a clean house, people would assume he was feeling okay on the inside. However, he admitted this was not always the case, but felt it was what other people expected – when they ask, "How are you?" they want to hear you say, "Fine".

Once he explained this, the other participants confirmed that they also felt this and were careful in their presentation, often in an effort to "convince" other people that they were okay, and in order to avoid being asked, "How are you?" and face the risk of truthfully answering, "I feel terrible".

Griebling *et al.* (2013) explain that photo elicitation places the power of research into the hands of the photographer as they are looking to illustrate strengths and challenges within their lives, then they share interpretations with interested parties. In turn, the interested parties, be they researchers, facilitators or peers, then engage with the photographer in an effort to learn and understand what the issues are – the photographer becomes an educator.

As well as avoiding stigma, photo elicitation can aid in the development of identity, exploration of the self, and clarification of roles by acting as an externalised medium for the expression of issues (Goessling & Doyle, 2009). Rice *et al.* (2013) found that photo elicitation was useful for helping younger adolescents who had experienced trauma prioritise wants and needs when care planning. The benefit of being able to externalise issues through images meant that participants could take photographs to represent what was personally important to them, and when the researchers looked across all images there were clear themes with regards to the importance of friends and family to reinforce identity. The results also highlighted the importance of considering environmental factors, how they reinforce identity and how the participants found the process engaging and empowering. Teixeira (2015) observed that the action-orientated way in which data is collected through photographs also encourages participants creatively to discuss solutions to the issues identified, thus suggesting that empowerment is also an outcome of this approach.

Because of the emancipatory potential of photo elicitation, it appears to be a useful technique to elicit information from hard-to-reach communities. Oliffe and Bottorff (2007) used the technique in a medical setting when working with men who were going through prostate cancer treatment. They found that the experience was a therapeutic one in that it allowed the participants to photograph aspects of their treatment, then to reflect, process and talk about what was occurring. It also allowed the men who participated to choose what would be discussed at each session by deciding what to photograph, thus the power was in their hands, and the interviewers felt that they were learning from the participants and became spectators of the participants' perspectives.

If the societal perception is that minority groups are closed off and stoic, then attempts to reach these groups may be tainted by this attitude; if traditional methods of data collection have proved fruitless, then introducing a visual aspect may have benefits and could elicit more information. The therapeutic value of photo elicitation was also highlighted by Newbury and Hoskins (2011) when feedback from their study revealed that the process had been "healing" (p.1070) for participants. Their study looked at problems associated with substance use and they found that photo elicitation helped to move away from the perspective that risk-taking behaviour is an individual's choice, towards a more holistic view that the environment and society we are raised in will also contribute; photo elicitation allowed participants to bring other aspects of their lives into the interviews. They also noted that the dynamics of communication was affected by the introduction of a photograph in that the researcher would sit side by side with the participant, as opposed to face to face, and the conversation and eye contact was directed at the image, rather than with each other. This appeared to give a sense of safety so that the participant could control the flow of information.

Stevens and Spears (2009) acknowledge that there are similarities between the practices of therapeutic photography and art therapy and suggest that the work of Carl Jung influences both. Jung worked with visuals in order to assist expressing emotional disturbances through art, believing that it was often easier to do this than to verbalise experiences. Where the practice of therapeutic photography coincides with Jung's work is through this visualisation and expression. Once a participant has chosen to objectify something in an image they have given it a form and brought it to the fore of their attention. They may share this image in a group, or with the facilitator, and that reinforces the existence of the issue and makes it easier to address and discuss this, rather than working with abstract thoughts and feelings. The result is that participants who might engage defence mechanisms, such as denial and rationalisation, may find it easier to express issues through visuals which they can then hold as an object and discuss the problem as if it was external to themselves (Graf, 2002; Chickerneo, 1993).

LABELS

Hannah was exploring her battle with depression and looked at some of her triggers that might be posing a risk to her mental health. However, during the exercise, which asked her to pictorially record a day in her life, she made another revelation.

During a trip to the supermarket, she photographed the aisle where alcohol was sold. At this point, she revealed to the group that she was an alcoholic. This was news to the group and it was clearly a big issue for Hannah; she had given a lot of thought about how to share this information with her peers. By capturing the issue in a photograph, she had objectified it, but also made it real and tangible, and could confront it. The issue was there for all to see and she could not deny her problem.

Her presentation appeared to change after she shared this information with the group, and she appeared to be happier, more at ease and conversational. One of her peers asked her, "Was it not difficult to take that picture?" to which she replied, "I only had to photograph the stuff, other people have to drink it!"

In another health-based study, Fitzgerald *et al.* (2013) used photo elicitation to look at obesity and tobacco use in Philadelphia and took Bronfenbrenner's (1992) ecological model to structure the results, using images and narratives to see where the impacting factors sat on the model. They found that photo elicitation gave good insight into the beliefs and priorities of the participants, but that there may have been a tendency for participants to focus on areas which lent themselves to be photographed, and this may have excluded other areas of discussion that were difficult to photograph. Despite this, abstract concepts were elicited in the discussion process.

In another study, Angus *et al.* (2009) found that using photography to elicit information and discussion was actually a barrier for some participants. This appeared to be attributable to the social class of the participant, the subject matter they were focusing on, and the life experience of the participant. They warn that photo elicitation might not be appropriate for certain subject matters, nor for participants who are uncomfortable with using technical equipment like cameras. They do state that this can be overcome in the interviewer–interviewee dynamic by simply asking the participant if there was anything they felt they could not capture in a photograph, and then see if the response might elicit further discussion. Dennis Jr. *et al.* (2009) warn that photo elicitation can also lead to an overwhelming number of images being produced and suggest that limits are set for participants so that the therapeutic benefit is not forgotten and consumed by the task of taking photographs. They also highlight another challenging area for this practice in that if illegal activities are part of the problem for the client, this is not an easy (or safe) thing to photograph and perhaps this requires a more abstract approach to capturing images for discussion.

Clark-Ibanez (2004) favours participants taking photographs for themselves, rather than using a pre-existing stock of images to facilitate discussions. She believes there is value in using pre-existing images, but warns there might be a tendency for the interviewer to choose images to be used that they like themselves, or they can read messages into themselves, whereas if a participant is coming in with fresh images that they have produced, the photographs have much more meaning. She illustrates this by drawing on an example from her experience where she interviewed a young person who had taken 38 photographs of her new kitten:

The content of the photos did not end up being as important. For Janice, moving to a new community and not yet knowing anyone were factors in her strong attachment to her kitten. What became more important (and interesting) was the conversation about how her parents let her have the kitten after moving from Watts to Oak Park: a mixture of being able to afford having pets and compensating for the loss of friends. For example, Janice explained her family's slightly improved economic situation that (sic) allowed her to have a kitten. (Clark-Ibanez, 2004, p.1513)

Harper (2002) describes three categories when using photographs to elicit discussion:

1. Photographs are used to record inventories such as objects, people and belongings.

2. Photographs record events along the life path and institutional landmarks like school, graduation, birthdays, weddings and celebrations.

3. Photographs capture social interactions, usually intimate moments that connect the self to culture and society.

Harper believes that using the three categories above of *inventory*, *institution* and *social* can help facilitate discussion and focus the conversation on one of these three areas. Whereas Ulkuniemi (2007) uses the categories of documentation, unity, interaction and identity-building to explore photographs in terms of relationships, Harper's categories appear to look at the cultural definitions of the image; because of the polysemic nature of photographs, this means that one image could actually fall into several different categories, which may be an obstacle if discussion is defined by category. Hedges (1972, in Graf, 2002) believes that categories might be too restrictive and advises that an effective facilitator using photo elicitation should work to establish a good rapport with the participants, have no preconceptions about images that would be presented, and work with both the photograph and the participant to elicit a discussion, appreciating that the participant will guide that process.

▓ TIME

For Rebecca, life as a single mother to three children was demanding and time consuming, but also immensely rewarding. She spoke of the joy they brought her and the games she devised to keep them amused. Most of the time she had to create amusement for them with no money, so she spoke of going beachcombing to find stones that her children could paint, or of using old fishing crates to "sledge" down the pier onto the sand.

Rebecca's "typical day" revolved around her children, but in this image she describes a visit to the local children's hospital to attend an appointment with one of her boys. Her mother accompanied her to the visit and went into the appointment with Rebecca's son, leaving Rebecca outside with her other son, Ray. Rebecca explained that this was a precious time as she got to spend some quality one-to-one time with Ray, a rarity in her situation. She went on to explain that her other son has suspected autism, hence the hospital appointment, and his needs tended to come first, which left her other two children to fend for themselves on occasion. In the image, she is playing with Ray, and photographed his shadow, highlighting the fact that he looked like a lion. This created a mix of emotions for her – guilt, anger and resentment, but alongside this there was also joy in the fact that she had three children whom she loved dearly.

The therapeutic value of taking photographs is also important, as the act of framing an image, pressing the shutter and printing off an edited image can all impact on the way in which a client views the world, as well as themselves. Cosden and Reynolds (1982) recognise that encouraging clients to engage in photography boosts self-esteem and has an impact on how they view the relationship between action and consequence because the process of photography involved planning the shot, anticipating the final image and viewing the finished product. They also suggest that taking photographs can bring withdrawn clients into closer contact with their environment, as well as other people, and the act of displaying images and receiving feedback can have a direct impact on self-esteem. Overall, they believe that because photography involves creative expression, mastering a skill, sequencing events within time and completing a task, the resulting impact on self-esteem makes it a therapeutic activity.

In terms of gathering information, photo elicitation is a method that changes traditional dynamics between the interviewer and the interviewee. It is more than simply an "aesthetic experience" (Coronel & Pascual, 2013, p.120) and actually provides a tool for exploring and expressing cultural, social, economic and power dynamics that impact on the life of the interviewee (Coronel & Pascual, 2013; Clark-Ibanez, 2004). This means that the interviewer has to be aware of their own preconceptions and be prepared to learn from the interviewee, and it also means transferring a large degree of responsibility to the interviewee for gathering information. From a research perspective, issues that arise from this approach may be dealt with through ethics committees, but from a professional perspective there is a need to consider how this approach aligns with the purpose of professional values, boundaries and intentions.

Working with photographs and the narrative

Photo elicitation can be a means of accessing the unconscious and it is also a useful method for exploring personal narratives and social experiences (Rice *et al.*, 2013; Fitzgerald *et al.*, 2013; Trainin Blank, 2009; Schwartz, 1989). This technique of exploring life stories and interpretation of previous events is linked to areas of professional practice through a strengths and narrative approach wherein the past has to be acknowledged, but interventions are forward facing and look at how the client can reinterpret events to move forward in the future (Payne, 2014). Strengths-based approaches tend to focus on positives and have been criticised as being dismissive of negative factors when clients are giving an account of the experiences and may wish to explore these (Payne, 2014). Narrative approaches allow a fuller exploration of issues and are closely linked to identity formation as individuals try to construct who they are in relation to contemporary society (Riessman & Quinney, 2005).

White and Epston (1990) developed narrative therapy from their work with families in which they recognised there were a number of influential systems at play which impacted on family members and the roles they adopt; each of these roles had expected behaviours which were influenced by societal factors. White and Epston were influenced by the work of Foucault (in Faubion, 1994) and Goffman (1961) who described a hierarchy of power which is used to exert control over individuals using techniques such as subordination, surveillance and demonstrating superior knowledge. This power delineation impacts on societal roles because they impose socially constructed norms through areas like politics, values, beliefs and gender expectations. White and Epston believed that identifying these societal expectations and examining how they impact on behaviour is the underpinning factor within narrative therapy. Personal narratives are simply a *representation* of the life lived, not an accurate reflection; as a result, the *interpretation* of past events may be problematic for the service user and may influence behaviour and self-esteem in a negative way; "the dichotomy between how the individual views themselves (and) how society defines a person of 'moral worth' within the culture" needs to be investigated (Gibson & Heyman, in Lishman *et al.*, 2014, p.310).

White and Epston (1990) explained that the narrative therapeutic process begins with empathy from the professional as the client tells their story. The professional should be looking for the *problem saturated* narrative, which is where the story is largely negative and focuses on events that have been detrimental to the client. The next stage is to externalise the problem by naming it, giving it an identity and then deconstructing the story around the externalised problem. Part of the process of deconstruction will involve exploring how society has impacted on the view of the problem and how that has consequently shaped the client's ability to cope. Ultimately, the aim is to get the client to explore exceptions and to create an alternative narrative based around the root cause of the problem (Gibson & Heyman, in Lishman *et al.*, 2014; White & Epston, 1990). Moxley *et al.* (2012) recognise the close links between narrative therapy and resilience, explaining that when a client identifies strengths used to cope with adversity this can enhance self-respect by recognising themselves as resilient problem solvers.

NARRATIVE THERAPY

For the practitioner, the key to narrative therapy is to help the client identify what the problem is, and then help them understand why that problem impacts negatively on them with regards to stigma, labelling and societal perceptions. To do this, the practitioner needs to begin by assisting in the externalising of the problem – helping the client see that the way they are feeling is because of the problem, as opposed to viewing themselves as the problem.

For example, it might be that depression is the problem, but the client views themselves as a failure, useless and demotivated. By exploring the problem, the practitioner can begin to talk about how depression makes them feel like a failure, makes them think they are useless, or makes them feel demotivated. Separating the problem from the person helps the client to understand that it is the depression impacting on them, rather than them impacting on the depression.

Photography can assist in the externalising of the problem. By externalising the problem, the practitioner and client are trying to name and define what the problem is. White and Epston (1990) suggest giving the problem a name to use in order to make it easier to speak about (for example, depression could be called "darkness"), but by giving the problem a form within an abstract photograph, the problem is literally externalised and can be held at arm's length and discussed. This can assist in the exploration of the problem, helping the client and practitioner explore further how society views the problem, and how this also impacts on the client's self-esteem and self-image.

Traditionally, narrative therapy has been a linguistic-based intervention but the value of adding a visual element into the practice is now being recognised. Riessman and Quinney (2005) describe the distinguishing features of narrative work being linked to the two elements of sequence and consequence: to tell a story you need to select the events, create a structure and connect the events, and then evaluate the overall meaning. Petersen *et al.* (2005) warn that verbally processing traumatic experiences and memories can be difficult for some clients – particularly those who experience alexithymia, which makes putting feelings and emotions into words very difficult – and therefore other forms of communication should be introduced into the process of narrative therapy, including photography. Moxley *et al.* (2012) used photography alongside narrative therapy in their research with homeless African American woman and found that using images helped to externalise the problem when the women were asked to look at areas that compromised resilience. Adding a visual element into narrative work appeared to allow service users to introduce metaphors for issues that might be difficult to directly address (Sitvast & Abma, 2012). In their work in health care, Sitvast and Abma (2012) recognised the value of using photographs to elicit the narrative and describe it this as *hermeneutic photography*, wherein the therapeutic relationship explores how meaning is constructed. The use of metaphors within images to represent other, deeper and unconscious meanings can be explored through photographs.

■ DISPLACEMENT

Jack was very mild mannered and spoke gently about most subjects, but when asked to explore something he disliked he chose to focus on recycling. It was not the ethos of recycling he was opposed to, in fact, he felt the action was necessary – what he objected to was how recycling was managed in his community, and specifically, by his council. He went on to explain that different bins were required for different items, yet no bin was provided for glass items and this was because the council did not recycle glass. The company that the council commissioned to manage recycling did not have the equipment to deal with glass, therefore it was not collected.

> Jack got angrier about this issue as he explored it, raising his voice and describing the council's attitude as "draconian and dictator-like". He said the council was there to serve the population, yet it seemed that the opposite was in effect, and the people had to bend to the will of the council.
>
> Jack was a carer for his wife, and he was also reliant on services from the council to help with care provision. The issue of recycling, and the attitude of the council to this service, appeared to permeate service provision across the local authority, and Jack had a chance to vent his frustration and anger at the council during this exercise. Recycling, for Jack, was just the tip of the iceberg – their care provision was a much deeper issue for him.

In another health sector, the use of photographs to underpin patient narratives proved beneficial when working with individuals with type 1 diabetes in that it provided a patient-centred approach and changed the consultation style between the physician and the patient. In their study, Smith *et al.* (2006) encouraged participants to use photography to aid communication in consultations to look at how they were managing their disease, and to allow for reflection on beliefs and behaviours as and when they arose.

When a client is recounting their life story, the narrative may conform to what society deems acceptable and normal, but adding a visual element into narrative therapy means that a self-initiated photograph may assist in the circumvention of defence mechanisms (Barbee, 2002). Photographs themselves can evoke narratives and can allow the professional to explore the story with the client, which emphasises the role of the photograph as a neutral third party in the therapeutic relationship (Parker, 2009). This is particularly useful in narrative therapy because it redresses the power balance in the therapeutic relationship and can facilitate the therapeutic alliance. Pink (2013) believes that exploring the narrative with the aid of visuals provides useful information to facilitate understanding about how clients experience social environments, but also warns that no singular narrative is offered up in any one image and that the professional must be willing to explore the meanings, which could be multiple. Ketelle (2010) believes that in exploring narrative with the benefit of photography, both are closely intertwined because both are socially constructed so that one informs the other, while Washington *et al.* (2009) observed that using a combination of narrative exploration and photography with minority groups had two distinct benefits. First, it *documented* experiences, and second, it helped identify where *strengths* were drawn from, thus making the outcome of the intervention that of empowerment. They also found that an additional effect of their study with African American woman who had experienced homelessness was that the use of images helped the participants give meaning to their homelessness experience and recognise it as part of their lives, but one that did not define their whole identity (Washington *et al.*, 2009).

Erving Goffman's work impacted on White and Epston's narrative therapy, and has helped professionals recognise the impact of stigma and labelling, particularly when working with marginalised communities, or members of those communities. Goffman (2009) wrote about *social identity* and *personal identity* and explained that social identity can lead to alienation and isolation if the larger population of the society deems the membership of a certain social category to be far from ideal. He went on to explain that personal identity is how each and every individual feels about themselves and that it impacts on the formation of a history or a biography to explain their uniqueness. When the effects of stigmatisation from social identity impact on self-esteem, personal identity is also affected. This viewpoint echoes the work of others such as Mead, Cooley, Bronfenbrenner and Winnicott who believed that, as we are social beings, identity is formed by observing and interpreting responses from others; we then incorporate this feedback from interactions into our identity (Crocker, 1999). Goffman (2009) underpinned his discussions by aligning his thinking with Erikson's (1963) writing and likened the development of social identity to the development of the ego across the lifespan; however, he has been criticised for neglecting to look at the formation of selfhood, and also for taking little account of motivation (Jenkins, 2008). Despite this, his identification of the impact of stigma on individuals in society facilitates professionals to recognise that negative outcomes may be the result of prejudice from society rather than individual shortcomings, and this knowledge can help to address self-esteem issues (Crocker, 1999; Crocker & Major, 1989).

TWO LIKES, ONE DISLIKE

An interesting exercise to encourage the exploration of the environment revolves around a game known as "Room 101". In it, the participants should be encouraged to photograph three things – two should be images illustrating something they like, and one should be something they dislike. Once they have three images, they show them to the other participants to see if they can guess which images are "likes" and which are "dislikes". Once this has been done, it is a good idea to encourage participants to elaborate on why they photographed the items they liked.

Then, each participant is left with the image representing a dislike, and they each need to argue a case for banishing that thing from the planet forever – confining it to Room 101. This is a fun exercise, but allows participants to engage in healthy debate as the other participants should be encouraged to explore alternative views to banishing the item. Once everyone has stated their case, all of the participants need to come to a consensus as to which item they have chosen to get rid of.

During a therapeutic photography group with women who were receiving support from a criminal justice service, the participants explored their immediate environment. One woman, Janet, produced the image above. She stated that this image represented a dislike, and when it came to argue her case she explained that the city she lived in was not a big one, and the police knew who the local trouble makers were. She said that this resulted in families being labelled as "bad" by the police, and if there was any trouble in the neighbourhood, then the police usually came looking for her and her family. The other participants recognised this issue and spoke about the labelling and stigma that they all experienced. They discussed what the world would be like if there were no police and explored a variety of crimes, looking at minor crimes that did not require punishment, through to major crimes that clearly demanded punishment.

During this exploration, Janet admitted that she had deserved to be caught and punished for her crime, and began to see why the police were an asset in the environment she lived in. There was balanced discussion which recognised oppression, but also the value of the police force. She ended her exploration of law enforcement by explaining how she took the photograph. She said that she had approached the police officer and asked if she could take his photograph. He had said, "No, but you can photograph my hat if you like", so she did. She said that she had a laugh with the policeman about her photograph, thanked him, and left. On reflection, she then announced, "I think that was the most positive interaction I have ever had with the police!"

Labelling theory is often associated with stigma in that once an individual is categorised into a certain role, the attributes of that role affect the self-esteem of the individual, which becomes a self-fulfilling prophecy as the individual begins to adopt the characteristics. An example of this might be when someone finds out they have a mental illness and believes they are going to be alienated, rejected and devalued by society, and begins to adopt this role (Link et al., 1989). Rosenberg et al. (1989) believe that self-esteem underpins human motivation in that every person wants to achieve self-maintenance or self-enhancement, and this is gained through three different sources:

1. From observing and interpreting responses of others.

2. From self-perceptions.

3. From social comparisons.

If an individual feels appreciated by other people, if they feel that their actions are effective and productive, and if they feel that they compare favourably to others, then self-esteem will be enhanced (Verhaeghe et al., 2008; Gecas, 1989).

Within therapeutic practice it is not only self-esteem that needs to be considered, but also self-efficacy. Bandura (1977) identified self-efficacy as one of the main factors which underlies behavioural change and stated that those with good levels of self-efficacy were able to believe in their ability to make and maintain change. This is closely tied in with self-esteem because human beings not only derive a sense of self from the reaction of others, but from self-evaluations of how actions and consequences of behaviour impact on self-development

(Gecas & Schwalbe, 1983). For self-esteem to be effectively developed, the power dynamics of the therapeutic relationship need to be considered. If the power balance is too unequal and the person trying to develop self-efficacy is at the lower end of that power scale, then they will look for positive feedback from the person who holds the power, and then use this positive feedback to enhance self-esteem. If the power dynamics are balanced, then the person developing self-efficacy may still be motivated by the feedback from others, but there should also be motivation from recognising the outcomes of their actions and how this can effect change in their life (Gecas & Schwalbe, 1983).

Bandura (1982) identifies four areas of experience in which self-efficacy is developed:

1. Enactive mastery (building confidence and skills).

2. Vicarious experience (seeing others overcome challenges).

3. Verbal persuasion (positive feedback from others).

4. Physiological arousal (understanding emotions and the consequences of them).

Ultimately, how an individual cognitively appraises and integrates these experiences will determine levels of self-efficacy. The last of the four areas of experience, physiological arousal, acknowledges the impact of anxiety on self-efficacy, which links back into psychoanalytical theories where this particular emotion drives the ego to protect the id by employing defence mechanisms.

This suggests that it is beneficial for professionals to consider self-efficacy when planning interventions. This should involve an assessment of the task in hand, as well as the individual's personal resources and constraints, and careful management of interventions can facilitate a positive change in self-efficacy (Gist & Mitchell, 1992). Bandura (1977, 1982) also recognises that self-efficacy involves outcome expectations and therefore it is important to consider motivation alongside self-efficacy. He believes that outcome expectations are impacted by the environment, and Gecas (1989) also suggests that, from a sociological perspective, individuals are actors within their own environments but need to take an active and creative view of themselves so that they can appreciate that they have a role in shaping and creating the world around them as well as being created by it. Bandura *et al.* (2001) recognise that cultural differences will affect self-efficacy beliefs, and Gecas also identifies that self-efficacy will be affected by social structure, gender, social stability and change, as well as development over the life course, but that any work to enhance self-efficacy has beneficial and therapeutic consequences. If an intervention can facilitate identification and discussion of cultural impacts then this suggests that poor self-efficacy could be redressed.

Summary

It has been suggested that helping a client to identify and externalise a problem makes it easier to begin to address and understand it (White & Epston, 1990). If objectified, this creates a third "entity" in the relationship between professional and client and establishes a triangulation (Janzen & Harris, 1986) that can provide stability, and in the case of photography, can be described as the neutral third party (Parker, 2009).

If professionals aim to facilitate change, they need to consider what contributes towards the motivation to change, and what hinders efforts to make change. To do this, psychodynamic theories can be considered alongside sociological factors, and the professional must recognise the powerful force that attitudes, beliefs and cultural values play on stigmatising and labelling clients, then work to address this in tandem with the client.

In doing this, self-esteem and self-efficacy need to be acknowledged as these factors will impact on self-concept and motivation. If therapeutic intervention is successful, it has also been suggested that empowerment is an outcome to be expected, and it is to this concept that the next chapter will turn.

Chapter 9

USING PHOTOGRAPHY TO MAKE CHANGES TO SOCIETY

Using skills from the previous chapters, this final stage looks at using photography to identify common issues and then empower groups to display the images to people who can make changes. This is underpinned by the work of Wang and Burris (1997), who initiated the approach and spurred on the photovoice movement. This chapter explores the concept of societal exploration and looks at the work of Paulo Freire and his writings about community empowerment to ascertain how this can be incorporated into therapeutic photography. To do this, the merit of group work is also discussed and examples from practice are used throughout to demonstrate how this approach can be put into operation. It is an approach that gives a voice and a sense of control to marginalised groups and communities in order for them to explore issues relevant to them, and then identify common themes within their images.

Photography to explore society

Griebling *et al.* (2013) propose a hierarchy of photographic methods based on the level of participation and the personal growth of the client, as well as the impact on the wider community. First on the scale, they feel that photographic methods document, investigate, evaluate and uncover. Photo elicitation is second on the scale, followed by the ability to challenge, and the third goal would be to empower. The technique of photovoice sits at the far end of this hierarchy.

Photovoice was developed by Caroline Wang and Mary Ann Burris who, in 1992, set up a project which they called "photo novella" (which later became known as "photovoice") to assist women in a Chinese village to photograph their everyday health and work routines, the underlying aim being to learn first-hand what challenges these women faced. Wang (1999) explains that this was underpinned by feminist methodology so that the programmes and policies could be developed *with* the women, as opposed to *for* the women. Allowing the women in the project to control the process of taking photographs in order to communicate the challenges they faced made them the experts of their problems as opposed to sending in researchers to confirm or deny hypothesised problems. The goal with photovoice is to find a common theme among the group of participants and present the findings to policymakers in order to facilitate change, a strategy which is claimed to have stimulated improvements as a result of a number of projects (Wang *et al.*, 1996; Wang *et al.*, 2000; Wang *et al.*, 2004). In the case of the Chinese rural community, photovoice was attributed to three policy changes aimed at day care, midwifery and education for girls, because the images illustrated to the policymakers the realities of the hardships the women were encountering (Ozanne *et al.*, 2013; Wang *et al.*, 1996).

Wang developed five overarching stages to help guide the photovoice process:

1. In collaboration with all of the participants, themes, topics and issues need to be identified so that there is a guiding "brief" for taking photographs, although she admits this is not always possible and that sometimes the researcher may have to be directive to encourage a theme to be focused on (Wang *et al.*, 1996).

2. All of the participants need to be trained so that they can use the photographic equipment, then go out and gather images with their cameras.

3. As a group, the images are presented and discussed, the purpose being to reflect on the underlying meanings and to critically analyse each other's work.

4. Narratives are shared and the participants learn from each other's experiences.

5. The message taken from these collated stories and experiences are shared with policymakers, usually by displaying the photographs taken during the project (Griebling *et al.*, 2013).

USING PHOTOVOICE

If you are using therapeutic photography with a group, photovoice is a useful technique to consider and forms the final part of the proposed programme within the Appendix. When using this exercise with a group of participants, it is important to get them to think about a theme to investigate. Ideally, it should be an issue that is important to all of the participants, and one that allows exploration of the good points, as well as the bad points.

Once a theme has been selected, the next thing to think about is how many images each participant should produce, and the timescale they will need to do this. Again, the group should come to a collective decision about a rough number of images so that everyone knows the limits and boundaries of the project. It is also a good idea to discourage participants to think in a 50/50 manner and view the set number of images to be split equally between the good points and the bad points – some participants might have many more good points to photograph than bad, and vice versa.

Photovoice is a project where participants gather images on an individual basis, and then after a certain amount of time, reconvene and explore the images they have taken, looking for common themes, issues and narratives.

The exploration stage is an opportunity for everyone to present, and to ask questions of each other. There will also be a large number of images on display, and it is worth considering what the participants would like to do with all of the images. If they have uncovered some interesting themes around the issue they have been exploring, they may wish to publicly display the photographs to inform other people about their findings, and their project. Given that the ethos underpinning photovoice is centred on empowerment, the decisions need to be driven by the participants wherever possible.

Throughout this chapter, you will find images which were part of a photovoice project with people who were living with mental health problems. They decided to explore a concept around mental health and called their project "My Safe Space". In their exploration, they wanted to capture things that gave them safety and things that jeopardised their safety. The result was a collection of images that documented what it was like to live with mental health issues, but alongside this the participants recognised that they were no longer isolated by their conditions and experiences as there were common issues among them all.

Photovoice has been used with a wide variety of minority groups, and Wang (1999) explains that the success of the intervention is due to some basic concepts. The images produced facilitate teaching, which can be in a formal sense to influence health and well-being, as well as social policy, or it can be self-directed learning and expanding personal knowledge about how we view ourselves. Because the main outputs from this intervention are photographs, the resulting images can help to educate participants about common issues, and in turn help to inform policymakers. If policymakers do not directly view the photographs, the participants should still feel empowered through the process and have an awareness of issues which can then perpetuate action. Community action lies at the heart of photovoice, and Wang believes it is the action of people coming together and sharing the stories behind their creations that makes photovoice an empowering intervention. There is also a sense that the participants are educating themselves and others. De (2015) noted that when young girls in an Indian slum were given cameras to participate in a photovoice project they felt they were getting the opportunity to explore their story through the photographs. They explained that photographers could have taken images that were similar to the ones they produced, but the girls all had narratives that underpinned the significance of the image, and the story they were telling was from the girls' perspective, therefore the viewer got a sense of "girls' issues" (De, 2015, p.34).

As well as feminist theory, photovoice is a Freirean process (Griebling *et al.*, 2013; Ozanne *et al.*, 2013; Duffy, 2011; Strack *et al.*, 2010; Catalani & Minkler, 2010; Carlson *et al.*, 2006). Paolo Freire recognised that marginalised groups often feel powerless to the extent that community participation is rare, and to effect social change the perspectives of these marginalised groups is vital (Duffy, 2011). Freire proposed that community change can only be brought about by engaging people in dialogue within the communities, encouraging critical reflection in a safe environment to look at why current issues are present, raising levels of critical consciousness to encourage action, and putting pressure on policymakers to initiate change (Strack *et al.*, 2010). Photovoice goes hand in hand with the Freirean process as the learners and teachers are seen as co-creators of knowledge, taking an egalitarian approach to creating knowledge through introspection, which is intended to guide participants through three levels of consciousness, which Freire identified:

1. At the base level, which Freire termed the *magical level*, participants assumed they had no voice, that they were inferior, and that this was the accepted norm.

2. The next level is termed the *naive level of consciousness* and at this stage participants view the social situation as having been corrupted, but instead of addressing issues of hierarchical injustice, they direct blame at their peers.

3. The final level, known as *critical consciousness*, sees a developing awareness of how individual assumptions can shape perceptions of reality, the result being a responsibility for making choices that either accept the status quo, or begin to make a change (Carlson *et al.*, 2006; Freire, 1998).

One of the main intended outcomes for participants involved in photovoice is that of empowerment. Wang and Burris (1994) aimed to empower the Chinese women they worked with in the photo novella project and identified that for empowerment to work there needed to be access to knowledge, decisions, networks and resources. Raeburn and Rootman (1998) identify control, participation and competence as characteristics of empowerment, and Duffy (2011) recognises that the definitions of empowerment are wide ranging and might encompass activities as diverse as learning a new skill, through to taking part in political action. Catalani and Minkler (2010) write that it is the element of engaging participants in critical dialogue with peers, using images that document strengths and issues within the community, which contributes to the outcome of empowerment within photovoice. They further state that as well as individual empowerment, the outcomes include enhanced community engagement and improved understanding of the needs of the community.

▨ STRENGTH AND RESILIENCE

In her exploration of "My Safe Space", Jane took a photograph of her bedroom (above). In it the room is ordered and nicely presented, and she explained that this represents a good day for her. To contrast this, she then presented the following image.

This photograph represents a bad day, and the beginning of a downward spiral. In the image, she used pillows to recreate the form of someone sleeping in the bed, and she explained that this is her when she is beginning to feel depressed, with the covers firmly over her head. She has also pulled the curtains so that they are closed and this represents shutting the day out. Closed curtains turned out to be a common theme among the participants as they all did that, yet they thought they were alone in their actions and did not realise that this was a common trait among them. The final statement within Jane's image is the phone, and the fact that it is off the hook so that she cannot be contacted.

The value within Jane's images was twofold. She had thought about her own triggers and realised that any of the factors she had captured in the image were signs that she needed to seek help for herself, but the fact that she was presenting her "findings" to her peer group was also informing and educating them on the importance of identifying triggers and developing an action plan to address them if, and when, they arise.

A number of studies suggest that the practice of photovoice should follow a structure known as SHOWeD (Griebling *et al.*, 2013; Catalani & Minkler, 2010; Gant *et al.*, 2009; Wilson *et al.*, 2007; Mitchell *et al.*, 2006; Wang, 1999) which is an acronym for:

- What do you **S**ee in the photograph?
- What is really **H**appening here?
- How does this relate to **O**ur lives?
- **W**hy do these issues exist?
- What can we **D**o to address these issues?

Griebling *et al.* (2013) also highlight that the PHOTO question can be used instead of the SHOWeD format which is structured like this:

- Describe your **P**hotograph?
- What is **H**appening in this picture?
- Why did you take a picture **O**f this?
- What does the picture **T**ell us about your life?
- What **O**pportunities does this provide to help improve the lives of the group in question?

Following these lines of questioning can highlight common themes and issues, particularly if discussed among the group of photographers who have taken the images. In a project run by Mitchell *et al.* (2005), photovoice was used to look at incidences of sexual abuse within Swaziland schools. Single sex groupings of children were asked to photograph areas where they felt "safe" and where they felt "not so safe". When the photographs were analysed by the groups there were a large number of images portraying the girls' toilets and bushes around the school area, all marked as "not so safe". The teachers were alarmed at the high number of photographs, but these areas were zones within the school where the girls were particularly vulnerable to sexual attack. In a further project, Mitchell *et al.* (2006) used photovoice to explore absenteeism among school-aged children and they referred to the results as "rich insider data" (p.274) as the participants were able to illustrate reasons for being absent without feeling interrogated.

The therapeutic benefits of engaging with photovoice were also highlighted by Aubeeluck and Buchanan (2006), who used the method to elicit views of informal carers for relatives with Huntington's disease. They noted that because the carers had time to capture issues as and when they arose, and because they had time to reflect on positive aspects of the caring relationship as well as negative aspects, the carers felt their needs were expressed more accurately and described the process as "therapeutic and cathartic" (Aubeeluck & Buchanan, 2006, p.109).

Loopmans *et al.* (2012) identify a number of advantages of using photovoice to communicate a message. First, they believe that photography is a very accessible form of communication, perhaps more so than writing, and only a very small amount of training is needed to produce images that communicate a message. Second, an unedited image taken straight from the camera gives "a direct and straightforward representation of the world" (p.702) and therefore adds visual clarity to communication. Third, they reiterate an observation made by Newbury and Hoskins (2011) when exploring photo elicitation: the way in which a photograph is viewed helps to redirect the dominant gaze in that the interviewer and interviewee will sit alongside each other to look at the photograph as opposed to sitting opposite each other, looking at each other, in a traditional interviewer–interviewee relationship. Finally, to support Wang and Burris's (1997) argument, they state it can be used to empower communities by exploring issues and options for future action. Moletsane *et al.* (2007) recognise the value of using photovoice to access stigmatised communities and engage them in social change, but they also recognise that using photographs to communicate a message includes significant elements of having fun, an important aspect when engaging younger people. They suggest that enhanced engagement leads to sustained attention and involvement, which ultimately leads to enhanced self-efficacy.

However, there will be occasions where it is not safe to take photographs. Wilson *et al.* (2007) used photovoice with an after-school programme to look at the strengths and issues in the communities where drug use and violence were rife. One group wanted to take images that represented the drug culture but this was deemed to be too dangerous so instead they were encouraged to write about images that they *could not* capture. Goodhart *et al.* (2006) had similar problems when using photovoice to empower students to advocate for their rights. They found that students were faced with unintended consequences when taking pictures of underage alcohol use and illegal drug use. Students were therefore advised not to take photographs that could harm themselves or others, which ultimately affected the honesty of the images used within this project. It is therefore important to ask the question, "Was there anything that you could not photograph?" at the discussion stage. Moletsane *et al.* (2007) found that the participants also got around this challenge by staging photographs and then explaining the meaning behind the photographs at the discussion stage.

Goodhart *et al.* (2006) recognised that there were challenges around confidentiality and privacy when photographing other people which had to be addressed from the outset so that civil liberties were not breached. They noted that engagement was affected if participants were not clear as to the purpose or method of using photovoice, and for optimal involvement the participants needed to opt into the project, rather than do so under compulsion. They also highlighted that the quality of equipment used would affect outcomes and engagement (but recognised that this would be dictated by finances). However, Loopmans *et al.* (2012) explain that if participants are only selected on their motivation to engage with photography, this potentially excludes those with low self-efficacy. They illustrate this point by noting that two male participants in their study of a deprived Scottish community expressed unease at using photography because they did not believe they were from the "correct social class" (p.713), but as they engaged with the process they realised the potential the medium had to initiate change within the community and at a political level.

Wilson *et al.* (2007) suggest that the success of their photovoice project with adolescents was affected by the participants' cognitive abilities and their age and stage of development. They state that the level of analytic thought required in the SHOWeD process may well have been beyond the capabilities of younger participants and highlight the work of Vygotsky's (1962) social constructivist theory to add validity to their observations. Gant *et al.* (2009) reflect on the process of photovoice and believe that the claims over the effectiveness of the technique are often unsubstantiated due to lack of empirical evidence. In an effort to provide quantitative data they researched civic engagement among youth by engaging them in a photovoice project and using a pre- and post-project questionnaire (Survey of Youth Engagement) to ascertain any changes in attitudes. They concluded that photovoice had minimal impact on the under-18s in terms of engaging them in the community, but a greater impact on the 18 and over group. However, as each participant was paid $500 at the end of the project, one may query the impact this had on the reported data post-project.

Loopmans *et al.* (2012) acknowledge that participants of photovoice may also self-censor their photographs if they know they are going to be displayed within the community in order to conform to community norms and privacy, which suggests there should not be a compulsion to display all images, and that the participants should be involved in the overall selection process at the end of the project to reduce any need to censor during the project.

ABSTRACT REPRESENTATION

Censoring images is a consideration, but before attempting a photovoice project, some of the exercises listed in the Appendix will give participants skills and experience in trying to represent issues and hard-to-photograph topics in an abstract manner. During the "My Safe Space" project, one of the participants produced the following image.

This unassuming spaniel received a chorus of "ooohs!" and "aaahs" from the peer group, but the photographer explained that the dog represented a threat to her safe space. She went on to explain that she had recently read a book about depression and it had used the term, coined by Sir Winston Churchill, of a "Black Dog" to refer to the illness. She had remembered this, and it had remained with her, so she was able to creatively represent the condition of depression by photographing her own black dog.

Catalani and Minkler (2010) conducted a review of literature in relation to health and public health where photovoice was used. They identified 37 articles and found that participation was variable, with only 27 per cent of studies reporting a high level of participation, although they do recognise that the articles included in the studies were vague on levels of participation. The average duration of a photovoice project was roughly four months but there were very few consistent practices across the articles. Eighty-five per cent of the projects involved an element of photo elicitation, where participants would be expected to talk about the meaning of the photographs. Most of the studies were rooted in feminist theory and Freirean ideology and, again, the outcomes of the projects tended to fall into three categories:

1. Enhanced engagement with the community.

2. Better understanding of the needs of the community.

3. Increased empowerment for the individuals involved in the project.

Catalani and Minkler (2010) suggest that empowerment stems from partnership, community participation, learning new skills through training, and through *researching* the environment, which leads to discussion and action. However, they also note that none of the studies looked at long-term empowerment and that there was an assumption that if empowerment was an outcome of photovoice then this would naturally have longevity. These factors suggest either an ad hoc approach to delivering photovoice, or the flexibility of photovoice to meet a wide variety of communities.

There is a risk of over-emphasising the importance and effectiveness of photovoice, and Mitchell *et al.* (2006) warn against promising too much to participants who choose to become involved with projects. If the outcome of empowerment is explicitly promised then expectations are raised, and when set in a climate where social and cultural change is slow, the lack of immediate efficacy at the end of the project may be counter-productive to any promise of empowerment. Wilson *et al.* (2007) underline the flexibility of the technique and suggest that efficacy results in listening to the participants in terms of what end goal *they* want to achieve, rather than setting a prescriptive outcome of targeting policymakers. In their work within a school, it was decided to target the school principal in order to effect change.

The relative simplicity of the process has appeal, and the scope of engagement across a wide range of communities is evident; if the means are both accessible and acceptable then engagement with a view to effect change has a motivating factor (Watson & Douglas, 2012). It has also been suggested that because of the Freirean underpinnings that foster group discussions and analysis, the potential for change across social ecology (individual, family, community, organisational and society) is high (Strack *et al.*, 2010).

Theory and society

The practice of photovoice is built on three core principles: it adopts a feminist perspective wherein it can be used to question oppression and inequality; it is built on a Freirean process that takes a pedagogical approach to address issues of powerlessness; and the outcome of the process aims to empower participants (Duffy, 2011; Catalani & Minkler, 2010; Carlson *et al.*, 2006; Wang, 1999).

Empowerment is a concept that many professionals embrace within their practice as it enables alliances within working, therapeutic relationships and aims to achieve greater understanding and change in the lives of clients by helping to understand social and personal obstacles (Payne, 2014). Empowerment also underpins the objectives of Freire's work, as well as feminist perspectives, and it is therefore important to consider how applicable these two approaches are to the professional ethos and values of client-based work, before looking at how empowerment in practice manifests.

Paulo Freire was a Brazilian philosopher and spent many years working in education. He faced hardship and adversity when growing up, which made him reflect on social class with regards to education in his country, and this formed the bedrock of his philosophical viewpoints. His most famous writings were published in *Pedagogy of the Oppressed* in 1968 but he wrote extensively about combating social inequities across his varied and turbulent life.

Freire (1990) largely wrote about education, but many of his writings addressed other professions. In his focus on professions, he highlighted issues that have applicability across a large number of health and social care sectors. He believed that professionals often took on the role of educator in their contact with clients, but to successfully perform this role the professional needs to be aware of how and why they practise. He explained that individual professional workers are not neutral agents and will have their own beliefs, personal values and political leanings, which they need to acknowledge. This means that professionals should not view themselves as specialist technicians, but instead they should attempt to work alongside their clients in a progressive manner. In order to be progressive, a professional needs to be aware of the gaps between their lives and the lives of their clients, as it is impossible to be progressive if the professional believes they are inherently *better* than the clients they work with. In order to close this gap, the professional must develop a critical curiosity to question themselves and the world around them, but also to foster this in the people they work with, and only then will a professional develop an effective knowledge of the problems within the society in which they work. From a pedagogical standpoint, the professional must not assume that they have all the answers, but instead try to listen to the questions posed to them by the client.

Freire's (1998) views are critical of the traditional model of pedagogy as a means of filling up the empty vessel (the student) with knowledge. He believed that this perspective is disempowering for the student and that a better way of approaching pedagogy is to view the student and teacher as co-creators of knowledge, both willing to learn from each other, and both willing to listen to each other. Only when the power balance is equalised can the student use their learning to achieve equilibrium between theory and practice so that informed action can be taken and freedom to feel complete as a human being is achieved, which Freire termed *praxis*. Critical consciousness is another outcome of the Freirean approach, which results in an awareness of issues and empowerment to take action to challenge those issues (Hare, 2004). Black and Rose (2002) believe a Freirean approach empowers clients to become active participants in developing their roles, rather than simply objects who allow people to control their lives, and that by engaging in critical debate and exploring subjective and objective reality, a transformation from dependence to interdependence can be achieved. The overall aim of the Freirean approach is to empower clients to be able to communicate issues that they are facing. In communicating these issues, they are helping others to learn about experiences they are facing, informing possible interventions, and becoming co-producers rather than passive consumers of professional services (Payne, 2014).

▨ LEARNING FROM OTHERS

Linda explored her safe spaces and spoke about the importance of family, and of attending support groups, but then she produced the image below. The photograph had captured an empty waiting room, and Linda explained that this was the psychotherapy department where she attended outpatient appointments. This was a big revelation as she had never discussed this with her peers before, but she was able to objectify her support structure and display this to the group. She explained that this was a space for her which she relied on and where she felt secure. She could come and speak to professionals about her condition, and this service was vital to her.

Linda later revealed that the experience of sharing this image, and her other photographs throughout the various tasks, had been empowering for her. She qualified this by explaining that she had learned from the other participants, and no longer felt alone in how she managed her mental health condition. Empowerment was the beginning of something new for her – she explained that she had never felt compelled to join a group before, but because of the photographic element of the tasks, she had been drawn to participate in therapeutic photography and she now felt that she would be more inclined to join another group after her experience with therapeutic photography, something she would never have previously considered.

When Wang and Burris undertook their first photovoice (photo novella) project their intention was to explore the perspectives of Chinese women and the issues they faced in accessing health care. They worked from a feminist methodology, developing support *with* the women (Wang, 1999). Many professional disciplines must also consider feminist perspectives in practice, with an aim to identify gender inequality, eliminate these issues and promote the well-being of women as they define it (Dominelli & Campling, 2002). An awareness of society's expectations of roles and responsibilities of females is essential to understand how oppression occurs due to social and political norms (Payne, 2014; Trevithick, 2012); if conformity to these societal norms does not occur then this can often be seen as a female failing. In therapeutic work with couples or families, it is not enough to simply look at traditional gender alignments and expect the male to be the breadwinner, while the female tends the children; instead, practitioners must adopt an empowering, anti-oppressive framework towards practice and try to address the social contexts that impact on the feelings of failure and oppression (Walker, in Lishman, 2015).

Trevithick (2012) highlights five main principles for professionals to consider when working from a feminist perspective:

1. There should be an acceptance that there are inequalities between genders and that these differences have a realistic impact on opportunities and life chances.

2. Much like the Freirean approach, professionals should have a general interest in and commitment to exploring issues with clients to build up knowledge and awareness.

3. Female clients should be encouraged to shift their thinking towards being motivated to do things for themselves rather than for other people, or for family members.

4. Power imbalances within the working relationship must be acknowledged, but working in an open, honest and reliable manner should reduce the gap.

5. In an effort to seek collective solutions to issues, ways of working that link personal issues to political issues should be enhanced, again mirroring the Freirean approach of working towards critical consciousness.

Hudson (1985) believes that taking a feminist perspective can be challenging and workers who do this leave themselves open to allegations of engaging their personal values, rather than professional values, and lacking objectivity when practising. However, Dominelli and Campling (2002) state that this is simply an argument to oppress the feminist movement, that a professional working from a true feminist perspective would never impose their ideology onto clients or colleagues, and that there should be complete acceptance of any female choice as to the individual level of involvement with the feminist agenda.

▓ REMINISCENCE

Ruth came from a large family and she explained that her identity was heavily influenced by this. She remembered getting on a bus as a young child with all of her brothers and sisters and hearing comments from the other passengers about the size of the family. This was not always a positive thing, as she went on to explore how the identity of her family subsumed her own personal identity and, years later, she went through a rebellious phase where she was determined to find her own identity and shake off the family expectations she had grown up with.

But her relationship with her mother had endured and she had always been close to her. She remembered the picture of Mary and Jesus hanging in the living room when she was growing up, and when her mother became too frail to live on her own, she moved into a care home and the picture followed her. It hung above her mother's bed until she passed away, and now Ruth had the picture in her own flat, hanging in the living room.

> For Ruth, the photograph of her mother's picture (above) represented memories and nostalgia which, in turn, represented a safe space for her. She loved reminiscing and remembering how things used to be, and this was shared by all of the other participants. One of the other group members spoke about how she regularly looked at old family photographs, just so she could reminisce and "get lost in the good old days", even describing how photographs of her grandmother evoked the smell of baking in her kitchen. These opportunities to reminisce also allowed the female members of the group to discuss their roles as daughters, mothers and, in some cases, grandmothers.

It is also difficult to ignore the power imbalance between professional workers and their clients, particularly in statutory settings, and White (1995) states that this makes practising from a feminist perspective challenging as there can be a tendency to deny the power imbalances within these relationships. However, Dietz (2000) argues that professional practice can benefit when feminism is paired with empowerment perspectives. She refers to the use of language and how problems are constructed by linguistics, which results in a professional tendency to over-pathologise. The terminology professionals use to define problems can borrow heavily from other disciplines, particularly professionals from social work and social care backgrounds, and risks becoming overly medical, resulting in the objectification of the *problem* at the expense of viewing it in context to take account of resilience and empowerment factors. This was the standpoint that Jo Spence took when working with self-portraits to regain her identity while going through treatment for breast cancer (see Chapter 4). As a result, some professionals only focus on the micro level of treatment, targeting interventions at the individual level rather than looking at the holistic picture and considering oppression at all levels. Dietz believes that empowerment through feminist practice involves a critical consciousness of the political environment, but also reconnecting through relationships that are built on trust and collaboration, and being allowed to explore narratives. The experience of telling the story can be a healing experience in itself because oppression can be explored and validated by an empathic listener. Indeed, Parton (2003) believes that incorporating feminist perspectives into practice moves the professional towards a constructive approach where attention is given to collaborative narratives; clients are encouraged to explore their narratives, externalise issues, and then create new ways of managing the challenges – a similar ethos to that which underpins narrative therapy (as explored in Chapter 8).

E. Summerson Carr (2003) suggests that conceptualising the aims of a feminist approach into the three broad categories of consciousness, identity and agency can help professionals align outcomes with those of empowerment in practice. Within professional practice and disciplines, consideration of empowerment is a two-way process that helps workers to consider social barriers that might stand in the way of clients achieving objectives, and gives information on how to challenge these, but it also helps workers to enable clients to become involved in the decision-making process, building capacity as well as self-determination (Payne, 2014).

Gutierrez (1994) believes that the process of empowerment involves an individual moving through four different stages:

1. Increasing self-efficacy and believing that change can come from within.

2. Understanding the Freirean concept of developing critical consciousness and the challenges faced.

3. Developing the ability to reflect on previous actions and use this information to inform future action.

4. Identifying with others who are facing similar experiences.

However, there is growing concern that the term "empowerment" has become a buzzword that is used to generalise outcomes of professional involvement without actually considering how professionals can work to truly empower clients (Leonardsen, 2007). Leonardsen goes on to explain that professionals can only work to empower if they are competent enough to identify the challenges of power dynamics and the complexity of issues facing clients, and that if they do have this ability then they should work to politicise their clients so that they develop the ability to act on situations. The simple way to achieve this is to begin with the question, "What is the problem?", but Askheim (2003) warns that many workers are caught in a dichotomy because to truly empower they must relinquish power and authority in their own roles, then be guided by the client as to how professional involvement should continue. This can pose a problem as the client's right to self-determination has to be considered alongside risks that their decisions might present.

Donaldson (2005) goes on to explain that there are therapeutic benefits to empowerment, particularly when working with groups. She feels that this is underpinned by Bandura's self-efficacy theory, but also Yalom and Leszcz's (2005) curative factors of group therapy. They identified 11 factors that they felt contributed to therapeutic change within groups:

1. *Universality* – recognition from other group members to validate struggles and shared experiences.

2. *Altruism* – satisfaction from helping others.

3. *Installation of hope* – belief in the efficacy of the group from both group facilitators and group members.

4. *Imparting information* – facilitators may begin by providing information in the hope that peer leaders will take over.

5. *Corrective recapitulation of family experience* – unconscious transference of familial experience onto the group, which needs to be identified by the facilitator so it can be understood by the members.

6. *Developing socialisation techniques* – through consciousness raising and interacting with a wide range of participants (peers and professionals), social skills will be developed.

7. *Imitative behaviour* – learning from the strengths of peers to develop self-esteem.

8. *Cohesiveness* – feeling a sense of belonging and developing from this interpersonal context.

9. *Existential factors* – developing intimacy through sharing experiences, but taking responsibility for one's own actions.

10. *Catharsis* – having a safe space to vent emotions and feelings, and feelings of relief through sharing and affirmation.

11. *Interpersonal learning and self-understanding* – through feedback from others, each member develops self-awareness and insight.

Breton (1995) believes that social action can only result from personal healing and that an individual has to address self-worth, which will impact on self-efficacy, and in turn may result in the ability to participate in collective action and engage in consciousness raising. Chapin and Cox (2002) also acknowledge that empowerment approaches need to consider the personal, interpersonal and political levels of practice, which suggests that individuals need to work out from an initial period of introspection, before progressing to considering peer involvement and the impact of the wider environment. Rappaport (1995) believes that incorporating narrative approaches into group work can enhance the goals of empowerment. She explains that individuals can find it difficult to sustain change without collective support, and from this collective support a communal narrative can develop which, once recognised, can either be sustained or changed.

■ PERSONAL GROWTH

Within the exploration of the "My Safe Space" project, the group was also solution focused, and there were a large number of images that highlighted coping strategies and ways of managing mental health conditions. Janet highlighted the importance of physical exercise for her and took a picture of a local outdoor swimming pool to show where she exercised.

The image was beautifully stark, as she had taken the photograph out of season when the facility was closed and she had managed to squeeze her camera through a gap in the fence. The other participants were very complimentary about the photograph and spoke about a sense of isolation, while at the same time, experiencing a sense of peace. It seemed to encapsulate many feelings and emotions that the group had been discussing.

The intended outcomes of therapeutic photography are to enhance self-esteem, self-efficacy and empowerment. Through Janet's involvement and engagement, she had produced a number of interesting images, but the colourful isolation and loneliness within her image of the swimming pool caught the attention of the group and demonstrated to her that she could produce interesting talking pieces through her photography, something which enhanced her self-esteem, as well as demonstrated self-efficacy. Learning that she was not alone and did not need to feel isolated was also empowering for her.

Summary

Empowerment is a nebulous concept that is difficult to quantify, but there is a suggestion that by opening up dialogue and identifying issues of oppression, this can raise levels of critical consciousness. Becoming aware of a problem is the first stage of being able to address a problem, and Freire (1998) identified this when he wrote about using education to empower communities. As critical consciousness is raised, it can be useful to share experiences with others, and this "strength in numbers" impacts on feelings of power, learning from others, identifying with others and taking action with others; these are all factors that can lead to enhanced feelings of empowerment.

For professionals working to encompass an empowering ideology, the power balance is again called into question, and it has been suggested that to be an effective therapeutic worker the professional needs to consider oppression from all angles (familial, peer, community, society), but also to be curious and willing to learn from clients. By becoming co-creators of knowledge, the power balance between the professional and client moves towards equilibrium.

Chapter 10

ADULTS WITH AUTISM: A CASE STUDY

Introduction

In this chapter, the ideas and theories presented in previous chapters are brought together and used within a group to demonstrate the efficacy and impact of therapeutic photography. Using the programme which is contained within the Appendix, a six-week group was conducted with five adults who were on the autism spectrum. The National Autistic Society estimate that 1.1 per cent of the UK population has autism, which means that approximately 1 in every 100 people has the condition, and this will also impact on the lives of family members and carers. Autism is a lifelong disability and, as a spectrum condition, it affects different people in different ways. This can mean that individuals require support with communication, care and other social skills, but may also mean that a person with autism can live independently with very little support. Asperger syndrome is also a form of autism and can mean that a person appears to have average (or above average) intelligence but may still experience issues with understanding and processing language.

A local organisation was approached and offered the opportunity to engage with a therapeutic photography programme. Five clients from the organisation opted into the programme.

This case study will begin by presenting a brief summary of the observed results from the group, then go into more detail about how the participants used photographs within the group environment and what issues they chose to explore. Throughout, extracts from observations will be presented, along with the original images and excerpts from the focus group interview held with the group at the end of the process. The final section will look at the observed outcomes from the experience.

The group was facilitated by the researcher and co-facilitated by a staff member, Janet, from the local organisation. The following is a brief summary of the participants:

- Charles: the only male participant. Lives independently in the city and has full-time employment but was allowed to take time off to attend the group. He is in his late 40s.

- Wendy: lives independently in the city. She is in her mid-20s.

- Sarah: lives in a rural village with her mum, her sister and a nephew (her sister's 2-year-old child). She is in her early 20s.

- Rebecca: lives in rural countryside with her mum and sister. She is in her early 20s.

- Tamara: Rebecca's sister. She is in her late teens.

Summary of outcome

The largest observed outcome for the group was the level of support the participants gained from one another, and the advice and assistance offered to those who were having issues. There were also observed impactors on self-efficacy, and the level of control (particularly around self-disclosure) that participants exercised was noticeable.

In terms of understanding the dynamics of individuals, group work was observed as being the biggest influence, which correlates with the high level of support observed in the outcomes. Within this, participants did spend considerable time exploring fears and strategies, which allowed advice to be offered to participants who were having problems. Family systems theory was also useful when looking at the support participants relied on, and Erikson's (1963) theories were also helpful when considering the age and developmental stage of each individual.

Identity was, by far, the main area explored through photography, and when looking at the individual results for each participant it was also clear that everyone focused on identity before any other issue. The other areas of exploration included isolation, role, family and creativity.

Group dynamics were challenging to begin with. Due to the nature of autism, social skills were varied and this meant that the first session was difficult to facilitate because of lack of verbal input from the participants. The oldest member of the group, Charles, offered the most information during the first session and began to talk about how challenging he found social situations.

> *Observation 1:* Charles explained that these images represented socialising and he said that this was something he could not do. He explained that he really did not like social situations and was not good at conducting himself within social situations and he recognised this was a "deficit" within himself.

This appeared to act as an opening for other group members because they seemed to realise that they were in a safe space where they could explore what it was like to have autism, and how it impacted on day-to-day living.

The second session was conducted in a local park and took the participants out of the familiar office-based surroundings. Feedback from the photographic exercise was conducted around a table in a cafe and the participants offered considerable detail within their narratives at this session. From session three onwards, participants offered much more depth to their narratives and the facilitator had to ensure everyone was given time to input into the conversation. It was also noted that participants liked to ask each other questions about the images which, at times, negated the role of the facilitator to guide the photographic enquiry.

How photography was used

Identity

Mead (1934, in Bagatell, 2007) believed that individuals form a sense of self through interaction with other people, therefore suggesting that identity formation is a complex, social phenomenon. Shakespeare (1996, in Bagatell, 2007) explains that for individuals with a disability, identity can also be defined by institutions and through identification with other people with similar conditions. However, Bagatell (2007) explored the pressures of identity formation for one young male with autism and acknowledges that identity formation is a challenge that everyone will face as they grow and develop, but for those with autism this can be compounded by lack of opportunities to participate in society, and lack of experiences to form relationships.

When looking at the narratives that the group attached to their photographs when exploring identity, there appeared to be similar trends. Charles disclosed his discomfort with social situations at the first session and called this a "deficit" within himself, stating that he viewed himself as the problem. He did go on to explain to the group that he had found ways to cope with familiar situations that required "routine reactions", but dreaded going into a room full of strangers. Yet he was sitting in a room full of strangers and offering insightful comments within 15 minutes of meeting them. The other group members offered little bits of information about themselves, such as a love of cartoons and creative expression, and insights into isolation, a theme which developed over the six weeks, but Charles was the person offering the most information from the outset.

Other participants soon found confidence to share information about themselves, which might have been because they could identify with each other as they had similar conditions, as Shakespeare (1996) suggests. The "self-portrait" exercise allowed participants to explore positive aspects of their characters, so both Rebecca and Sarah had photographed themselves engaged in creative activities, but Tamara decided to explore the exercise in a bit more depth.

Observation 2: Tamara said that this represented the way she saw the world, "through different eyes". She said that this represented her autism and that sometimes she could be receiving so many messages at the same time; whereas other people could focus on one part, she could not. She also said that she wanted to incorporate reflections from the past into the photograph because she did reflect on the past quite a lot and she wanted to get this into her image as well.

This was the first time a photograph like this had been presented in the group. The thought that had gone into producing it, the meaning within it, and the narrative attached to it were insightful, creative and, according to the group feedback, powerful. Tamara used an image to convey the challenge she had in filtering information, and all of the group members appeared to identify with this. Tamara was the youngest member of the group and was still at school, so some of her later images in future exercises focused on challenges she faced in that environment, and it was clear from her narratives that she was struggling with her diagnosis of autism. However, in the "self-portrait" exercise she was asked to identify a positive aspect of her self, and she decided that the fact that she viewed the world in a different way from other people might be a positive. For Tamara, this was a significant step in addressing her negative experiences.

Later in the group experience, Wendy offered Tamara (and others) advice and guidance, but in the early stages of the group she did not want to display any of her photographs. Wendy appeared to be one of the more confident members of the group, so the fact that she did not wish to display her images was surprising, but she was happy enough to talk about what she had photographed. She explained to the group what she had photographed for her self-portrait.

> *Observation 3:* Wendy said that the image was a picture of her hiding her face with her hair and that this represented how she shut out the world by hiding behind her hair, but went on to explain that when she was little she believed her hair provided a magical bubble around her, which protected her.

Her narratives often referred to her childhood and her upbringing, and she also liked to explore her creative side. As she did this, she was aware that others had similar experiences and this encouraged her to share more.

> *Observation 4:* Wendy said that she often saw faces in lots of things and asked if that was normal. There was silence from the rest the group. Charles then admitted that he saw faces in transport and the eyes were often the car headlights, and then Sarah commented that she saw faces in clouds. Wendy said that she saw monsters in clouds and this led to quite a good discussion about where people saw other things within objects. This perhaps brought the group a bit closer

together as they could see that some of the creative thoughts that they had were shared by other participants.

The fact that Wendy did not want to show her photographs in the first sessions did not appear to offend or upset any of the other participants, and it was reiterated to the group that they should feel in control of the information they chose to share at all times, so Wendy was exercising her choice not to display her images. This changed by week four and she was confident enough to exhibit her images along with all of the other participants.

Rebecca was always willing to share her images and they mostly focused on family life. Rebecca was Tamara's older sister and they both lived at home with their mother. Rebecca's narratives told of a safe, loving environment at the family house where she enjoyed time with her dog, her family, cartoons and fantasy role-playing games on the computer, which she acknowledged was a form of escapism. Her photographs and narratives portrayed Rebecca as being afraid, or unwilling, to try to engage with wider society outside the family home, and for her it was a big step to come to the therapeutic photography group. She had experienced growing up through school in a rural community, being different from the other children, and could now escape into her own comforts of cartoons and computer games, whereas Tamara was still going through the school system. Rebecca did make attempts to address other issues in her life during the group and displayed the following photograph.

Observation 5: Rebecca went next and was asked what it was about bins that she did not like and she explained that it was the contents of rubbish bins but also what they carry on them, specifically germs. She said that the germs caused her obsessive compulsive disorder (OCD). She explained that the OCD ruled her life and the bins were the

focus of the OCD. Rebecca admitted that getting rid of bins would get rid of her stress. There was some questioning from Charles and Wendy about the nature of OCD, and Tamara said that there was no logical explanation for the thought pattern behind OCD. Charles was investigating what might happen if Rebecca used different types of bins to store the rubbish and whether that might help her feel safer from the germs but Rebecca was adamant that she had tried different types of bins, including an automatic bin which opened when you waved your hand over it, but she thought that the germs were jumping up from the bin onto her hand when she waved her hand over it.

Here Rebecca was telling the group about something that dominated her life, another aspect of her psychological make-up that controlled her everyday actions. The group was curious about this and asked appropriate questions to find out more about the condition, and Charles went as far as to offer solutions to help Rebecca. In this scenario, she was the focus of attention and interest, her peers were offering support, and this appeared to empower her to educate the other participants about OCD and the challenges it presented – from a photograph of an unassuming wastebin rose an opportunity to educate others about aspects of her identity.

Sarah's background was also similar in that she was in her early 20s, lived at home with her mother, and had a close relationship with her sister and her son (Sarah's nephew). Again, her images and narratives told of a loving family environment but she did reveal the history of family issues, and her diagnosis of autism to the group.

Observation 6: We then looked into the importance of family occasions within photographs and highlighted that most family photograph albums contain images from periods of celebration. More telling were photographs Sarah had taken of her little nephew Joshua. When looking at these photographs she was able to explain that she had not wanted Joshua in her life to start off with but now he was here he was the most important thing to her. She said that the routine that she had experienced before Joshua came along had been challenged, and she had had to adapt to a new routine, but she was managing this. She also explained that when they found out her sister was expecting a baby her reaction had led to the diagnosis of autism, so she felt thankful that Joshua came into her life because he helped in her diagnosis.

This meant that Sarah had gone through secondary education without a diagnosis of autism. In her story, she conveyed a sense of confusion – she did not know why she reacted negatively to her sister's pregnancy, she did not understand why routine was important to her, but when the diagnosis came she appeared relieved. She finally had an explanation for the behaviour which she found so incomprehensible and scary. Her late diagnosis had alienated her from relationships outside the family home, as another image explains.

Observation 7: Sarah said that these two ducks represented safety and that one duck was looking after the other duck and keeping the other ducks away from it. The group asked who this represented and Wendy asked if it was the way Sarah felt towards her nephew, but Sarah said it was probably how she felt about her own mother and how her mother protected her.

Her mother had been a protective factor throughout her life, and the routines she spoke of still gave the impression that her mum helped maintain these. She talked about her birthday celebrations and explained the "traditions" they followed, and she explained that they went on outings and activities together; there was a sense that the therapeutic photography group was something she was doing on her own for the first time. As a result of her upbringing and late diagnosis, she felt isolated.

Observation 8: In Sarah's image was a lonely white bench and she explained that it was supposed to represent loneliness. Wendy asked her, "Is that how you feel?" Sarah replied that it was sometimes how she felt but it was commented on that the bench looked thick, solid and prominent and although it was alone, it was a solid presence.

The group looked for positives in her narrative, yet all recognised the experience of isolation that became incorporated into their exploration of identity.

Isolation

Tamara was also struggling with isolation and during the exercise which asked the participants to record a typical day in their lives she captured a number of emotive images to highlight her experiences. She explored her experience of travelling to school in a taxi with two other young people.

Observation 9: Tamara said that the taxi picked up two other children who also had learning needs and she had no conversation with them or the taxi driver. She said it was an hour of silence in which she stared out of the window. She was obviously very negative about the experience and did not feel that it was an enjoyable experience. When asked if there were better ways of getting to school she said that even on the bus she would feel isolated and simply stare out of the window.

She was labelled as being different and categorised as having a "learning need" and was therefore transported with other children with a similar label, albeit not a similar condition. This reinforced the fact that she was not the same as others, and this experience continued at school where she spent time in the playground on her own, wondering what it would be like to be "normal" (or "neurotypical", the term Charles kept using in referring to other people). Her narrative went on to explain her isolation at lunchtimes, where she photographed her hand holding a chocolate egg.

> *Observation 10:* Tamara said that at lunchtime she sat on her own and ate her lunch by herself. She explained that two years ago there were two other people at the school who offered to sit with her but they soon stopped doing this because there were long silences, so now she accepted the fact that she had to sit by herself.

The group appeared to recognise this experience and the pressure of being sociable with other people. Charles had already highlighted this as an issue for himself but every group member had experienced this when interacting with society. Tamara then displayed her next image (this has been edited to focus on a close-up to preserve anonymity).

> *Observation 11:* Tamara explained that when she looked at this photograph she recognised that she looked blank and that she felt numb and she did not like taking self-portraits, so this was a difficult portrait for her to take. She then said, "I looked into my eyes and I wonder if I am covering up for something. I know the eyes are the route to the soul but I often fear that I wear a mask."

Tamara had not been asked to take a self-portrait for this exercise, this was her choice, but she was using the image to analyse herself, to try to find out what she was hiding. At this point, Wendy spoke up.

> *Observation 12:* Wendy then turned to Tamara and said that she was a lovely person with a great personality and that she had not met the right group of people to be friends with yet. She recognised that school was not the best environment for her, and Tamara was really touched by this feedback from Wendy. This was a really touching moment in the session and the support Wendy gave to Tamara was quite overwhelming.

The group had sensed that the youngest member needed hope. Wendy offered her personal wisdom and reassured Tamara that things did get easier. Wendy did not portray a perfect future – she explored her experiences of isolation in her own images – but she also highlighted her coping strategies.

> *Observation 13:* Wendy's next image was of chairs piled up on tables and she said that this represented rejection (from Starbucks). She said that she was sitting there and the tables and chairs were being stacked around her but she did not know whether they were a sign for her to go, or barricades for her to stay, so she ended up staying anyway. It did make her feel isolated but she then remembered that she used a technique to block negative thoughts when she started thinking negatively and that this worked for her.

She also explained that she had motivational statements on her front door so she could read them as she left her flat every morning and, for her, this was a way of challenging negative thoughts. She also photographed her own shadow in another image and described this as "her company", but within her narratives was a sense that she had experienced the challenges Tamara was living through and had learned to cope, and although she still experienced isolation, she often did so through choice.

Charles also explored isolation in his images and took photographs that he described as "voyeuristic", which captured members of the public in social situations. He photographed a couple having a chat in a coffee shop (but ensured the image was out of focus so that they could not be identified); he photographed people sitting on a wall with their backs to the camera; and he photographed an older man walking down the street, again, with his back to the camera. When exploring these images, he spoke about wondering what their "neurotypical lives were like". He explained that he analysed every person he came into contact with to study how they acted, what they did, but ultimately, how they socialised. Again, Charles returned to his "deficit", and Wendy stepped in once more.

> *Observation 14:* Wendy went on to say that Charles should be proud of his differences and not try to be the same as everybody else and Charles explained that by looking at neurotypical behaviour he was not trying to emulate it, but rather understand it.

For Charles, socialising was a science he was trying to decode, and this awakened the curiosity of the group and they pressed him for more information.

> *Observation 15:* Charles was then asked if it made him feel happy or sad and he said that that was a very good question and it depended what kind of mood he was in. If he was feeling cynical then it made him happy that he was not like a neurotypical person, but sometimes he did feel frustrated that he could not socialise in ways that other people could.

Like Wendy, Charles also identified coping strategies and spoke about online support networks he had come across, including one called "The Wrong Planet" forum. In the focus group feedback, Charles spoke passionately on the issue and ended up in tears.

> *Focus group transcript 1: Charles:* "I use a forum, two forums called 'Wrong Planet' and 'Aspie Village', and I've used 'Aspie Village' for six or eight years now and I have met other people through that. But that's a UK, Northern Ireland, minimum age so that's about 18, so I don't know if you qualify *(to Tamara)*, but that's basically how I've learned everything about autism… I get emotional about 'Aspie Village' – *(shouts)* it's my life blood! Without it I wouldn't be here in the first place."

The group (particularly Wendy and Charles) were keen to impress on Tamara that there were ways of learning to live with autism. Sarah was quiet on the subject but acknowledged her own experiences, and Rebecca also recognised her isolation when she spoke about the safety of home and her new medication. Tamara was encouraged by the group narratives and there was an attempt to try to identify positives within the final exercise.

Observation 16: Tamara said that these colours were all individual and all bright colours but when placed together they made a beautiful pattern. She then explained that in a film that she had watched about Moses there was a scene in the film where somebody had pointed to a thread in a weaving and had said something along the lines of "so the colour brightly shines, it can never see its purpose in the pattern of the grand design". Tamara went on to explain that this was about recognising that sometimes people can get lost in the crowd and that we are all individual and all have special qualities and they should be allowed to shine through. She did say that she was trying to be positive in this and that she had thought about what Wendy had said a couple of weeks ago about positivity and said that within it you recognise that everybody is unique and that we are all made up of different shapes and sizes and that we all have a place in the wider plan.

Role

As well as isolation, other aspects of having autism were explored through the participants' images. This had the effect of sharing coping strategies with one another, and this sharing of experiences reinforced that what they were experiencing was not out of the ordinary for people who are on the autism spectrum. Wendy recognised issues that Charles was experiencing when thinking about socialising and offered advice to the group.

Observation 17: Wendy said that she recognised this too, but that she had developed some strategies to deal with these situations and that she would actually listen to people because she recognised that people liked to talk about themselves. She also mentioned that there were groups of people who liked to talk about other people and reflect on sad or tragic events. She referred to it as a "formula of conversation".

One issue that Wendy did focus on in a bit more depth was similar to that raised by Tamara in her self-portrait, in that she explored the problems that sensory overload created for her. Wendy was a good influence on the group as she did talk about problems, but also explored solutions.

Observation 18: Everybody, all the participants, recognised what Wendy was talking about and they discussed various ways to deal with the situation to try to switch this overload off. Wendy explained that she used her personal stereo headphones to block out sounds and often would not actually be playing any music in them but just using them as a block, and she recognised that people found this strange. She also said that it was like Superman and his superpowers in that having sensitive hearing was actually a superpower that could be channelled into creative things like art and music.

The group went on to explore other autistic traits such as a fascination with water, fondness for sensory toys (such as textured stress balls), obsessiveness with technology (particularly computers), and a difficulty in identifying emotions. This latter trait was evident in one particular exercise, the "emotions" exercise, which asked the participants to represent six different emotions in an abstract way. Wendy struggled with this task and kept returning to the facilitator for guidance on how she should be doing the exercise. It appeared that she could not connect the name of an emotion to a visual representation of it. However, she paired up with Charles for the exercise and he provided further guidance as they walked around the park, and she managed to produce six images. The other participants managed the emotions exercise without further guidance, and Wendy was inquisitive during the feedback, asking why certain pictures had been taken to represent an emotion. This appeared to highlight differences in people's autism.

Another difference was recognised through discussion of one of Tamara's images. She had photographed a clock to represent something she disliked.

Observation 19: Tamara explained that time was "pure evil, it's arrogant, it stares at you and says 'you need me', 'I control your life'". She explained that she spent a lot of time at home and the concept

of time was quite imprisoning. She argued a very eloquent case about how we were bound by the concept of time and how it dictated what we do and when we do it. She said that time impacted on attendance and she could often be late but she asked what was so bad about being late. She explained it wasn't so much time itself but clocks. She acknowledged that time was a natural phenomenon and in days gone by people would meet at certain times of the day, like sundown or sunrise, but now we are so bound by the rigid nature of the clock. She said that she always lived in the present whereas her sister lived in the future and her sister was always thinking about what was going to happen next and was always looking at the clock to tell her what should be happening when.

In her explanation, Tamara explored the difference between her and her sister, but Charles was adamant that he needed time, and clocks, to help guide him through his day. He worried that he would be late, and this initiated another discussion exploring how he could be late if time had been abolished – there would be no such thing as lateness. Wendy was quite enthused at the prospect of having no time and the issue divided the group in their opinions. This discussion underpinned the individual nature of autism and challenged labelling of the condition. For the participants, it was an opportunity to explore their own identities, which was a point that was raised in the focus group feedback by Sarah and Rebecca.

> *Focus group transcript 2: Sarah:* "It's the first time I have like actively talked about the whole autism thing. I have never been in a group where, kinda, everyone is. Ehm, it's still very new and I don't know a lot so it's like, finding out things, like, look back and it's like oh 'that's why I did that'."

> *Focus group transcript 3: Rebecca:* "I like the fact that I like ehm, I am not the only one going through all this, and I like the fact that we all like, ehm, communication, ehm, I realise that I am not like the only one going through these kind of problems."

Applications to theory

Exploring fears and strategies was a significant element of the analysis of the images, and because of the group dynamics, this was an opportunity for the group to learn from one another, discuss their own experiences, and share strategies for dealing with future situations. Wendy was forthcoming with her own strategies and discussed her motivational statements (including "a smooth sea never made a strong sailor" and "mistakes are proof that you are trying") as well as her use of physical activities to provide a sense of "being normal" wherein she could channel energies into something positive. Wendy appeared to have confidence in her abilities, but she also had vulnerabilities and was able to express these as well. In one of her images, she photographed a flight of stairs and explained that these represented "one step at a time", which was similar to another photograph taken by Sarah with the associated observation.

Observation 20: The next image was a children's playground toy wooden bridge and it had a series of steps on chains. Sarah said this represented "watch your step", "just go slow". Charles immediately found affiliation with this photograph and said that he completely understood what she meant by being cautious and going slowly. He said that he has had to do this when building up relationships with other people so that he doesn't get hurt. He kept repeating today that he was not in a good place at the moment and was struggling with friendships and relationships.

Charles went on to reflect on his own images and had photographed a cobbled street and spoke about the representation of "structure and order" which he craved in life, but he believed this was unobtainable in relationships. Wendy also identified with this when she spoke about her fascination with sensory toys, and how she liked to arrange them in a certain manner because she also craved structure and order. When Rebecca spoke about her love of role-playing games, she explained to the group the concept of building up the characteristics and strengths of each character, which Charles referred to as "keeping yourself safe". Their experiences had taught them that the world was not a place to be entirely trusted outside the family home, and they shared their caution with one another.

There were also opportunities to share other insights, such as creativity and laughter. The group liked to question meanings and metaphors in the images.

> *Observation 21:* Charles said that this looks as though the flowers were standing to attention, something had caught their attention and they were standing upright, alert. He said it was almost like a cat's ears pricking up and then somebody else suggested it could be like a submarine's periscope poking out of the sea or a soldier standing to attention.

And there were also opportunities to have fun and be inventive with the tasks, which Wendy demonstrated when capturing the emotion of "anger".

> *Observation 22:* Anger was represented by a photograph of a banana tree which had no bananas on it and she said that as a banana tree that would make you feel quite angry.

Family systems

Family was a dominant feature within the group, with the participants exploring the importance of family members, involving them in taking photographs, and, in the case of Rebecca and Tamara, participating together. Sarah shared information about her sister's work in a craft shop, the problematic birth of her nephew, and the protective actions of her mother, and explored the matriarchal environment in which she lived. Minuchin (1974) recognised that no matter how dysfunctional a family is, they will always try to maintain a homeostasis so that rules and norms that have been established underpin behaviours. As this relates to all families, not just dysfunctional ones, there was evidence of this when Sarah explored the news and consequent arrival of her nephew. She did not receive the news well, and in terms of family systems theory, the homeostasis of the family was being jeopardised, but as this was compounded by the diagnosis of autism, the effects were magnified for her.

Rebecca and Tamara also used the project to explore their differences and discuss the way that one focused on the present, while the other focused on the future. During the "emotions" exercise there was further opportunity to analyse emotional reactions.

> *Observation 23:* Tamara went next and she admitted from the outset that she had struggled to get a photograph of *anger* and clearly stated that it was because she was not an angry person. There was a bit of laughing between her and her sister Rebecca, and the group picked up on this and had a chat about Tamara's anger. Tamara asked Rebecca if she was angry and Rebecca said that she perhaps wasn't but Tamara admitted she perhaps gets angrier at objects than people.

Rebecca and Tamara had different roles within their family too; Tamara was "protected" by her mother, but also by Rebecca. In one of the final exercises, Tamara brought in an old family photograph and in her narrative she gave further analysis of their roles (the image has been edited to preserve anonymity).

> *Observation 24:* In Tamara's next picture was an old photograph of her and her sister. Rebecca is standing behind her, with her hands on Tamara's shoulders and she said that Rebecca had been a big inspiration to her all of her life and she always looked up to her and

she saw her as a guiding angel. Rebecca explained that she had to put her hands on Tamara's shoulders because she moved so much when she was a little child and this was the only way of keeping her still. I asked Rebecca how she felt about being called an angel and she said that it was very nice and she also viewed Tamara as an angel but joked that the family often called her the little devil because she was always quite mischevious when she was younger.

No information was given about their father, but in other images their mother also featured. Minuchin (1974) identified family subsets, where members will form a clique together for stability and security, and there are signs of a solid subset in the images displayed by both Rebecca and Tamara, one of which showed a glass paperweight with an image of Rebecca, Tamara and Mother engraved onto it with the words "All for one" printed underneath. When this was being displayed by Rebecca, Charles commented that it was very touching to see a family so close, and that he wished his family had been like that with him.

Charles did not say much more about his family directly, but indicated that there had been issues in the past. He photographed a restaurant and explained that this was where he celebrated his 21st birthday, but stated that this was a long time ago. It appeared to have happy memories for him. In the final exercise, he photographed a graveyard and explained that he got to spend time on his own here, and that one day he and his family would all be in the graveyard permanently and they would "all get some peace and quiet".

Wendy also gave some insight into her family, but mostly from when she was growing up. During the "emotions" exercise the following observation was noted:

> *Observation 25:* Wendy explained what she had taken and said that she had photographed the waterfall as well but this was to represent *joy* and *sadness* because she had memories of playing here with her brother when she was a little girl and the pair of them used to jump from one rock to another, so there was a lot of memory tied up in that image.

Wendy did not elaborate to the group on why this created sadness for her. It could be that this was a reminder of childhood innocence which could never be regained, or perhaps her brother was estranged or deceased, but the group did not ask and she did not offer this information. On a one-to-one basis, it may have been appropriate to ask her to expand on this, but because the group did not enquire further there was possibly an opportunity missed to encourage Wendy to share more after she gave them an opening.

Erikson and Bronfenbrenner

Erikson (1963) did not write about autism directly, so perhaps caution is required when applying his stages to the group, yet at the core of Erikson's writings was the fact that societal influences shape development, and from the narratives of the participants there would appear to be issues when it comes to integrating with society. The photographs representing "watch your step" and "one step at a time" represented cautious attitudes that may well have developed from childhood experiences where outcomes of Erikson's stages may have been inclined towards negative experiences (such as shame and doubt, inferiority, role confusion and isolation). Isolation was explicitly explored throughout the sessions, and Charles also indicated that trust needed to be built up when he entered new situations.

However, there were also narratives that demonstrated positive outcomes when related to Erikson's stages. Creativity was an outlet for many of the participants and Tamara even went as far as to state that she had taken art classes in school and was good at the subject. She demonstrated self-efficacy and this suggests that her pride in her abilities impacted on her ego identity.

Certainly, Erikson's stages could help to identify specific areas where a participant may feel challenged in social situations, but it is perhaps worth returning to Bronfenbrenner's model which underpins where the issues for the group members lay. The microsystem and the mesosystem both seemed relatively problem free for the participants, but when looking at the exosystem and the subsequent levels there were signs that challenges occurred in these areas. The participants discussed labelling, attitudes, beliefs and general awareness of the condition. When they collectively produced photographs for the final exercise, which was entitled "the positives and challenges of autism", they discussed what could be done with the information they had gained from the exercise. Suggestions included displaying the images in the City Art Gallery, putting a selection of the images in a newsletter, and having an exhibition at the university. The reason they stated for these approaches was that they wanted to inform and educate as many people as they could about what autism is and what it is like to live with the condition. Within these actions, they were addressing issues in the exosystem and the macrosystem and trying to change attitudes.

Observed effects and outcomes

Support

Because the participants worked within a group, it was not surprising that one of the commonly observed phenomena was that of support. As Sarah and Rebecca both acknowledged, this was the first time they had been involved in a project where everyone had autism, and it was an opportunity to share and learn. Participants explored each other's situations and offered advice where appropriate. Charles offered solutions to Rebecca's aversion to rubbish bins by talking about lids that opened automatically; Wendy explored sensory overload and offered the group some of her techniques; Tamara used the group to find hope for her situation in dealing with school.

The fact that autism can be a hidden disability was also noted within the group, and this was raised by the participants themselves.

> *Observation 26:* Charles was reflecting on his inability, in his eyes, to socialise and Tamara asked him, "Is it because you don't look like you have a problem?" To which he said that that was partly the case but also he had been diagnosed quite late in life as having autism.

This question led on to an exploration of labelling, particularly around Tamara's situation at school, and whether this helped or hindered attitudes towards autism. Charles gave a personal perspective and felt that the label of autism had helped him in creating understanding and explaining his behaviour. He felt that he could finally understand "why he was like he was" because of the label.

Out of all of the participants, Tamara seemed to gain most support from the others. This might have been because she was the youngest and all of the other participants had lived through similar experiences to those she was now encountering. In the final exercise, Tamara presented the following image with a complex narrative (the photograph has been edited to preserve anonymity).

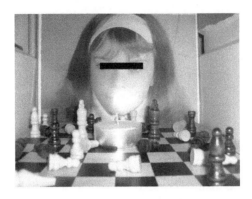

Observation 27: Tamara's third photograph was a very powerful image which she obviously spent a lot of time setting up. At the back of the picture was an old photograph of her and she explained that her eyes looked different in the old photograph. She said that the eyes represented her split personality and that it was split between her true self and her autistic self. In front of this photograph was a chess game and she said that chess represented two sides of a fighting war, relating to her split personality. She explained that war was messy and this was represented in a chess game but that in chess, when pieces get taken, they get removed to the side of the chess game. In this photograph she had scattered the taken pieces onto the board as well. The chess pieces were also placed incorrectly and she said that this was what it was like to have autism; it was messy and full of the casualties of the battle between the two personalities. Placed in the middle of this chaos was a candle that was not lit and she said that candles represented death and were lit when we needed to remember the dead but this one would not be lit until she died and then, when she died, she hoped people would remember the war that was going on inside her head.

The other participants were invited to comment on Tamara's picture and narrative and Wendy stated that she could completely understand the casualties within Tamara's head but offered advice about trying to accept differences, rather than fight them. She also gave Charles some useful advice when he said that Tamara's photograph had "struck a nerve".

Observation 28: Charles then said that he recognised aspects of that within himself but had to find coping strategies to help him through situations when he felt that his head was a dangerous site. He then said that the photograph had "struck a nerve" with him and that he often just had to "hang on for help", at which point Wendy said it was important that he asked for help if he needed help because often people could not guess that he needed help.

The experiences that each individual took to the group, then shared through their images, narratives and feedback, had positive effects on all of the participants. The focus group captured the value of the shared experience, the importance of a safe place to share, and the value of reciprocity, as Charles and Wendy explained:

> *Focus group transcript 4: Charles:* "For me it has been a very positive experience. For me it's probably the only positive experience of the week that I feel safe and inclusive, to use the word, and all the people who have made that for me, I hope I have given something back to other people, and that's why I like it, and it's been very good for me, almost more powerful than…in the larger scale of things it is still very small, but in the small…it depends how you look at it, it's been quite powerful in some ways."

> *Focus group transcript 5: Wendy:* "That other people have…well…I was looking at the thinking patterns of other people and I noticed a lot of similarities, or like, I dunno, like, in the analysis and like, looking ehm at meanings of things, like in your chess photo *(to Tamara)* and your (children's) bridge one *(to Sarah)* and other ones."

Self-efficacy

As soon as the group began, all of the participants were producing photographs, and this was noted in week one by Charles who spoke about the "immediacy of photography". He went on to explain that he really liked taking photographs but also felt that he was not "artistic"; however, he felt that photography helped him access "creativity", which for him was different from being "artistic".

Because of the nature of the exercises, there was no "correct" way to produce an image for each task, and Wendy did struggle with this initially. She produced some interesting images, but she questioned herself because others had taken literal interpretations for early tasks, whereas she had been more abstract in her approach. This meant that she needed to explain what each image represented, which was actually the purpose of the exercise, but she was one of the first participants to realise this and initially felt she was doing something wrong because the meaning in her images was not immediately apparent. By week two, the other participants were also being more abstract in their choices, which alleviated Wendy's fears. The participants actually began questioning each other about how they had taken photographs; in particular, Tamara's self-portrait received a considerable amount of analysis but she was unwilling to share how she had taken the picture, stating that it was "her secret". Tamara appeared to be pleased that her image had received such attention, and took pride in producing a talking point.

There was also exploration of changes in people's circumstances that demonstrated a command of their autism. Wendy explored coping strategies with other group members, and there were also discussions about receiving the original diagnosis and the relief people had felt as it helped them understand their behaviour. In another discussion, Tamara explored a fear she once had about rats and told the group that she could not even listen to stories where there might be a rat in it because she was so afraid, but recently had managed to overcome this and watched *Cinderella* (which had rats in it). It was important for Tamara to highlight this because she was the participant who had been struggling the most with her experiences of isolation at school, but by her own admission, things change and can get easier.

There were also examples of feedback given to participants by each other that highlighted skills and positive characteristics. In the final exercise, Sarah explored the positives of living with autism and displayed a photograph of her engaging in crafts.

Observation 29: In her seventh and eighth photograph was a craft kit, which consisted of a mosaic design in which she was building up the pattern of a flower. Charles asked if this represented attention to detail and Sarah said that it did. Rebecca commented that Sarah was creative.

Not only did this experience give Sarah a sense that she was able to produce something worthy of praise, it also impacted on her self-esteem to know that others found her creative. The photographs gave the participants an opportunity to be expressive and creative and focus on aspects of their own personalities that they wanted to highlight. Charles made the following statement during the focus group:

Focus group transcript 6: Charles: "I actually thought it was going to be a more technical course, from a technical point of view, then I realised it was, well, I said, well actually, I think it is 'therapeutic' camera… therapy…therapy with a camera as opposed to the other way round, but it creates positive interactions which kind of helps, which has done a lot more, it's quite powerful in that sense, given where I come from, my confidence levels…pretty shot to pieces basically."

Using images helped Charles socialise with the group, control what he displayed, and also control what he said about each image in relation to himself. He stated that there had been an impact on his confidence levels because of the positive interactions, which suggested that the experience had been beneficial for his self-efficacy and self-esteem.

Self-disclosure/control

It was notable how much information the participants chose to share through their photographs, and some of the information was quite personal. Out of all of the participants, Wendy shared the most information about herself through using photographs to make self-disclosures. During the "day in the life of…" exercise she shared information about her computer use and stated that she could be "quite obsessive" when it came to using the internet. She went on to explain that she had now chosen not to have internet access at her flat so that she could exercise control over her usage and would only go to the library to go online. Despite her self-imposed limitations, she was still actively involved in a social media group about autism, regularly updating it and looking at other people's comments about her posts.

Wendy went on to talk about her feelings towards her stepfather and admitted that the most stressful times with him were when she could hear him eating (a condition known as misophonia). She admitted to the group that her sensitivity to sensory overload did impact on this scenario, but noted that it was worse if she was feeling stressed. In the final exercise, where participants photographed "the positives and challenges of living with autism", she explored her volatile nature in two photographs.

Observation 30: Wendy's second photograph was a fried egg in a pan and she said that she had wanted to photograph a scrambled egg but had just bought this pan and wanted to use her new pan for the photograph – therefore, it was a fried egg. She said this was often how her head felt, which was why she wanted to do a scrambled egg. Her next image was of a boarded-up building with a sign that said "dangerous site/keep out" and she said that this also felt like her head but then said that this probably represented her head before she had been prescribed medication. When asked if this meant she was a danger to other people she said no, she was a danger to herself.

Wendy was the only participant who disclosed the fact that she was on medication, and she acknowledged that it was helping her, given that without it she would be a danger to herself. She went on to tell the group that she had expected to be dead by the age of 24, but was not, so she decided to "try to be amazed by the world" around her.

Other participants used photographs to make disclosures, but were always in control of the information they shared, such as Rebecca's image of a bin in relation to her OCD, Sarah's images of her nephew with regards to her jealousy, and Charles's images of people socialising with regards to his "deficit". Because Rebecca and Tamara were sisters and had attended the group together, the researcher asked if using photographs had revealed anything new in their relationship.

> *Focus group transcript 7: Rebecca:* "Some of it reaffirmed, some of it is a bit, like, out there, with some of the pictures Tamara said and the way she told lots of different things, there's maybe a little out there that I didn't know before."

Wendy also offered further insight into the use of photographs and the associated narratives. She began explaining why she had wanted to attend the course.

> *Focus group transcript 8: Wendy:* "...therapeutic photography" so I thought that it's something else, another thing that could be ehm helpful, and like the way you structured it, ehm, like as a means of communication, so it's ehm, sometimes people find that if you have to do like verbal communication, like talk about things that's perhaps more challenging than if you're like, if you have a photo, and then... does that make sense? You can do it through that or like writing, like other mediums."

Wendy recognised that, for some, verbal communication was not the strongest form of communication they had and felt that there were other ways to foster a relationship where information could flow.

She praised the use of photographs but also felt that there was scope for other mediums to be used to facilitate communication.

Self-esteem

Due to the group dynamics, there was considerable feedback given to participants from the other group members about the content and narrative of each image. No negative feedback was observed. The interest that participants took in each other's images appeared to give everyone a sense of pride in their work. When the group began in week one, Sarah told the researcher that she had only taken photographs in her garden before, and in week two she was taking abstract images to represent emotions.

> *Observation 31:* Joy was represented by fish in the pond. Charles particularly liked this photograph. He stared at it for a while and really expressed a lot of interest in it. He said that he was fascinated by "the light, the water, and the fish" and he said it appealed to him "on all three of these levels". He also added that the fact that it contained fish was very calming as well.

Sarah appeared to appreciate this feedback from Charles and as the weeks progressed these observations became more commonplace. During the focus group feedback the co-facilitator made the following statement:

> *Focus group transcript 9: Janet:* "Can I just say, I thought it was fascinating to see pictures of…of things that you would sort of just be walking down the street and sometimes just miss, but if somebody took that photo actually explained what it was all about, it actually is quite powerful. It can be quite emotional as well, especially people that say they are rubbish and they're not any good, but that's through your eyes, through someone else's eyes they are really quite, sort of, eye opening and exciting and interesting."

Her observation took account of the fact that some of the participants would apologise before showing the image, stating that they were not very good, but every image received feedback and comment which affirmed the inclusion. This encouraged the participants to be creative as the weeks progressed and, although there was never a sense of competitiveness between participants, there was obvious satisfaction when an image received praise from the group.

However, there were also moments of self-doubt. This was perhaps to be expected at the start of the process as participants were still finding the confidence to engage in each activity, but in week four Wendy approached the researcher after the session to ask if she was being "too domineering" within the group. Wendy had a sense that she was being too challenging towards other group members but the researcher explained that he had not felt this and explained to her that she was one of the more confident members of the group and was able to bring her experiences to the younger members. This appeared to reassure her and she continued to question the images over the remaining weeks in an appropriate, non-confrontational manner.

Empowerment

With the five autistic participants, it was difficult to ascertain aspects of empowerment until the final week where they collectively looked at "the positives and challenges of living with autism". After each participant had displayed and talked about their images they collectively looked at the themes that had emerged and decided that there had been a lot of emphasis on isolation, the journey through diagnosis, friendships and socialising, and there was also an overarching sense of hope.

The project had brought these individuals together and asked them to bring issues and observations each week to discuss, and through the images and narratives the participants learned about aspects of other people's lives, but also learned that some of their experiences were common and "normal" within the autistic community.

Charles and Wendy both stated to the researcher that it had been refreshing to meet a professional who did not assume they were the expert on the situation and was prepared to listen and learn from the participants. They both felt that this would be beneficial in all their contact with professionals, as an individual with autism is the best expert on their situation.

As the youngest member of the group, Tamara received considerable support from the other participants and revealed a lot of information about her current situation. In the focus group feedback, she summarised her experience with the following statement:

> *Focus group transcript 10: Tamara:* "Well, talking about experts *(to Charles)*, you said ehm they should know more than you, actually a saying in my school has a picture of a wee caterpillar on a leaf and it says 'An expert at anything started out as a beginner'."

For her, this had been a learning experience, but also gave her hope for the future, and the belief that things would get better. At the very least, she had access to three new people (and her sister) who had had similar experiences and challenges, potentially providing strength in numbers should they ever decide to meet again and try to educate society about living with autism. It might be bold to believe that the group could challenge their oppressors in a Freirean sense, but the group did appear to have been transformative given that they had defined issues that impinged on their lives, and also shared understanding with others to empathise with various perspectives. Transformative experiences can be empowering if individuals gain a sense of their values, strengths and abilities to cope with adversity (Bush & Folger, 1994) and this appears to align with the observed outcomes from this group.

■ Chapter 11 ■

VOICES FROM PRACTICE

This final chapter brings together descriptions of experiences from practitioners who are using therapeutic photography within their own practice. What is demonstrated in these synopses is the variety and scope of the impact of using photographs with clients, and this should encourage further creativity, exploration and innovation in future practices. In some descriptions, there appears to be a fine line between the practice of therapeutic photography and phototherapy, and where possible, the authors have identified and commented on these two disciplines. It is worth bearing in mind that phototherapy should be delivered by a trained counsellor or therapist within a protected, therapeutic framework. However, most of these descriptions give accounts of the applicability of therapeutic photography.

Coping with breast cancer through photos

Antonella Cunsolo

I was involved in running a workshop of great emotional relevance which involved some patients from the Humanitas Cancer Centre of Catania hospital, giving them the opportunity to express themselves and their emotions during group therapy sessions.

The aim of the project named "I don't die" was to talk about the patients' experience and life through photographs; photographs were used as a therapy, revealing through them the women's fight against breast cancer.

The project sessions

The workshop was divided into three main sessions: the first one led to the narration of the personal history of each patient and the sharing of how they had coped with the traumatic event. During this session, we used a mixture of images selected by me, and photographs taken by the patients.

The second session was characterised by the photoshoots. Each patient posed according to the photographic project they had outlined in order to express the message and the feelings they wanted to transmit through their pictures.

The third session was dedicated to the selection of the self-portraits produced in the previous session. Particular attention was given to the personal experience elicited by the chosen pictures and to the witnesses and feedback on what the project had meant to the patients.

The importance of sharing experiences

During the process, I witnessed an intense therapeutic path in which the patients were deeply emotionally charged. Using photos, the patients immediately had the opportunity to share their own experiences and emotions, being aware that all of them were living the same difficult traumatic event, and that was considered priceless. The photos that each patient selected conveyed their personal experience and that enhanced the process of elaboration of the traumatic event. By the creation of a place that was both mental and real, mediated by the photographic tool, the patients were allowed a moment of weakness in which they could express their fears and anxiety without any restrictions. Moreover, the project fostered the creation of a strong relation of mutual help among the patients, whose bond proved to be a supplementary aid in facing their clinical pathway.

The group of women showed great enthusiasm and involvement, having had the opportunity to work on their own image, deeply transformed by the cancer. The photographs intentionally did not show the visible signs of the scars caused by the surgery, but emphasised the beauty and the pride of a woman, things that a scar can never blur.

The power of optimism

Last but not least, was the desire expressed by each patient to promote a positive and hopeful message. This was summed up by Daniela, one of the patients who participated in the project:

At the beginning, we were simply strangers who were meeting around a desk, and only as the project went on did I deeply realise the meaning of it. The aim of the project wasn't simply about taking snapshots, but through a sharing process we have created pictures that represent us, that dig into our heart, that bring out what we have suffered, our pains, our will to fight and our victory. Sharing our experience, we have rapidly become a close and cohesive group. Bringing out our inner pains, we have partly treated some open wounds caused by the cancer.

At the end of this project an exhibition was organised, followed by the publication of a photo book.

Dr Antonella Cunsolo is a psychologist, psychotherapist, photographer and President of the association Art'è Benessere in Catania, Italy.

The self-portrait experience – transforming pain into art, or "shit into diamonds"

Cristina Nunez

I have photographed myself since 1988, after my heroin addiction as a teenager. I didn't know what I was doing back then, I thought it was an expression of vanity, so I kept it secret, but in moments of pain I realised that taking self-portraits made me feel better. This practice also stimulated my creative process and allowed me to become a professional artist and start photographing others in 1994.

In 2005, I created my method, The Self-Portrait Experience, and started to teach self-portrait workshops around the world – in prisons, mental health centres, universities, high schools, museums and companies – so that people could learn to transform their emotions and inner life in artworks, or better, turn their "shit into diamonds". Discovering that I could be useful for others and getting their positive feedback has stimulated a permanent and inextinguishable "inner fire," which drives me to produce project after project and I feel I am constantly on a mission that I will never give up, no matter the hardship and the numerous obstacles.

My method consists of two parts: on the one hand, the production of self-portraits following different exercises to explore all aspects of our lives (me, me and the other, me and the world); on the other hand, a methodology of perception and choice of the works in order to create an inner dialogue and to build a personal, autobiographical art project. Self-portraits are produced both with me in my studio – what I call collaborative self-portraits – and by participants at home with their own cameras.

But we produce "self-portraits", not selfies. The selfie is mainly a public image, produced to be published on social media and thus controlled to build the image we want to show of ourselves, and mostly produced quickly with a smartphone. We delete a lot of selfies in which we do not recognise ourselves.

The self-portrait as produced in my method is the result of a creative process, and an inner dialogue with oneself, far less controlled than the selfie, generally produced with a camera and allowing more time between the initial idea and the selection of the artwork and its publication or usage in an art project.

As Bond and Woodall (2005) state, in the self-portrait artwork we are, at the same time, author, subject and spectator. Each of these roles makes an empowering statement: the author says, "I am the creator of this image"; the subject says, "I am, I exist"; and the spectator says, "I look at myself, I see myself". The powerful dynamics between the three roles trigger the creative process and stimulate our unconscious to speak with the language of art. By objectifying our emotions and pain – our dark side – we open up for catharsis and renewal. The self-portrait, according to Tournier (1986), is the only possible image of the creator of that image, in the precise moment of creation. Thus, it is the portrait of our creative self, or what I call our higher self.

During my workshops in the last eight years, I have produced more than 4000 collaborative self-portraits, which has allowed me to work on independent research on how the creative process can give expression to the personal and collective unconscious, as in Jung's (2001) theory of the human psyche. It is extremely surprising how the subjects, concentrated in the expression of a chosen emotion, unknowingly incarnate iconographies which are part of our cultural memory – emotions, as the German art historian Aby Warburg stated, can work as a vehicle for cultural memory – and how our visions about the image tend to be closely related to the subject's life story.

At first, the subjects do not recognise themselves in these images but working on the in-depth perception with the help of the method's artistic criteria, they start to recognise their own emotions, needs, values and life stories, so they take possession of this "other in me". The visions, archetypes, iconographies and myths triggered by the powerful image help the subject to change their perception, to see something opposite and to discover that as they look more closely at an image, they will continue to see different emotions and attitudes, different expressions of the self. It is a sort of training to make our perception flexible, which demonstrates the multiplicity and plasticity of human identity and proves that each one of us possesses a huge potential to be anything or anybody.

Cristina Nunez lives and practises in Barcelona, Spain.

Promoting intentional seeing

Sophie Bjorkquist

Living in or visiting a city, one comes to notice where tourists flock and take photographs. We've all seen it, swarms of people snapping away, frantically trying to "capture" a new environment often without taking the time to actually *see* it. These days, in our extremely visually saturated world, sometimes we can become overwhelmed and desensitised due to the flood of images we are bombarded with from social media to advertising and so on. In addition, with the progression of digital photography and smartphone cameras, we no longer have to wait to view our image, as it used to be with analogue, or worry about the number of images we have left to take. This has caused a lack of intention and created mindlessness when photographing, which is unfortunate because I see each aspect of photography from shooting to processing to printing to viewing as having its own separate but equal potentially therapeutic advantage for the person taking the photograph. For example, to begin with the first aspect of shooting or vision, during that moment when you click the shutter (or press the button) if you pause and take the time to ask yourself, *Why am I choosing to take a photo of this? What does this mean to me and say about who*

I am? then it is inviting some of that thought back into the equation. These questions bring back the intentionality which used to be much more heavily connected to photography.

In an attempt to deliver these ideas to the world and the people, I went to Trafalgar Square in London, because I know many tourists visit that location every day. I asked volunteers to use a disposable camera to take a photograph of whatever they liked in the square. After they took the photo, I asked the volunteer to write a short statement as to why they chose to photograph what they did. By asking someone to think about and consider what they are photographing more deeply, I thought it would add another layer of processing for them. Some of the volunteers then engaged with me in a dialogue as to why they chose that scene and how it connected to their lives – past, present and future. The idea was that it would simply plant a seed for the next time they took a photograph, and encourage them to revisit the questions they asked themselves in Trafalgar Square, such as *Why am I choosing this? What does this say about me?* and in essence therapeutically begin to know themselves better and be better as a direct result of photographing.

Sophie Bjorkquist received her Bachelor of Fine Arts in Photography from the School of the Art Institute of Chicago and is attending graduate school at Antioch University Seattle studying clinical mental health counselling and art therapy.

Photo Explorations and Resilient Souls
Cathy Lander-Goldberg

My work has primarily been about using photography and writing to help girls and women strengthen their voices and learn more about themselves.

I have been working with youth since the late 1980s when I began volunteer teaching photography with adolescent females at a residential treatment centre. In 1993, I founded Photo Explorations, which offers workshops for organisations and schools interested in helping girls and women use photography, writing and collage to increase self-awareness and strengthen their voices. The workshops have been offered in a variety of community settings such as libraries, schools and art centres. My workbook, *Photo Explorations: A Girl's*

Guide to Self-Discovery through Photography, Writing and Drawing (2015) includes assignments from my workshops and is recommended for girls aged 9–15. It gives photography and art assignments followed by writing prompts about the images. The intent is for girls to better understand themselves, strive for a balanced life and set meaningful goals for the future.

I am also working on The Resilient Souls Project, a powerful travelling exhibit of portraits and writing celebrating the individual strength and beauty of spirit in a diverse group of women. This display is a 20-year follow-up to a photo and literary exhibition I did in the mid-1990s entitled Resilient Souls: Young Women's Portraits and Words.

At that time, I had the honour of working with young women from various backgrounds who had overcome personal challenges in their lives. They were brave and generous by writing and sharing their stories as we worked together to create beautiful self-portraits to represent their perseverance in the hope of encouraging others. This was pre-internet, when private matters tended to stay private. The original exhibit explored issues such as disability, mental health, unhealthy relationships, illness, adoption, pregnancy, immigration, eating disorders, school problems, violence and grief. Two decades later, we have revisited these women's continued journeys, including their low points, their triumphs and their growth, as they approach middle age.

Copyright Cathy Lander-Goldberg, The Resilient Souls Project

This project gave participants an opportunity for personal development through writing and storytelling and reflecting on their histories. The photographs of their external selves provided concrete symbols that represented their inner power.

The exhibition concludes with a self-portrait backdrop to give viewers the option to use these same tools of storytelling and visual imagery to take self-portraits and possibly post their own stories of overcoming obstacles in their lives on social media.

Cathy Lander-Goldberg, MSW, LCSW has practised as a licensed clinical social worker since 2003 and as an individual and group psychotherapist specialising in issues related to girls and women. She frequently incorporates expressive therapy techniques into her clinical practice.

Body image

Grace Gelder

I started the project with Aphra two years ago after she emailed me to enquire about a photoshoot. "I think that working with you would be very helpful in improving my body image and coming to terms with the way I look when I'm not starving myself", she wrote. I'd often worked with women who had issues with their appearance but never anyone who had been diagnosed with an eating disorder. I agreed to meet with Aphra to chat and see if it felt like a process that we would both be able to navigate with clarity and healthy boundaries.

During our first meeting, we talked about our ideas and each asked the other questions about ideas and intentions for the shoots. It was important to me that Aphra understood that I'm not a qualified therapist and that she already had a professional support system in place outside our sessions. We agreed that it would be a step-by-step creative collaboration and that her input would be an important part of our sessions.

During our first shoot, we did some simple head and shoulders portraits and I directed her as she was nervous. It felt important that we looked through the pictures together and that Aphra chose the photographs she liked herself. Viewing them together also meant that if there were any that she didn't like I would be there to offer my comments and check she was okay before leaving.

The most interesting part was the conversations that followed. Because Aphra loved some of the pictures, she was more comfortable talking about her experiences and we had a great discussion about mirrors. In one eating disorders unit that she had been in there were no mirrors, so for the six weeks while she was regaining a healthy weight she didn't see herself at all. She spoke about the difficulty in returning to a world full of reflective shop windows and mirrored public toilets. From this conversation, we decided that the next shoot would include a mirror.

Most of the shoots were relatively short as I sensed it would be best to focus on one theme at a time, unless the flow of events insisted otherwise. What interested us both were the conversations that happened before or after each session as these often led to a subject matter that would then be incorporated into the next shoot. It felt as if the photography was a conversation starter and while we were building a collection of beautiful images, they weren't the only goal of the sessions.

Aphra and I met six times over two years, and we were asked to be part of a launch event at Switch House, the new Tate Modern building. This provided us with a great opportunity to reflect on the process from start to finish, including some of the moments when it was hard for Aphra and how there were times when her experience of seeing the images after a photoshoot was more difficult than others. Aphra's bravery and commitment to recovery shone through during the question and answer sessions and enabled us both to feel confident in the process we had co-created.

Grace Gelder has an MA in Photography and works as a freelance photographer and workshop facilitator in London. She has developed a range of workshops around the theme of identity and is regularly called on to work with people who are uncomfortable in front of the camera. She sees photography as a powerful tool for storytelling and self-expression.

Therapeutic photography or phototherapy?

Mark Luyten

I offer two examples from my work as a psychotherapist, which use photography to explore family systems and to raise aspirations.

Example 1

One of my clients complained about the absence of her father in her life, as if he had rejected her (and some other children – the girls – as well). She did not understand why this was the case.

I asked her to bring along some family photograph albums to our session. She did and was quite amazed to find a great number of photographs of her and her father: sitting on his lap, in his arms, reading together in an armchair, playing in the garden. There were many pictures showing a warm and committed relationship. This confused my client very much. It did not confirm her perception of the absent, distant and non-committed father who deliberately avoided contact.

However, we noted that at the age of 7 the continuous flow of photographs stopped. What had happened there? The next photograph of her and her father was a picture taken on her wedding day. In the months following this session she investigated the family history. She found that her father and her mother had relationship difficulties in that period. Her father wanted to invest in the family business and develop it internationally, but her mother did not agree because she feared it would damage their family. This discussion resulted in a kind of parental job description. Her father would invest in the family business and include his two oldest sons in the process, her mother would concentrate on the household and the education of the smaller children in which the father would not participate. The younger children would be directed away from the family business. Talking to many people who knew her father, she learned that it was a very difficult decision for him. He talked about all his children and seemed to know a lot about their lives.

This work changed her perception about her father, but also about family relations, particularly with her mother. She contacted her older brother, offered her services and now plays an important role in the family business. The photographs of her and her father are manifestly present in her office reminding her of the original legacy. They changed not only her life, but the lives of many other family members as well.

Example 2

Marc is a 53-year-old man with an IQ (intelligence quotient) of about 70. His intellectual disability makes him dependent on daily help, for instance when he needs transportation. I was asked as a photographer to hold some workshops about photography with Marc and his colleague, Dirk, whose disability was more severe. I was not involved in their lives as a therapist.

Both were very enthusiastic photographers and with a camera in their hands they came into a kind of ego state where they seemed to function on a higher level.

In the workshop, I gave Marc an assignment. I suggested he must make a series of pictures so that I could see how his typical day went. In the next session, he showed me several pictures in which he was always present. He travelled on public transportation from his house to the institution, telling his mother it was a requirement of the task. He had never done that before; everybody assumed he couldn't do this. On the bus, he had asked his fellow passengers to take his picture for him. These were complete strangers whom he mobilised to assist. Nobody thought he was that socially skilled. He did the same in the institution, in his workplace, and at home. He explained that if he wasn't satisfied with the result when he viewed the images people had taken for him he had these assistants take another picture, and another one. He was very excited about it. The last picture portrayed him sat behind a computer, with a serious face watching the screen, his right hand on the mouse. "This is the funniest one," he said. "Now everybody thinks I can read and write!" His humour shone through as well.

Because of this experiment, opinions about Marc shifted. The social skills training he was engaged in was intensified by the team. He became more independent and at his workplace he was given more responsibility.

Photography played a very important role in these changes. Marc's position changed, and the perception of people in his environment also changed. The treatment targets changed, the bar was set higher, and in the institution the professionals took note of the process and worked to encourage Marc to live a fuller life. The target became assisted independent living.

There is a similarity between these two stories. In example 2 we call this therapeutic photography, but in example 1 it is phototherapy because I was also using my skills as a trained therapist. But I am still the same professional, proposing experiments, so to me the difference is irrelevant.

Mark Luyten is a psychotherapist who has trained in relational therapy and Gestalt therapy. He works in his private practice in Aalst, Belgium.

Shooting Oot And Aboot

Allan Finnie

As part of our curriculum, we provide a photography group on Wednesday mornings called Shooting Oot And Aboot, where we go out in the minibus to different interesting locations within Aberdeen and Aberdeenshire. The participants are ten service users with a varied level of support needs; on this particular activity we have two regular staff, a one-to-one support worker and a volunteer.

When we started this group, our intention was to provide education on how to be a better photographer, which we provide individually. To be honest, I had some trepidation taking on this task. I have always been interested in photography on the creative side, but would never class myself as an expert. It was a learning curve for me as well as the service users, and I learned with them rather than being the teacher, leaving the technical aspect to my colleague David. After finding out more about photography as a therapy I now know through experience of running this group that learning the technique for capturing better pictures is a bonus, but as a therapeutic tool it excels, and the technical skills of photography are not the most important thing.

Elliot

One of our service users who attends the photography group has autism (I shall call him Elliot). Elliot is a 29-year-old Romanian. His mum has expressed how she finds his behaviours very difficult to deal with; activities he has taken part in before have never been successful. He attends our sport and boccia group and staff have found great difficulty in sustaining his attention; he could always be found wandering around, at times appearing very anxious, finding it hard to make friends and preferring to be alone.

Elliot's mum appeared to be at her wits' end trying to find activities that would interest him; he always preferred his own company and spent a lot of time in his room. I asked if he would be interested in doing some photography, which would get him out and about.

As Elliot comes from Romania he has taken a great interest in location and wants to know where he is going and the name of the place, which has become very important to him. When I let him know, he checks the pronunciation to get it right. I offer to write it down for him. "No, no," says Elliot, "I will remember," which he does. In fact, when we look back at his portfolio, Elliot can tell me when the picture was taken and where. He tends to take photographs of landmarks, a statue maybe, or any plaque he can find which perhaps relates to the particular location. He always takes six pictures, no more and no fewer, and brings them to me for discussion. I have discovered that he enjoys colour and will count with me how many colours he has captured within his picture.

On his return home, his mum has said how excited Elliot is to show off his work. The importance of the location becoming clear, Elliot takes great pride in telling his mum where he has been, which are places he has discovered himself, places his mum does not know exist and she has never been to. In a sense, Elliot is educating his mum about the surroundings which are now their home, and it is something he can have a conversation with her about.

Elliot's mum has commented on how much more communication there is between them and how much their relationship has grown since starting the photography group. They have something to discuss, a product to look at and be proud of.

One of the highlights for Elliot was the pride he felt when he saw for the first time a picture he had taken in Johnston Gardens, a local park in Aberdeen. It was of a bright blue arched walk bridge with beautiful red bushes shining clear in the background. A truly special piece, this was mounted in a black frame with a cream surround and was to be his exhibit for the forthcoming exhibition. It was explained to him that it would be up on the wall for all to see and someone may even buy it. Elliot kept repeating over and over, "Someone will buy my picture!"

When his mum was told I don't know who was more excited; in fact, someone did buy the picture, someone Elliot and his family knew well. It was Mark, his care manager, who was very impressed with everyone's work as he knows most of our members. Mark now has Elliot's framed picture in pride of place in his home, possibly a talking point for any visiting guest.

From time to time we do experience many different behaviours but we have managed to tap into Elliot's interests. When planning our trip for the following week, Elliot always suggests the airport and heliport and the day we went there Elliot was snapping away with his lens through the wire fence. He took far more than his normal six photographs. "It's time to go now, Elliot," I said. "Please, five more minutes," he answered. We were all on the bus enjoying watching Elliot taking his helicopter pictures and sharing them when I eventually got him back on the bus. His social skills have much improved and he has now made good friends within the group.

We try to have an exhibition once per year, the money going to buying ink and frames for the following year. I have found this can boost the interest in taking the best photographs they can as there is an end result. For example, we had a week-long exhibition one year at the Arts Centre in Aberdeen. The first night we had an advertised cheese and wine reception where friends, family, carers, peers and the public could come to see the exhibition. It looked very professional, with correct lighting shining onto the exhibits, and the service users took full ownership of this, escorting people round, explaining not only their own picture but their fellow group members' pictures too. One service user, an 18-year-old man with Down syndrome who has poor communication and mobility, took immense pleasure in discovering that his photograph of an iron bicycle ornament taken in a garden at Footdee, located at Aberdeen Beach, sold four times over. His parents were so proud.

All of our group choose what they would like to exhibit. This is done indoors in bad weather where everyone can sit down and discuss one person's portfolio. This often starts up good conversations and individual praise. Without knowing whose portfolio we are discussing, I can always tell from their own personalities and likes who has taken the photograph.

Allan Finnie is co-founder of a registered charity, Create Aberdeen, providing community-based activities for adults with additional support needs in Aberdeen, Scotland.

Camp Camera

Kelly Gauthier

Using photographs with children is a fantastic medium and a magical gateway to conversation. During my 15 years as the owner and operator of Camp Camera, I was introduced to a great many children who were experiencing difficulty socialising, managing their emotions and expressing themselves in a way that would lead to further conversations or understanding. There seemed to be a verbal disconnect somewhere that photography mended and elevated. When these children were given a camera and asked to take photographs of things that described who they were and what they liked, something beautiful happened. Communication was no longer an issue, as these children couldn't wait to talk about themselves and their pictures, and socialisation just happened naturally as the children started noticing similarities between themselves and their stories. Thanks to photographs, friendships blossomed and a new language emerge.

Kelly Gauthier is an art and photo therapist for Picture Yourself Well. She is also owner and operator of Camp Camera and Creative Dating.

Noah's story
Sophie Lizoulet

The autism spectrum diagnostic was established when Noah was 20 months old. Since I got pregnant, I kept a diary but I never thought of relating our story through another medium. Noah had a very troubled life: five day-care centres and five schools. His father and I divorced when he was 5 years old, but luckily we get along very well. And between me and his dad, Noah went through nine house moves. He is 17 years old. There are two sides of the therapeutic effect of photography on Noah's life.

First effect

Because Noah loves computers and tablet devices, six years ago he started to go through the photo library on our home computers. He enjoys looking at them often. This helps him to put all the pieces of his life together. He asks many questions with regards to the pictures: How old was I when...? Where was this taken? I remember this... and so on. Two years ago, we created a wall of pictures just in front of his bedroom door. These are Fuji Instax small photographs, printed out from our smartphones. They are memories of our friends, and events we shared. Dates and places are written on them. Photography is always a good start for a conversation between us. And little by little Noah gives more details about them. At first it was where and whom. Now it is what he saw, ate, experienced, liked and disliked.

Second effect

It all started in May 2014, when I decided to relate Noah's story through a photographic journal. Noah was 14 years old. It happened as a photographic assignment for the photography workshop I was enlisted in. The purpose was always for it to be shown to the public. Noah knew it all along. I started to take pictures of our everyday life: Noah's activities, our vacations, school and so on. Pretty soon, I discovered that having the camera in my hand made me unavailable to help him. And actually, he didn't need my help. Noah was much more autonomous than expected. I wasn't giving him the opportunity to gain autonomy. I was too protective of him. It felt great!

The other discovery was more difficult to observe: the camera was almost hurting him physically. I could see how annoyed he was. So I gave him the camera and asked him to take pictures. He enjoyed it a lot and was very good at it. He got used to having the camera everywhere – in the house and outside. In January 2015, the video projection of our work was presented to 300 people. Noah was present and everyone could see how happy and proud he felt about the project.

Even today we continue to photograph our life, just not as much. Noah is now the school photographer; his work has been posted through the Nos, Why Not? Agency social network. Not only did photography help Noah put his story together, it also helped me to understand he was much more capable and autonomous than I imagined. And finally, it is giving him an opportunity to develop a hobby for which he gains recognition. Recently, Noah was the topic of a journalism student video assignment for UNESCO (United Nations Educational, Scientific and Cultural Organisation). One can observe that the only moment Noah is smiling in the video is when the camera is in his hands. Photography in autism works like PECS (the picture exchange communication system) with a personal approach, so it has a lot of potential as a therapeutic approach with this particular group.

Born in Belgium, Sophie Lizoulet has a Master of Science in Mass Communication from Boston University. She created Happy People House in 2015, a place for creative well-being development.

Photovoice

Tiffany Fairey

Photovoice projects are more commonly thought of as social action rather than therapeutic interventions. The approach supports communities and groups to "voice" concerns and issues through images and in turn put these images back out into society, using them to advocate for change, to raise awareness with public audiences and within communities, and to push for policy and attitudinal change. The images produced by participants are used in the press, in exhibitions, in publications, as postcards and on websites. For those involved in projects, seeing audiences look and listen to what they have to say is often an emboldening, validating and transformative experience.

Therapeutic forms of photography are at the core of photovoice processes that seek to harness the capacity of the photographic image to act as a catalyst to dialogue, self-reflection and self-expression. For some, the "public" aspect of photovoice projects does not sit comfortably alongside what could be considered the more "private" therapeutic side of the personal creative process; for others, the public sharing of their images enriches and amplifies the experience. Some groups, who have already identified that they want to share their stories and to speak out about issues, quickly take ownership of the photovoice process. Others, who may be more vulnerable or who come from more fragmented communities, need to work at a pace that suits them to come to explore and understand the processes involved.

For photovoice practitioners, it is crucial to not make too many assumptions in advance about how people may or may not react to working with photography and what they may or may not want to do with their images. The "voice" in photovoice projects is not a given but is something that emerges; it is developed, cultivated, negotiated and claimed through photographic, individual and group processes. It is through deciding what to shoot and how to shoot, in sharing and talking about your images, deciding what you want to say and how you want to represent yourself and your concerns that the individual and group "voice" emerges. This can be personal, uncertain and often private work and it cannot be assumed that it will be suitable for public display and advocacy.

Most often in groups there is a mixture of people – those who enjoy and gain the most from a more personal, group-based creative experience, and others who embrace the opportunity to use photography to speak out to people beyond the workshop walls. Many fall somewhere in between – they are keen to share their images but it is an unknown, challenging, even intimidating, process that requires a leap of faith. This variety can make photovoice projects ethically challenging. Practitioners need to be highly sensitive to the range of tensions and issues that can arise and be careful to ensure that the public element of the project is an enabling and empowering experience for those involved and, most importantly, that those participating are appropriately supported and informed. Photography holds huge potential as a therapeutic tool but it is key that practitioners are aware of its limits and of the complexities that can arise when vulnerable people use images to speak out.

One person I worked with on a therapeutic photography project argued that perhaps it is better when photography projects are not even defined as "therapeutic" at all. For him, the therapeutic impact should be incidental – a by-product rather than the focus of the activity. As a former mental health service user and now a mental health support worker, he argued that many of the people he worked with had been through so many different kinds of intervention and forms of treatment that the value of photography as he saw it was "time out" from all of that. Photography allowed him to consider his experiences from a totally different perspective.

Tiffany Fairey is a researcher, practitioner and educator specialising in participatory visual media and is a co-founder of Photovoice.

One-to-one work

Ailsa Rainnie

Working in a rural environment means one important thing – you have to be more creative than those working in environments that have access to great resources and services. For me, therapeutic photography has enabled the young people and families I work with to take control of their lives and invite me, as a worker, into their lives through the medium of photography. The Scottish government's Getting It Right For Every Child (GIRFEC) framework that we work within appears to the practitioner to be a framework that promotes and supports a person-centred approach yet many of the available assessment tools can hinder this. This in turn can strike an all too familiar service-led approach as opposed to a person-centred one.

Therapeutic photography allows the young person to explore their interpretation of their world and what is positive or negative for them. I learn the most from young people and families utilising a tool we adapted called the Feelings Wheel – it asks people to explore certain emotions from a list placed on a wheel. Some emotions I took for granted; for example, I thought surprise was always a positive emotion until experience showed me otherwise. I worked with a young person who had taken a picture looking across the water encompassing all the surroundings in a rural location. In my opinion, the picture was beautiful and made me feel positive. For this young person, the feeling of "surprise" did not have the same interpretation. She used the photograph to explain that surprise was not welcome and created uncertainty and suspicion – the content of the image was not really relevant, she was simply using it to explore her experiences of being "surprised". That day will always be the most powerful piece of work I have participated in and certainly opened a door to the young person's world that I would not otherwise have accessed.

Therapeutic photography is a gift to practitioners and through its use will often lead the practitioner to learn so much more about the individual than was first expected. It allows the individual to express how they are feeling and control the conversation. Working within care and protection can lead to highly emotive situations. Not all children are at an age and stage where they are able to discuss verbally how they are feeling but through photography they can visually explore their surroundings, and themes can be looked for within the images.

I found that therapeutic photography enabled me to incorporate theories and relate them to practice, for example when using a strengths-based perspective. I found this most noticeably within the exercise "How I see myself" and "How others see you". I carried this out as part of one young person's assessment. The young person's parents could not agree on where he would live and he felt trapped between them and their acrimonious relationship. The impact on the young person was tipping the situation into a child protection issue. When I asked him to take a picture of how he felt he was seen by his parents, he took a picture of his own reflection in the water and exclaimed that he could not see himself and it was all blurry. He felt as though this was how his parents saw him, that he was there but they couldn't really see him. For a 10-year-old to be able to identify through photography how he felt his parents saw him was very powerful for me, and helped me in ensuring that a person-centred plan was in place. With the consent of a young person, photos such as this one can be shared during multi-agency meetings and when working with the parents to help emphasise that the child should be placed at the centre.

Ailsa Rainnie is a social work practitioner who graduated from Robert Gordon University. Ailsa was nominated and won the Newly Qualified Social Worker of the Year in 2017 because of her innovative approach to working with clients.

My photo therapeutic diary: my body's voice
"The relationship with my body, food and society through the eyes of my camera"
Almudena González Valenzuela

"All together, let's take a picture!" That sentence, for years, had been torture for Almudena. She would panic and run away. No images of her existed in a photographic album for very long, not even from her sister's wedding. Photography was her enemy at that time, but later, surprisingly, even without her being consciously aware of its power, it became her saviour. Its light was crucial in her own path of self-healing, allowing to her observe a clear mirror of herself covered before by dark reflections of fear and disgust. As a result, photography became her primary sense through which she could (and still can) listen, observe, taste, hear and feel the beauty of existing in this world in harmony with her body.

When I was 22 years old, out of pure coincidence, I took a photography course in London. It was then that the dialogue between me, my body and my camera began. During the course, I felt a profound need to talk to my camera. All my school projects had developed based on a series of self-portraits, which in time started to make more sense to me. Those pictures were telling me how I was torturing my body, they were speaking to me, they were the mirrors of my emotions, fears, loneliness and, eventually, hope.

Then, with time, those series of portraits became part of my diary, and the creation of a book. During that process, seeing the pictures of my body around me, touching them, writing to them and judging them, allowed me to find a sacred place where, privately, I used to hide, talking and listening to Almudena.

Over time, seeing how I overcame my relationship with my body and food empowered me, making me more confident, giving me the chance to live in this world. The images reflected the voice of the suffering and pain I felt. They also reflected the start of positive changes I have made in my life, which has led me to better relationships with my body, society and especially my family.

During those years, I kept those photographs in silence. Only my best friend, who was behind the camera, who supported me all the time, was aware of my journey, nobody else. I was embarrassed to share them. However, with time, this process also began to change. Slowly, I began to open my diary to people around me, and especially to my parents. The diary was a testimony to them, confirming to them that their daughter was no longer suffering; it was a proof of my recovery. And then slowly I began trusting other people to view it, and as a result, I became more distanced from that time, more present to the actual moment, more grateful for my new self, my new life.

Almudena González Valenzuela lives in Spain.

The healing power of therapeutic photography

Deborah Cluff

First, it should be established that therapeutic photography is about the personal experience of photographing, your relationship to the images, and gaining personal insights. The focus is photography as communication – it is not about photographic techniques. Therapeutic photography is helpful to photographers but one need not be a photographer to do it. No technical expertise with cameras or photography is necessary. Any camera will do. Some of the most compelling photographs are taken with smartphone cameras! It has been said that all photographs are self-portraits. Despite great efforts and ingenuity in the worlds of science, art and academia to attempt to experience phenomena in a pure state, the honest conclusion is that there is no clear way to fully separate the observer and the observed.

Based on these tenets I created "integrative photography", which consists of an interactive, directed set of activities that is designed to encourage participation in the world of phenomena while also witnessing one's self in various contexts (described further below). With the success of these techniques and a growing interest in therapeutic photography, I later created a public therapeutic photography group. Each week, members brought their photos to the group digitally and I used a projector to put the images onto a large screen. With permission from each photographer, we observed and contributed our own perceptions of the images, expanding the ways in which we idiosyncratically perceived them. According to participant feedback, the group's value rested in the safety to share personal images and the sense that others cared enough about the images to consider them deeply, offering unique associations.

Integrative photography uses photography as a medium for self-knowledge and expression. Integrative photography is not intended to provide analyses of photographs per se. It focuses on the experience of photographing, one's relationship to the images, gaining insights through reflection, and being witnessed. There is no critical aesthetic judgement and no agenda to evade environmental influences. An integrative photography session consists of a guided exploration of photographs taken each week. Based on what is revealed and discovered in the photographs, exercises for the following session are assigned or developed collaboratively. Clients make meaning of their own work and find that looking at their lives through photographs provides them with an opportunity to see from a more observing perspective – to witness the self.

With respect to sessions, it is useful, however, to recognise themes and patterns; the perception of another person may illuminate blind spots and make room for new ways of seeing. As an example, the first exercise of integrative photography is to notice what you are noticing. Noticing requires an alertness that is gentler than vigilance and more energetic than looking. It is possible to drive home on the same streets hundreds of times over the course of years and not notice the specific details of your route. If the mind is focused on the destination or too intently on the traffic ahead, if the eyes and ears are fixated on only the things that pertain directly to the drive home and what happens next, a form of tunnel vision dominates the psychic and sensual field. The type of noticing involved in spotting what may be dismissed or even invisible to an agenda-driven mind becomes accessible when the senses are open and receptive to the unexpected and the subtle. Clients are asked to have a camera on hand at all times until the following session – a period of one week – and to photograph anything that attracts visual attention. A main point of this exercise is to become conscious of what one pays attention to on a daily basis. The following is an abbreviated excerpt from a larger case study to provide a more direct experience of integrative photography.

Brief case study: "Psyllo" was a 28-year-old volunteer with no history of psychopathology other than mild but persistent undiagnosed depression (also known as dysthymia). He was assigned the "notice what you're noticing" activity, as discussed above. The series of photographs obtained from the first exercise consisted of indoor shots, taken from a limited number of angles (e.g., looking down on self, down on objects, at eye level). In reviewing the first series of photographs together, Psyllo stated that he felt his photographs were "boring", in that they lacked variety, that he travelled in a limited space, and engaged in a small range of activities day to day. This simple observation led to a transformation as it became clear to him that he "wanted to get out more".

Psyllo's next series of photographs visually represented a breakthrough in his visual field of interest. These shots displayed his private context (bedroom), love for his dog, and personal interest (fish breeding). These represented ways of indirectly self-disclosing and sharing how he saw himself. All of these shots were taken from above his head, as if from the perspective of an observer or his observing self. These few literal self-portraits conveyed what I interpreted as an intention of communication in his eyes. In looking at Psyllo's first album, I observed that most of the photos were taken indoors with certain patterns, themes repeating throughout. There was an emergence, with the self increasingly included in the frames. He began with indirect shots, through reflected surfaces, that limited exposure of his physical self to a foot (or feet). As the sessions continued, Psyllo moved from images of himself clothed, taken from above, focused on the face and communication, to vulnerable, unselfconscious upper body self-portraits. The series began to feel less about communication with others and more about self-exploration. Angles and uncommon postures in his later photographs suggested a curiosity about the way he looked. There was a sense that these views of self were new to Psyllo.

With respect to the work of integrative photography – as we cannot remove all filters of perception we have accumulated – all material is considered communication from the self. Physics tells us that simply the act of observing something changes it. Integrative photography uses this principle, along with many others, as a tool for personal transformation. The value of insight cannot be overstated; however, this work is to engage with our insights in ways that make a difference in our minds and hearts as well as the actual lives we live.

Deborah Cluff, PhD, lives and practises in the USA.

Group work

Lucia Cumposta

Introduction

I've been working as an executive coach for some years now. I mainly work with teams and leaders in small and medium companies, and I've always been also involved in voluntary service to non-governmental organisations and other local organisations.

Photography is a lifelong passion for me, but until 2012 I never thought it could also be an excellent tool to fit into my daily work. I decided to complete my studies with Points of You Israel on the use of therapeutic photography in coaching and personal development processes, and soon afterwards I attended the introductory course with Judy Weiser during the Perugia Social Photo Fest in Italy.

By the end of 2013, I proposed to introduce therapeutic photography to enhance the process of social and labour reinsertion of groups of immigrant women.

For nearly seven months I worked with different groups, two of them composed of ex-prostitutes who had been the subject of extensive work. The vulnerability of these groups made necessary the presence of a psychologist as a support during my interventions, which I appreciated and considered important, since I'm not a psychologist and an unexpected or violent reaction from any of the participants was possible and had to be managed in the proper way.

Common ground for all groups

During the previous meetings with social workers and psychologists I was informed of the different phases of the projects for the recovery, support and creation of work opportunities and other aspects, including legal ones, concerning the labour and social reinsertion of the participants. About 70 per cent of women were from Africa and Central/South America, 15 per cent from east European countries and 10–15 per cent were Spanish. Some of the psychologists explained that during the personal interviews and the group meetings many women couldn't express their feelings, felt ashamed to ask questions and tended to keep silent. This was especially true for the ex-prostitutes. I was asked to assist in helping women to uncover their personal values, address the wrong beliefs and overcome self-sabotaging habits, which sometimes clashed with their own culture and the traditional education they had received in their countries.

Playing with snapshots

The main idea for me was to make women play, relax and not be scared about the personal interviews. After introducing myself and explaining in a simple and clear way what a coach is and does (using the example of a basketball or football coach), I used the same strategy I use with every single group: first make them play, using colourful balls, words and numbers.

Then I put down many different photos (black and white, and colour) and let them choose the first one that captured their attention. I made sure there was an inclusive range of subjects (black and white people, men and women, children, animals, old people, different landscapes), in order to deepen the projective process and give better results. Most of the women chose more than one photo, which was quite indicative to me of their need to keep the feelings that had arisen from the images in their hands. "If you choose just one, is like taking all the other emotions away from you," said one of them.

In observing the photographs, I let them talk about likes and dislikes of elements of the pictures – lights, shadows, colours, movement, stillness, landscape. Most of them chose images in some way related to good memories from their childhood and that was the perfect way for them to be reminded of the values and abilities they had hidden or forgotten. The evocation of the past isn't only a nostalgic phase, but it can often be an acknowledgement of skills that could be recovered as a starting point to plan a different future through new initiatives and actions, hope and courage (self-esteem reinforcement).

All my questions were intended to guide the women to a vision of a different present, leading to a different future, made possible by catching the most significant and valuable details coming from the pictures during the projective process and allowing them to remain in participants' daily lives. I thought that it was also important to give a "title" to the pictures, since the use of a specific word or sentence can be an additional emotional anchor.

This is why I gave each of the women a notebook, as I always do with my coachees. I made some copies of the photos and in the last two meetings I asked them to choose the preferred ones and stick them in their notebooks. I put colouring pens and markers at their disposal to allow them to write down words, personalise their notebook and, most of all, to make them draw their personal picture of the future. Surprisingly, all the drawings were done using light colours, some of them clearly influenced by the photographs they had chosen.

In our wrap-up meeting, during the follow-up of the whole process, all the women said they loved working with photos because they could show their feelings and emotions, change their focus and consider new viewpoints about their lives. Some of them were really surprised (and glad) for the opportunity to talk spontaneously and said they felt much more confident, aware of their strengths and ready to undertake a new life project.

Lucia Cumposta lives and practises in Barcelona, Spain.

Therapeutic photography helping us in the smartphone age

Mark Wheeler

For many reasons, we may find words, written or spoken, less useful than pictures. We instantly connect with pictures that show ourselves, rather than with anonymous pictures.

From cave paintings to contemporary social media, we have used images as a primary source of direct communication for as long as there is evidence for human activity. There has never been an easier, quicker approach to making and disseminating images than those available to us now.

In care and therapeutic contexts

Whether caring activity is predominantly in the domain of physical, or psychological needs, the use of photographs is both physically and psychologically affecting. Whether professionally caring, or caring for a loved one, how do we know we are being helpful?

Photographs to enhance activities of daily living

We see before we speak. Images reach deeper than words and photographs of all kinds are an invitation to look, even when the image is already familiar. To help someone who is experiencing cognitive or memory deficits, we might post laminated cards of cartoon images around their bedroom, bathroom and kitchen, to help remind them of their activities of daily living:

- Get out of bed

- Wash my face

- Brush my teeth

- Brush my hair

- Put on my school clothes

- Go down for breakfast.

There are standard sets of such cards available, featuring simple drawings of people undertaking these activities. Better still are similar cards featuring photographs of us (for example, performing our basic morning routine), because we connect with the image more deeply, even though we are unconscious of the connection process. This technique was initially piloted with young people living in a community residential setting. Most of those young people completed more of their morning routine tasks than they had with the standard pictorial reminder images.

The young people were interested in the pictures of themselves. They had posed for the pictures, chosen the pictures from many proofs and had helped to put the images in place.

Developments in technology offer opportunities for a second level of prompting. For example, a tablet, programmed with alarms and the same pictures, can replace verbal prompts from helpers, with electronic prompts. We are all sensitive to movement (eyes are merely detectors of movement) so the changing image on the tablet screen, backed up by a chosen audio prompt, draws attention to the image on the screen. In my professional experience, families have found that this makes the "getting up" routine more successful and more likely. We all feel empowered by not having to be nagged to perform tasks, and this improves everyone's mood in the morning.

Photographs to soothe and reduce anxiety

We imagine that the things we see can also see us and this experience informs the growing sense of attachment we develop in our early years. Later, we try to use words to enhance our explanation of the world. For some, these words never come, or the words are inadequate; others express their experiences through sign languages, such as Makaton, that bypass the complicated brain pathways of speech. These pathways include Broca's and Wernicke's brain regions, the motor and the primary, secondary and tertiary auditory cortexes, criss-crossing the hippocampus and corpus collossum in at least two brains (one talking and one listening). Those experiences that occur before we have language to understand them are embedded in incoherent, incomprehensible, sometimes upsetting memories.

Pictures reach deeper and carry more implications of attachments to loved ones. Photographs elicit more direct emotional experiences than words and therefore enrich, deepen and intensify social care interventions.

We only see what we look at. There is a choice made by the photographer and a choice made by the viewer. The presentation of images has evolved from the cave painting to Instagram and Snapchat.

Some phone apps only offer a limited time to view images on the recipient's device, which prevents bewildering galleries of old images cluttering our phones and makes this an ideal vehicle for "picture prompts". One young adult, vulnerable early each morning to self-harm and suicide attempts, was living in difficult circumstances. Face-to-face contact was difficult to achieve, but brief daily messages reminded her that she was being thought about, which enabled her to get on with her life. Photographs of artefacts created in therapy sessions, or, for example, of the trees outside the facility, could be used to intensify such interventions and may render words superfluous.

Exchanging photographs using phones or tablets as part of communication about care can reduce the power imbalance between the "carer" and the "cared for" person. It can offer a beautiful example of social constructionism as the communication (for example, sending a carer an image of the task someone needs help with) is created in the potential space between carer and cared for. The use of photographic images in communication can enhance their understanding of each other, while reducing the limitations and disadvantages imposed by language. The image is concrete and explicit.

Practitioners may also consider using photographs therapeutically as a tool for preparing people for anxiety-provoking experiences, such as injections or medical investigations. Photographs can be used as "steps" in the process of desensitisation for procedures we have to face.

Therapeutic photography is now the most widely practised intervention in promoting our collective mental health, as we increasingly share images and respond to them, on our phones and in social media. As we live lives that offer less time in the actual company of those who matter to us, we can maintain our attachments by sharing photographs of our experiences, of where we are and what we see.

Mark Wheeler is an art psychotherapist, who has been using therapeutic photography for over 30 years with adults, young people and families. Mark has been a service user himself, benefiting from therapeutic photography, and is currently principal art psychotherapist and clinical supervisor at Nottinghamshire Healthcare NHS Foundation Trust.

The One Project

Bryce Evans

The One Project is the photography community for people suffering from depression and anxiety. We provide a private online platform and help you learn how you can better express, understand and overcome these issues with therapeutic photography.

I started The One Project in 2011 when I began using photography and creative writing as a way to break the silence around the severe depression and anxiety I was struggling with. Through this process, I developed a unique set of techniques that provided a step-by-step guide to make it easier to *start* talking and break the silence through photos.

Over the last six years, The One Project has reached people in over 128 countries and already built a community of more than 1100 people on its online platform. Through the stories that have been told on the website, we are helping people to see that they are not alone in these issues and are connecting them with others who can relate to them and provide support.

We are approaching one trillion new photos per year. The photos will be taken for many different reasons and used in different ways, but each and every photograph is an expression. It is representing a unique perspective of the world, a voice and a moment. Those photos may be telling a story that has never been told before or helping someone through a struggle that may seem unbearable, something they don't have the words for. A photograph can help express that. Many people are doing this already and unconsciously helping themselves with the power of therapeutic photography, but may not be getting the full benefits without understanding what they are doing. The most beautiful part of all of this is how these photos are helping us connect with each other, instantly across the world, and building empathy for our fellow human beings. The majority of people struggling with depression and anxiety have access to the tools and resources that they need, but stigma and silence prevent any recovery or growth.

Photography is powerful, especially for mental health, because it is non-verbal communication and allows people to express what is difficult to put in words. In the case of issues like depression and anxiety, it also provides a safer way to express thoughts or emotions in a general way (or "below the surface" of the photo) so that you are able to release them and see them from a third-person perspective, without having to personally admit to dealing with those issues yourself. It's a way to "test the waters" and see how people may react to that, while anyone who can relate and may have been through something similar will connect with it, providing, it is hoped, a very healing conversation.

Our mission at The One Project is to change how we see and talk about depression and anxiety through therapeutic photography. We believe that through simple education and providing a safe space online, people will be able to have profound experiences of healing and connection that will help them start the process of overcoming these issues.

Bryce Evans is founder of The One Project and lives in the USA.

The Therapeutic Photography Programme

This Appendix provides an outline of the six-week programme that was used with a number of different groups in the writing of this book. It is included here as a template for structuring exercises for those who are interested in delivering their own therapeutic photography programmes.

Day 1

The first session is structured so that participants can begin to work with images, talk about what pictures mean for them, and start to take photographs to represent things in their environment. It is an opportunity for a group of participants to get to know one another and to become more familiar with the equipment they are using to capture the images.

Pick a picture

This exercise gets the participants thinking about likes and dislikes, and is a good ice-breaker. Spread a large number of photographs, magazine clippings, postcards and so on over a table and ask the participants to choose one or more images that appeal to them. Once they have selected an image they then have to explain to the group why they have chosen the one or ones they have gone for.

Once all participants have presented their reasons, they then have to give the image a name/title – they can discuss with others to come up with a name/title they are happy with.

Photography scavenger hunt

The participants are restricted to the room they are in. Each one has to pick a certain number of sticky notes, each one with an instruction about something they have to photograph. Suggestions include:

- A happy face

- Something from your pocket

- Something that makes you smile

- Something green

- Something with a number on it

- The Queen

- Someone making a funny face

- Someone's tongue

- A pair of shoes

- Something blue

- Something red

- Someone's eye.

The purpose of the exercise is to encourage participants to engage with their environment and to begin to explore and think creatively, and also to be critical.

Once everyone has taken their photographs they have to present each image in turn and the other group members must guess what they had been instructed to photograph.

This can then lead to a discussion about how people will interpret different things from different photographs, leading to the point that *there is no right or wrong way to take a photograph* – the important thing is to listen to the person who took it and get their interpretation.

Photographs with meaning

This simple exercise asks participants to locate an image on their phone or camera (or perhaps a photograph they carry with them) that they would be upset to lose or discover had been deleted. Ask each participant to explain what the photograph is and why it means so much to them.

This can lead onto a discussion about the *power of photographs to create memories and meanings*. There is also an opportunity to discuss how we learn as infants, relying on our visual brain, and how visual learning is so important to our development.

Self-portrait

Ask the participants to do a self-portrait. This does not have to be a traditional "selfie" where someone tries to look "perfect". The participants can interpret the remit however they want, but the image must contain something about them that they like. Therefore, the participants are encouraged to think positively about themselves and identify something they like about themselves. Suggestions include:

- My hair

- My smile

- A tattoo

- My shoes

- An aspect of my personality.

Each participant will then present their self-portrait to the rest of the group and say what it is they like about themselves. This can lead to a discussion about how we present ourselves in public, and on social networking sites.

Day 2

This session begins by inviting the participants to show their self-portraits and discuss the content. The session is structured around encouraging the participants to think creatively about how to express ideas and emotions that might be difficult to capture in an image. The group spend time trying to represent emotions in photographs, learning that there are safe ways to capture complex subject matter.

Self-portrait

Continue feedback from self-portrait exercise.

Six emotions

Naming emotions is important for developing children, but for those affected by poor attachment and trauma, this might be neglected. This exercise asks the participants to explore the six main emotions and sets the challenge of taking a picture to represent each one. The picture should not include any people; instead, each participant has to think creatively and represent the emotions in an abstract manner.

The six emotions are:

- Fear

- Sadness

- Anger

- Surprise

- Joy

- Love.

Each participant then presents their images in turn and explains why each represents the emotion chosen. This can lead to a discussion about how we deal with particular emotions, what was difficult to photograph, and what might be omitted.

How I see myself – how others see me

This exercise builds on the abstract element of finding objects to represent other things. Each participant is asked to produce two images. In the first, they must take an abstract image that represents how they view themselves. Then, the second image must be an abstract image that represents how they think other people see them.

Again, each participant then explains their two images to the group.

Relationships

The final exercise can be set as homework. Building on the abstract nature of photography, each participant is asked to consider the people most important to them in their lives. For each person, they have to take an abstract image of how they view that person. These images are to be presented to the group with an explanation.

Day 3

The focus so far has been on internal aspects of character and personality, but now participants are encouraged to explore their immediate environment and consider how they relate to it.

Two likes, one dislike

Ask the group to go out and explore the environment. They must come back with three photographs – two must be of something they like, and one must be of something they do not like.

When they all return, they must show their three images and everyone has to guess which of the three images shows the thing the person dislikes. Participants will be encouraged to talk about why they like what they have photographed.

Room 101

Leading on from the previous exercise, each participant must try to banish the thing they dislike from the face of the earth by placing it into the mystical "Room 101". They must explain what it is they dislike about their image and why it should be banished from the world forever. Everyone gets to say which item should be voted into "Room 101". This can be an interesting discussion and allows everyone to explore opinions and come to a collective decision.

Set up activity: A day in the life of...

This is the project for the coming week. Every participant now has to think about their own lives and consider what a documentary team might focus on if they were filming the participant over the course of a day. The participants must take photographs over one day to document a typical day in their life.

The next session will begin by giving each participant time to present their photo documentary.

Day 4

By now, the participants should have developed skills to be able to explore themselves and their environment through photography. This session looks at the images produced in the project entitled "A day in the life of..." and then asks the participants to set a theme for their final project. The ethos behind this is that the participants should feel empowered to decide a topic, explore it, and then decide how they might be able to challenge any issues which may arise.

Present activity: A day in the life of...
Each participant will be given an opportunity to present their photographs from the exercise set last week. This is an opportunity for participants to engage in their narratives and learn from each other some of the common issues they face. The facilitator should think about social issues that impact on the participants.

Hopes and fears
Because all of the other tasks have focused on the past and present, this exercise asks the participants to consider their future. What have they learned? Where do they see themselves in two years' time? What would they like to achieve? Any aspect of the future can be considered, but ideally they must take one picture to represent how they see their future. They can then feed back to the group.

Discussion about how to present images
Ask the participants to think about how they might like to display some of the images they produce. Would local papers be interested? Are there display spaces they can use?

Set up activity: Photovoice
Give an overview of this activity. Photovoice involves the group selecting a theme to investigate using photographs. They have a given timescale to take a set number of images around a theme which the group decides on. After that period of time, the group come together and everyone takes turns to display their images and discuss why they have taken them. As the group explore, common themes and issues should emerge.

At the end of the experience, the group can decide what to do with the photographs and explore opportunities for informing others about the themes they have uncovered. This might involve putting on a photographic display, contacting a local newspaper, or simply sharing the images with a wider group of people (such as family and friends). Ask the participants about themes they might like to choose for their project and ask them to document the issue over the next two weeks. The aim is for the participants to do this individually and then compare results when they come together at the end of the project to look for similarities and differences.

Day 5

This is the final session, which takes place a fortnight after day 4, and represents a chance for the participants to explore the findings from the photovoice project. It is also an opportunity to review all of the images taken across the duration of the six-week course.

Present activity: Photovoice

This is a chance for all the participants to present their photographs from the past two weeks. There is no set format for how to do this but it is suggested that everyone gets a chance to present all of their images before the group look for common themes.

It is a good opportunity to discuss images, but the focus should be on what to do with the images, or about the common message – can an article be written for a newspaper using the images to back up the message? Can the images be displayed to let other people see how the group feel about a particular issue?

It may be that the group need time to select images to be displayed.

Overview of the course

Summarise what the participants have been doing over the past few weeks looking at self-portraits, relationships, photo elicitation and photovoice, while linking into the three areas of self-esteem, self-efficacy and empowerment.

Feedback

Ask the participants to take one photograph that summarises their feeling about the course.

References

Agarwal, N. *et al.* (2015) "Participatory action research with college students with disabilities: Photovoice for an inclusive campus." *Journal of Postsecondary Education and Disability*, 28(2), 243–250.

Ainsworth, M.D.S. *et al.* (2014) *Patterns of Attachment: A Psychological Study of the Strange Situation.* Hove: Psychology Press.

Ainsworth, M.S. (1989) "Attachments beyond infancy." *American Psychologist*, 44(4), 709–716.

Alexander, S.A., Frohlich, K.L. and Fusco, C. (2014) "Problematizing 'Play-for-Health' discourses through children's photo-elicited narratives." *Qualitative Health Research*, 24(10), 1329–1341.

Anderson, K. and Overy, K. (2010) "Engaging Scottish young offenders in education through music and art." *International Journal of Community Music*, 3(1), 47–64.

Angus, J.E. *et al.* (2009) "Context and cardiovascular risk modification in two regions of Ontario, Canada: A photo elicitation study." *International Journal of Environmental Research and Public Health*, 6(9), 2481–2499.

Arendt, J. (2011) "[In] Subordination: Inmate photography and narrative elicitation in a youth incarceration facility." *Cultural Studies, Critical Methodologies*, 11(3), 265–273.

Askheim, O.P. (2003) "Empowerment as guidance for professional social work: An act of balancing on a slack rope." *European Journal of Social Work*, 6(3), 229–240.

Aubeeluck, A. and Buchanan, H. (2006) "Capturing the Huntington's disease spousal carer experience: A preliminary investigation using the 'Photovoice' method." *Dementia*, 5(1), 95–116.

Bagatell, N. (2007) "Orchestrating voices: Autism, identity and the power of discourse." *Disability & Society*, 22(4), 413–426.

Baldry S. and Kemmis, J. (1998) 'Research note: What it is like to be looked after by a local authority?', *British Journal of Social Work*, 28, 129-36

Bandura, A. (1977) "Self-efficacy: Toward a unifying theory of behavioral change." *Psychological Review*, 84(2), 191–215.

Bandura, A. (1982) "Self-efficacy mechanism in human agency." *American Psychologist*, 37(2), 122–147.

Bandura, A. *et al.* (2001) "Self-efficacy beliefs as shapers of children's aspirations and career trajectories." *Child Development*, 72(1), 187–206.

Barbee, M. (2002) "A visual-narrative approach to understanding transsexual identity." *Art Therapy*, 19(2), 53–62.

Barthes, R. and Howard, R. (1987) *Camera Lucida: Reflections on Photography.* London: Vintage.

Bartholomew, K. and Horowitz, L.M. (1991) "Attachment styles among young adults: A test of a four-category model." *Journal of Personality and Social Psychology*, 61(2), 226–244.

Beckett, C. and Taylor, H. (2010) *Human Growth and Development*. London: Sage.

Bednar, R., Wells, M. and Peterson, S. (1995) *Self-Esteem: Paradoxes and Innovations in Clinical Theory and Practice*. Washington DC: American Psychological Association.

Berman, L. (1993) *Beyond the Smile: The Therapeutic Use of the Photograph*. London: Routledge.

Bernard, K. and Dozier, M. (2010) "Examining infants' cortisol responses to laboratory tasks among children varying in attachment disorganization: Stress reactivity or return to baseline?" *Developmental Psychology*, 46(6), 1771.

Black, B.L. and Rose, S.M. (2002) *Advocacy and Empowerment: Mental Health Care in the Community*. Abingdon: Routledge.

Bond, A. and Woodall, J. (2005) *Self-Portrait, Renaissance to Contemporary*. Catalogue to the exhibition in the National Portrait Gallery from October 2005 to January 2006. London: National Portrait Gallery.

Borden, W. (2000) "The relational paradigm in contemporary psychoanalysis: Toward a psychodynamically informed social work perspective." *Social Service Review*, 74(3), 352–379.

Bowen, M. (1993) *Family Therapy in Clinical Practice*. Lanham, MD: Jason Aronson.

Bowlby, J. (1969) *Attachment and Loss, Volume 1: Attachment*. London: Hogarth Press.

Bowlby, J. (1979) *The Making and Breaking of Affectional Bonds*. London: Tavistock.

Bowlby, J. (1980) *Attachment and Loss, Volume 3: Loss*. New York, NY: Basic Books.

Bowlby, J. (2008) *Attachment*. New York, NY: Basic Books.

Bowlby, J. and Parkes, C.M. (1970) "Separation and Loss within the Family." In: E.J. Anthony (ed.) *The Child in his Family* (pp.197–216). New York, NY: Wiley.

Braye S. & Preston-Shoot, M. (1995) *Empowering Practice in Social Care*, Buckingham, Open University Press

Bretherton, I. (1991) "The Roots and Growing Points of Attachment Theory." In: C.M. Parkes, J. Stevenson-Hinde and P. Marris (eds) *Attachment Across the Life Cycle* (pp.9–32). London: Routledge.

Breton, M. (1995) "The potential for social action in groups." *Social Work with Groups: A Journal of Community and Clinical Practice*, 18(2–3), 5–13.

Bridges, W. (2004) *Transitions: Making Sense of Life's Changes*. Cambridge, MA: Da Capo Press.

Bridges, W. (2009) *Managing Transitions: Making the Most of Change*. Cambridge, MA: Da Capo Press.

Bronfenbrenner, U. (1986) "Ecology of the family as a context for human development: Research perspectives." *Developmental Psychology*, 22(6), 723–742.

Bronfenbrenner, U. (1992) *Ecological Systems Theory*. London: Jessica Kingsley Publishers.

Bronfenbrenner, U. (2009) *The Ecology of Human Development: Experiments by Nature and Design*. Cambridge, MA: Harvard University Press.

Brookfield, H., Brown, S.D. and Reavey, P. (2008) "Vicarious and post-memory practices in adopting families: The re-production of the past through photography and narrative." *Journal of Community & Applied Social Psychology*, 18(5), 474–491.

Burnard, P. and Morrison, P. (1992) *Self-Disclosure: A Contemporary Analysis*. Aldershot: Avebury.

Burnham, J.B. (1968) *Family Therapy: First Steps Towards a System Approach*. London: Tavistock.

Burns, R.B. (1984) *The Self Concept: Theory, Measurement, Development and Behaviour*. London: Longman.

Bush, R.A.B. and Folger, J.P. (1994) *The Promise of Mediation*. San Francisco, CA: Jossey-Bass Publishers.

Cappello, M. (2005) "Photo interviews: Eliciting data through conversations with children." *Field Methods*, 17(2), 170–182.

Carlson, E.D. Engebretson, J. and Chamberlain, R.M. (2006) "Photovoice as a social process of critical consciousness." *Qualitative Health Research*, 16(6), 836–852.

Carr, A. (2003) *The Handbook of Child and Adolescent Clinical Psychology: A Contextual Approach*. Hove: Routledge.

Carr, E.S. (2003) "Rethinking empowerment theory using a feminist lens: The importance of process." *Affilia*, 18(1), 8–20.

Carter, B. and McGoldrick, M. (1988) *The Changing Familiy Life Cycle: A Framework for Family Therapy*. New York, NY: Gardner Press.

Carter, E. and McGoldrick, M. (1999) *The Evolving Family Life Cycle: Individual, Family, and Social Perspectives*. New York, NY: Allyn & Bacon.

Catalani, C. and Minkler, M. (2010) "Photovoice: A review of the literature in health and public health." *Health Education & Behavior*, 37(3), 424–451.

Chapin, R. and Cox, E.O. (2002) "Changing the paradigm: Strengths-based and empowerment-oriented social work with frail elders." *Journal of Gerontological Social Work*, 36(3–4), 165–179.

Chickerneo, N.B. (1993) *Portraits of Spirituality in Recovery: The Use of Art in Recovery from Co-Dependency and/or Chemical Dependency*. Springfield, IL: Charles C Thomas Pub Limited.

Christiano, D. (2008) *A Baby's View of Birth* [online]. Available from www.parents.com/pregnancy/giving-birth/labor-and-delivery/a-babys-view-of-birth, accessed 7 May 2015.

Clark-Ibanez, M. (2004) "Framing the social world with photo-elicitation interviews." *American Behavioral Scientist*, 47(12), 1507–1527.

Cohen, P. and Ainley, P. (2000) "In the country of the blind? Youth studies and cultural studies in Britain." *Journal of Youth Studies*, 3(1), 79–95.

Collier, J. and Collier, M. (1986) *Visual Anthropology: Photography as a Research Method*. Albuquerque, NM: UNM Press.

Combs, J.M. and Ziller, R.C. (1977) "Photographic self-concept of counselees." *Journal of Counseling Psychology*, 24(5), 452–455.

Cooley, C.H. (1902) *Human Nature and the Social Order*. New York, NY: Scribner.

Coronel, J.M. and Pascual, I.R. (2013) "Let me put it another way: Methodological considerations on the use of participatory photography based on an experiment with teenagers in secondary schools." *Qualitative Research in Education*, 2(2), 98–129.

Cosden, C. and Reynolds, D. (1982) "Photography as therapy." *The Arts in Psychotherapy*, 9(1), 19–23.

Crocker, J. (1999) "Social stigma and self-esteem: Situational construction of self-worth." *Journal of Experimental Social Psychology*, 35(1), 89–107.

Crocker, J. and Major, B. (1989) "Social stigma and self-esteem: The self-protective properties of stigma." *Psychological Review*, 96(4), 608–630.

Daniel, B. and Wassell, S. (2002) *Assessing and Promoting Resilience in Vulnerable Children: Adolescence*. London: Jessica Kingsley Publishers.

De, A. (2015) "Creating own histories: Adolescent girls in Mumbai's Bastis use photography as a tool of documentation and advocacy." *Space and Culture, India*, 3(1), 30–47.

DeCoster, V.A. and Dickerson, J. (2014) "The therapeutic use of photography in clinical social work: Evidence-based best practices." *Social Work in Mental Health*, 12(1), 1–19.

Dennett, T. (2009) "Jo Spence's camera therapy: Personal therapeutic photography as a response to adversity." *European Journal of Psychotherapy and Counselling*, 11(1), 7–19.

Dennis Jr., S.F. *et al.* (2009) "Participatory photo mapping (PPM): Exploring an integrated method for health and place research with young people." *Health & Place*, 15(2), 466–473.

Diamond, H.W. (1856) "On the application of photography to the physiognomic and mental phenomena of insanity [abstract]." *Proceedings of the Royal Society of London*, 8, 117.

Dietz, C.A. (2000) "Responding to oppression and abuse: A feminist challenge to clinical social work." *Affilia*, 15(3), 369–389.

Dominelli, L. and Campling, J. (2002) *Feminist Social Work Theory and Practice*. Basingstoke: Palgrave.

Donaldson, L.P. (2005) "Toward validating the therapeutic benefits of empowerment-oriented social action groups." *Social Work with Groups*, 27(2–3), 159–175.

Drinkwater, M. (2008) *Photography and Mental Health* [online]. Available from www.communitycare.co.uk/2008/01/16/photography-and-mental-health-a-relationship-kick-started-by-hugh-welch-diamond, accessed 9 September 2016.

Duffy, L. (2011) "'Step-by-step we are stronger': Women's empowerment through photovoice." *Journal of Community Health Nursing*, 28(2), 105–116.

Duval, S. and Wicklund, R.A. (1972) *A Theory of Objective Self Awareness*. New York, NY: Academic Press.

Duvall, E. (1977) *Marriage and Family Development* (5th edn.). Philadelphia, PA: JB Lippincott.

Early, T.J. and GlenMaye, L.F. (2000) "Valuing families: Social work practice with families from a strengths perspective." *Social Work*, 45(2), 118–130.

Erikson, E.H. (1963) *Childhood and Society* (rev. edn.). New York, NY: W.W. Norton.

Fairbairn, W.R.D. (1952) *Psychoanalytic Studies of the Personality*. London: Psychology Press.

Faubion, J.D. (1994) *Power: Essential Works of Foucault 1954–1984. Vol. 3*. London: Penguin Books.

Feder, E. and Feder, B. (1981) *The Expressive Arts Therapies*. Englewood Cliffs, NJ: Prentice Hall.

Fishbane, M.D. (2001) "Relational narratives of the self." *Family Process*, 40(3), 273–291.

Fitzgerald, E.A. *et al.* (2013) "Community-generated recommendations regarding the urban nutrition and tobacco environments: A photo-elicitation study in Philadelphia." *Preventing Chronic Disease*, 10, E98.

Folke, C. (2006) "Resilience: The emergence of a perspective for social–ecological systems analyses." *Global Environmental Change*, 16(3), 253–267.

Fonagy, P. (2003) "The development of psychopathology from infancy to adulthood: The mysterious unfolding of disturbance in time." *Infant Mental Health Journal*, 24(3), 212–239.

Freedman, J. and Combs, G. (1996) *Narrative Therapy: The Social Construction of Preferred Realities*. New York, NY: W.W. Norton.

Freire, P. (1970) *Pedagogy of the Oppressed*. New York, NY: Pantheon.

Freire, P. (1990) "A critical understanding of social work." *Journal of Progressive Human Services*, 1(1), 3–9.

Freire, P. (1998) *Pedagogy of Freedom: Ethics, Democracy and Civic Courage*. Oxford: Rowman & Littlefield.

Freud, S. (1957) "Mourning and Melancholia." In: J. Strachey (ed.) *The Standard Edition of the Complete Psychological Works of Sigmund Freud*. London: Hogarth Press.

Freud, S. (2001) *The Complete Psychological Works of Sigmund Freud*. London: Random House.

Fryrear, J.L. (1980) "A selective non-evaluative review of research on photo therapy." *Photo Therapy Quarterly*, 2(3), 7–9.

Gant, L.M. *et al.* (2009) "Effects of photovoice: Civic engagement among older youth in urban communities." *Journal of Community Practice*, 17(4), 358–376.

Gaskill, R.L. and Perry, B.D. (2011) "Experiences, and their impact on the developing brain." *Handbook of Child Sexual Abuse: Identification, Assessment, and Treatment*, 29.

Gecas, V. (1989) "The Social Psychology of Self-Efficacy." In: W.R. Scott and S. Blake (eds) *Annual Review of Sociology* (15th edn.) (pp.291–316). Palo Alto, CA: Annual Reviews Inc.

Gecas, V. and Schwalbe, M.L. (1983) "Beyond the looking-glass self: Social structure and efficacy-based self-esteem." *Social Psychology Quarterly*, 46(2), 77–88.

George, C., Kaplan, N. and Main, M. (1985) "The Berkeley adult attachment interview." Berkeley: Unpublished protocol, Department of Psychology, University of California.

Gerhardt, S. (2006) *Why Love Matters: How Affection Shapes a Baby's Brain*. London: Routledge.

Gibson, A. and Gibson, N. (2016) *Human Growth, Behaviour and Development: Essential Theory and Application in Social Work*. London: Sage.

Gibson, N. (2017) "Therapeutic photography: Enhancing patient communication." *Journal of Kidney Care*, 2(1), 46–47.

Gilligan R. (2000) "Adversity, resilience and young people: The protective value of positive school and spare time experiences." *Children and Society*, 14, 37–47.

Gilligan, R. (2004) "Promoting resilience in child and family social work: Issues for social work practice, education and policy." *Social Work Education*, 23(1), 93–104.

Gist, M.E. and Mitchell, T.R. (1992) "Self-efficacy: A theoretical analysis of its determinants and malleability." *Academy of Management Review*, 17(2), 183–211.

Glover-Graf, N.M. and Miller, E. (2006) "The use of phototherapy in group treatment for persons who are chemically dependent." *Rehabilitation Counseling Bulletin*, 49(3), 166–181.

Goessling, K. and Doyle, C. (2009) "Thru the Lenz: Participatory action research, photography, and creative process in an urban high school." *Journal of Creativity in Mental Health*, 4(4), 343–365.

Goffman, E. (1959) *The Presentation of Self in Everyday Life*. Garden City, NY: Double Day.

Goffman, E. (1961) "On the Characteristics of Total Institutions." In: D. Cressey (ed.) *The Prison* (pp.43–84). New York, NY: Holt, Rinehart and Winston.

Goffman, E. (2009) *Stigma: Notes on the Management of Spoiled Identity*. New York, NY: Simon and Schuster.

Goodhart, F.W. *et al.* (2006) "A view through a different lens: Photovoice as a tool for student advocacy." *Journal of American College Health*, 55(1), 53–56.

Graf, N.M. (2002) "Photography as a therapeutic tool for substance abuse clients who have a history of sexual abuse." *Counselling and Psychotherapy Research*, 2(3), 201–208.

Graham, M. (2004) "Empowerment revisited – social work, resistance and agency in black communities." *European Journal of Social Work*, 7(1), 43–56.

Griebling, S. *et al.* (2013) "From passive to active voice: Using photography as a catalyst for social action." *International Journal of Humanities and Social Science*, 3(2), 16–28.

Gutierrez, L.M. (1994) "Beyond coping: An empowerment perspective on stressful life events." *Journal of Sociology & Social Welfare*, 21, 201.

Haley, J. (1967) "Toward a Theory of Pathological Systems." In: G. Zuk and I. Nagy (eds) *Family Therapy and Disturbed Families* (pp.11–27). Palo Alto, CA: Science and Behavior Books.

Hammond, L.C. and Gantt, L. (1998) "Using art in counseling: Ethical considerations." *Journal of Counseling & Development*, 76(3), 271–276.

Hare, I. (2004) "Defining social work for the 21st century: The International Federation of Social Workers' revised definition of social work." *International Social Work*, 47(3), 407–424.

Harper, D. (2002) "Talking about pictures: A case for photo elicitation." *Visual Studies*, 17(1), 13–26.

Harrison, B. (2002) "Photographic visions and narrative inquiry." *Narrative Inquiry*, 12(1), 87–111.

Hazan, C. and Shaver, P. (1987) "Romantic love conceptualized as an attachment process." *Journal of Personality and Social Psychology*, 52(3), 511–524.

Hesse, E. and Main, M. (2006) "Frightened, threatening, and dissociative parental behavior in low-risk samples: Description, discussion, and interpretations." *Development and Psychopathology*, 18(02), 309–343.

Hills de Zárate, M. (2012) "Narrative, photographs and the experience of memory." *ATOL: Art Therapy Online*, 1(4), 1–19.

Hirsch, M. (1997) *Family Frames: Photography, Narrative and Postmemory*. Cambridge, MA: Harvard University Press.

Holmes, T.H. and Rahe, R.H. (1967) "The social readjustment rating scale." *Journal of Psychosomatic Research*, 11(2), 213–218.

Honess, T. and Yardley, K.M. (2003) *Self and Identity: Perspectives Across the Lifespan*. London: Routledge.

Howe, D. (1995) *Social Work and the University*. Dublin: University of Dublin, Trinity College, Department of Social Studies.

Howe, D. (1998) "Relationship-based thinking and practice in social work." *Journal of Social Work Practice*, 12(1), 45–56.

Howe, D. and Campling, J. (1995) *Attachment Theory for Social Work Practice*. London: Macmillan.

Hudson, A. (1985) "Feminism and social work: Resistance or dialogue?" *British Journal of Social Work*, 15(6), 635–655.

Huss, E. (2012) "What we see and what we say: Combining visual and verbal information within social work research." *British Journal of Social Work*, 42, 1440–1459.

Iwaniec, D. and Sneddon, H. (2001) "Attachment style in adults who failed to thrive as children: Outcomes of a 20-year follow-up study of factors influencing maintenance or change in attachment style." *British Journal of Social Work*, 31(2), 179–195.

Janzen, C. and Harris, O. (1986) *Family Treatment in Social Work Practice*. Itasca, IL: FE Peacock Publishers.

Jenkins, R. (2008) *Social Identity*. London: Routledge.

Johnson, R. (1999) "The use of photographs in mourning and bereavement and the anthropology of art." *Anthropology & Medicine*, 6(2), 231–241.

Jung, C.G. (2001) *On the Nature of the Psyche*. London: Routledge.

Kasabova, A. (2014) "Rethinking the perceived self: Samples from Facebook." *Acta Universitatis Sapientiae, Film and Media Studies*, 9(1), 209–228.

Ketelle, D. (2010) "The ground they walk on: Photography and narrative inquiry." *The Qualitative Report*, 15(3), 547–568.

Kindberg, T., Spasojevic, M., Fleck, R. and Sellen, A. (2005) "I saw this and thought of you: some social uses of camera phones." *CHI'05 Extended Abstracts on Human Factors in Computing Systems* (pp.1545–1548). New York, NY: ACM.

Kopytin, A. (2004) "Photography and art therapy: An easy partnership." *International Journal of Art Therapy*, 9(2), 49–58.

Kubler-Ross, E. (1970) *On Death and Dying*. London: Tavistock.

Leonardsen, D. (2007) "Empowerment in social work: An individual vs. a relational perspective." *International Journal of Social Welfare*, 16(1), 3–11.

Link, B.G. *et al.* (1989) "A modified labeling theory approach to mental disorders: An empirical assessment." *American Sociological Review*, 54(3), 400–423.

Lishman, J. (2015) *Handbook for Practice Learning in Social Work and Social Care: Knowledge and Theory* (3rd edn.). London: Jessica Kingsley Publishers.

Lishman, J., Yuill, C., Brannan, J. and Gibson, A. (2014) *Social Work – An Introduction*, London, Sage.

Loewenthal, D. (2013) *Phototherapy and Therapeutic Photography in a Digital Age*. London: Routledge.

Loewenthal, D. (2015) "The therapeutic use of photographs in the United Kingdom criminal justice system." *European Journal of Psychotherapy & Counselling*, 17(1), 39–56.

Loopmans, M., Cowell, G. and Oosterlynck, S. (2012) "Photography, public pedagogy and the politics of place-making in post-industrial areas." *Social & Cultural Geography*, 13(7), 699–718.

Main, M. and Solomon, J. (1986) "Discovery of an Insecure-Disorganized/Disoriented Attachment Pattern." In: T.B. Brazelton and M.W. Yogman (eds) *Affective Development in Infancy* (pp.95–124). Westport, CT: Ablex Publishing.

Mallon, B. (2008) *Dying, Death and Grief: Working with Adult Bereavement*. London: Sage.

Marris, P. (1986) *Loss and Change* (revised edn.). London: Routledge.

Martin, R. (2009) "Inhabiting the image: Photography, therapy and re-enactment phototherapy." *European Journal of Psychotherapy and Counselling*, 11(1), 35–49.

Marxen, E. (2009) "Therapeutic thinking in contemporary art: Or psychotherapy in the arts." *The Arts in Psychotherapy*, 36(3), 131–139.

Maslow, A.H. (1943) "A theory of human motivation." *Psychological Review*, 50(4), 370–396.

McBrien, J.L. and Day, R. (2012) "From there to here: Using photography to explore perspectives of resettled refugee youth." *International Journal of Child, Youth and Family Studies*, 3(4.1), 546–568.

McGilchrist, I. (2009) *The Master and his Emissary: The Divided Brain and the Making of the Western World*. London: Yale University Press.

McGoldrick, M. and Carter, B. (1999) "Self in Context: The Individual Life Cycle in Systemic Perspective." In: B. Carter and M. McGoldrick (eds) *The Expanded Family Life Cycle: Individual, Family, and Social Perspectives* (3rd edn.) (pp.27–46). Boston, MA: Allyn & Bacon.

Mead, G.H. (1934) *Mind, Self and Society from the Standpoint of a Social Behaviourist*. Chicago, IL: University of Chicago Press.

Merleau-Ponty, M. (1962) *Phenomenology of Perception [Phénoménologie de la Perception]*. London: Routledge and Kegan Paul.

Mikulincer, M. and Shaver, P.R. (2008) "Adult Attachment and Affect Regulation." In: J. Cassidy and P.R. Shaver (eds) *Handbook of Attachment: Theory, Research, and Clinical Applications* (pp.503–531). New York, NY: Guilford Press.

Milford, S.A., Fryrear, J.L. and Swank, P. (1984) "Phototherapy with disadvantaged boys." *The Arts in Psychotherapy*, 10(4), 221–228.

Minuchin, S. (1974) *Families and Family Therapy*. Cambridge, MA: Harvard University Press.

Mitchell, C. *et al.* (2005) "Taking pictures/taking action! Using photo-voice techniques with children." *ChildrenFIRST*, 9(60), 27–31.

Mitchell, C. *et al.* (2006) "'Why we don't go to school on Fridays': On youth participation through photo voice in rural KwaZulu-Natal." *McGill Journal of Education,* 41(3), 267–282.

Mitchell, C., de Lange, N. and Nguyen, X.T. (2016) "Visual Ethics With and Through the Body: The Participation of Girls with Disabilities in Vietnam in a Photovoice Project." In: J. Coffey, S. Budgeon and H. Cahill (eds) *Learning Bodies: The Body in Youth and Childhood Studies* (pp.241–257). New York, NY: Springer.

Mitchell, J. (1986) *The Selected Melanie Klein.* New York: Viking Penguin.

Modlin, H. (2015) "Child and youth care through a constructive-developmental lens." *Scottish Journal of Residential Child Care,* 14(1), 1–11.

Moletsane, R. *et al.* (2007) "Photo-voice as a tool for analysis and activism in response to HIV and AIDS stigmatisation in a rural KwaZulu-Natal school." *Journal of Child and Adolescent Mental Health,* 19(1), 19–28.

Moxley, D.P., Washington, O.G. and Calligan, H.F. (2012) "Narrative insight into risk, vulnerability and resilience among older homeless African American women." *The Arts in Psychotherapy,* 39(5), 471–478.

Newbury, D. (1996) "Reconstructing the self: Photography, education and disability." *Disability & Society,* 11(3), 349–360.

Newbury, J. and Hoskins, M. (2011) "Relational research and the use of photography in understanding substance use among adolescent girls." *Procedia – Social and Behavioral Sciences,* 30, 1067–1070.

Newman, S.D. (2010) "Evidence-based advocacy: Using photovoice to identify barriers and facilitators to community participation after spinal cord injury." *Rehabilitation Nursing,* 35(2), 47–59.

Noland, C.M. (2006) "Auto-photography as research practice: Identity and self-esteem research." *Journal of Research Practice,* 2(1), 1–19.

Nunez, C. (2009) "The self portrait, a powerful tool for self-therapy." *European Journal of Psychotherapy and Counselling,* 11(1), 51–61.

Oakes, P.J. (1987) "The Salience of Social Categories." In: J.C. Turner (ed.) *Rediscovering the Social Group* (pp.117–141). New York, NY: Basil Blackwell.

Ogden, P. (2009) "Emotion, Mindfulness, and Movement." In: D. Fosha, D.J. Siegel and M.F. Solomon (eds) *The Healing Power of Emotion: Affective Neuroscience, Development and Clinical Practice* (pp.204–231). New York, NY: W.W. Norton.

Oliffe, J.L. and Bottorff, J.L. (2007) "Further than the eye can see? Photo elicitation and research with men." *Qualitative Health Research,* 17(6), 850–858.

Orlinsky, D.E., Grawe, K. and Parks, B.K. (1994) "Process and Outcome in Psychotherapy." In: A.E. Bergin and S.L. Garfield (eds) *The Handbook of Psychotherapy and Behavior Change* (4th edn.) (pp.270–378). New York, NY: John Wiley & Sons.

Ozanne, J.L., Moscato, E.M. and Kunkel, D.R. (2013) "Transformative photography: Evaluation and best practices for eliciting social and policy changes." *Journal of Public Policy & Marketing,* 32(1), 45–65.

Parker, L.D. (2009) "Photo-elicitation: An ethno-historical accounting and management research prospect." *Accounting, Auditing & Accountability Journal,* 22(7), 1111–1129.

Parkes, C.M. (1988) "Bereavement as a psychosocial transition: Processes of adaptation to change." *Journal of Social Issues,* 44(3), 53–65.

Parkes, C.M. and Prigerson, H.G. (2010) *Bereavement: Studies of Grief in Adult Life.* London: Routledge.

Parkes, C.M., Stevenson-Hinde, J. and Marris, P. (2006) *Attachment Across the Life Cycle.* London: Routledge.

Parton, N. (2003) "Rethinking professional practice: The contributions of social constructionism and the feminist 'ethics of care'." *British Journal of Social Work*, 33(1), 1–16.

Payne, M. (2014) *Modern Social Work Theory*. Basingstoke: Palgrave Macmillan.

Payne, S., Horn, S. and Relf, M. (1999) *Health Psychology: Loss and Bereavement*. Buckingham: Open University Press.

Perchick, M. (1992) "Rehabilitation through photography: The power of photography as physical & emotional therapy – Contribution of Josephine U. Herrick's volunteer service photographers' organization to teaching photography to wounded World War II servicemen." *PSA Journal*, 13–15.

Petersen, S. *et al.* (2005) "Narrative therapy to prevent illness-related stress disorder." *Journal of Counseling & Development*, 83(1), 41–47.

Phillips, D. (1986) "Photography's use as a metaphor of self with stabilized schizophrenic patients." *The Arts in Psychotherapy*, 13(1), 9–16.

Pink, S. (2013) *Doing Visual Ethnography*. London: Sage.

Popa, N.L. and Stan, L. (2013) "Investigating learning space with photography in early childhood education: A participatory research approach." *Revista de Cercetare și Intervenție Socială*, 42, 248–261.

Prins, L. (2013) "Photographs in therapy." *Therapy Today*, 2, 28–31.

Raeburn, J. and Rootman, I. (1998) *People-Centred Health Promotion*. Chichester: John Wiley & Sons.

Rappaport, J. (1995) "Empowerment meets narrative: Listening to stories and creating settings." *American Journal of Community Psychology*, 23(5), 795–807.

Rice, K., Primak, S. and Girvin, H. (2013) "Through their eyes: Using photography with youth who experienced trauma." *The Qualitative Report*, 18(52), 1–14.

Riedel, E. (2013) "My African journey: Psychology, photography, and social advocacy." *Psychological Perspectives*, 56(1), 5–33.

Riessman, C.K. and Quinney, L. (2005) "Narrative in social work – A critical review." *Qualitative Social Work*, 4(4), 391–412.

Rogers, C.R. (1951) *Client-Centered Therapy: Its Current Practice, Implications, and Theory*. Boston, MA: Houghton Mifflin.

Rogers, C.R. (1959) "A Theory of Therapy, Personality, and Interpersonal Relationships as Developed in the Client-Centered Framework." In: S. Koch (ed.) *Psychology: A Study of Science* (3rd edn.). New York, NY: McGraw-Hill.

Rosenberg, M., Schooler, C. and Schoenbach, C. (1989) "Self-esteem and adolescent problems: Modeling reciprocal effects." *American Sociological Review*, 54(6), 1004–1018.

Ruch, G. (2005) "Relationship-based practice and reflective practice: Holistic approaches to contemporary child care social work." *Child & Family Social Work*, 10(2), 111–123.

Saita, E. *et al.* (2014) "The clinical use of photography: A single case, multi-method study of the therapeutic process." *Research in Psychotherapy: Psychopathology, Process and Outcome*, 17(1), 1–8.

Sartre, J. (2008) *Being and Nothingness*. London: Routledge.

Schore, A.N. (2000) "Attachment and the regulation of the right brain." *Attachment & Human Development*, 2(1), 23–47.

Schore, A.N. (2001) "Effects of a secure attachment relationship on right brain development, affect regulation, and infant mental health." *Infant Mental Health Journal*, 22(1–2), 7–66.

Schwartz, D. (1989) "Visual ethnography: Using photography in qualitative research." *Qualitative Sociology*, 12(2), 119–154.

Shakespeare, T. (1996) "Disability, Identity and Difference." In: G. Barnes and G. Mercer (eds) *Exploring the Divide* (pp.94–113). Leeds: Disability Press.

Sharland, E. (2006) "Young people, risk taking and risk making: Some thoughts for social work." *British Journal of Social Work*, 36(2), 247–265.

Sitvast, J. and Abma, T. (2012) "The photo-instrument as a health care intervention." *Health Care Analysis*, 20(2), 177–195.

Smith, B.K. *et al.* (2006) "Facilitating narrative medical discussions of type 1 diabetes with computer visualizations and photography." *Patient Education and Counseling*, 64(1), 313–321.

Smith, J.A., Flowers, P. and Larkin, M. (2009) *Interpretative Phenomenological Analysis – Theory, Method and Research*. London: Sage.

Sontag, S. (1977) *On Photography*. London: Macmillan.

Sorokowski, P. *et al.* (2015) "Selfie posting behaviors are associated with narcissism among men." *Personality and Individual Differences*, 85, 123–127.

Spence, J. (1986) *Putting Myself in the Picture: A Political, Personal, and Photographic Autobiography*. London: Camden Press.

Spence, J. and Holland, P. (1991) *Family Snaps: The Meaning of Domestic Photography*. London: Virago.

Stern, D.N. *et al.* (1998) "The process of therapeutic change involving implicit knowledge: Some implications of developmental observations for adult psychotherapy." *Infant Mental Health Journal*, 19(3), 300–308.

Stets, J.E. and Burke, P.J. (2000) "Identity theory and social identity theory." *Social Psychology Quarterly*, 63(3), 224–237.

Stetsenko, A. and Arievitch, I.M. (2004) "The self in cultural-historical activity theory: Reclaiming the unity of social and individual dimensions of human development." *Theory & Psychology*, 14(4), 475–503.

Stevens, R. and Spears, E.H. (2009) "Incorporating photography as a therapeutic tool in counseling." *Journal of Creativity in Mental Health*, 4(1), 3–16.

Strack, R.W. *et al.* (2010) "Framing photovoice using a social-ecological logic model as a guide." *Health Promotion Practice*, 11(5), 629–636.

Stryker, S. (1980) *Symbolic Interactionism: A Social Structural Version*. Menlo Park, CA: Benjamin-Cummings Publishing Company.

Stryker, S. and Burke, P.J. (2000) "The past, present, and future of an identity theory." *Social Psychology Quarterly*, 63(4), 284–297.

Sudbery, J. (2002) "Key features of therapeutic social work: The use of relationship." *Journal of Social Work Practice*, 16(2), 149–162.

Suttie, I.D. (1999) *The Origins of Love and Hate*. Abingdon: Routledge.

Tajfel, H. and Turner, J.C. (1979) "An Integrative Theory of Intergroup Conflict." In: W.G. Austin and S. Worchel (eds) *The Social Psychology of Intergroup Relations* (pp.33–47). Monterey, CA: Brooks Cole.

Teixeira, S. (2015) "'It seems like no one cares' – Participatory photo mapping to understand youth perspectives on property vacancy." *Journal of Adolescent Research*, 30(3), 390–414.

Tournier, M. (1986) *Petites proses*. Paris: Gallimard.

Trainin Blank, B. (2009) "Different strokes: Art and photo therapy promote healing." *The New Social Worker*, Spring, 14–15.

Trevithick, P. (2012) *Social Work Skills and Knowledge: A Practice Handbook* (3rd edn.). Maidenhead: McGraw-Hill International.

Turner, J.C. *et al.* (1987) *Rediscovering the Social Group: A Self-Categorization Theory*. Cambridge, MA: Basil Blackwell.

Ulkuniemi, S. (2007) "Exposed lives: Dialogues between viewers and installations about family photography." *International Journal of Education through Art*, 3(1), 43–55.

Ulkuniemi, S. (2009) "Breaking the frames – snapshooting the genre of family photography and ways of using it." *European Journal of Psychotherapy and Counselling*, 11(4), 385–396.

Van Dijck, J. (2008) "Digital photography: Communication, identity, memory." *Visual Communication*, 7(1), 57–76.

Verhaeghe, M., Bracke, P. and Bruynooghe, K. (2008) "Stigmatization and self-esteem of persons in recovery from mental illness: The role of peer support." *The International Journal of Social Psychiatry*, 54(3), 206–218.

Vygotsky, L. (1962) *Thought and Language* (E. Hanfman and G. Bakar (eds and trans.)). Cambridge, MA: MIT Press.

Vygotsky, L.S. (1980) *Mind in Society: The Development of Higher Psychological Processes*. Cambridge, MA: Harvard University Press.

Walton, G. and Niblett, B. (2013) "Investigating the problem of bullying through photo elicitation." *Journal of Youth Studies*, 16(5), 646–662.

Wang, C.C. (1999) "Photovoice: A participatory action research strategy applied to women's health." *Journal of Women's Health*, 8(2), 185–192.

Wang, C.C., Cash, J.L. and Powers, L.S. (2000) "Who knows the streets as well as the homeless? Promoting personal and community action through photovoice." *Health Promotion Practice*, 1(1), 81–89.

Wang, C. and Burris, M.A. (1994) "Empowerment through photo novella: Portraits of participation." *Health Education & Behavior*, 21(2), 171–186.

Wang, C. and Burris, M.A. (1997) "Photovoice: Concept, methodology, and use for participatory needs assessment." *Health Education & Behavior*, 24(3), 369–387.

Wang, C., Yuan, Y. and Feng, M. (1996) "Photovoice as a tool for participatory evaluation: The community's view of process and impact." *Journal of Contemporary Health*, 4(1), 47–49.

Wang, C.C. *et al.* (2004) "Flint photovoice: Community building among youths, adults, and policymakers." *American Journal of Public Health*, 94(6), 911–913.

Warfield, K. (2014) "Making selfies/making self: Digital subjectivities in the selfie." Paper presented at the International Conference on the Image and the Image Knowledge Community, Berlin.

Washington, O., Feen-Calligan, H. and Moxley, D. (2009) "Helping older African American women who are homeless through visual images and creative strategies." *Visual Culture & Gender*, 4, 7–20.

Watson, M. and Douglas, F. (2012) "It's making us look disgusting…and it makes me feel like a mink…it makes me feel depressed!: Using photovoice to help 'see' and understand the perspectives of disadvantaged young people about the neighbourhood determinants of their mental well-being." *International Journal of Health Promotion and Education*, 50(6), 278–295.

Weiser, E.B. (2015) "#Me: Narcissism and its facets as predictors of selfie-posting frequency." *Personality and Individual Differences*, 86, 477–481.

Weiser, J. (1984) "Phototherapy – becoming visually literate about oneself." *Phototherapy*, 4(2), 2–7.

Weiser, J. (1986) "Ethical considerations in phototherapy training and practice." *Phototherapy*, 5(1), 12–17.

Weiser, J. (1988) "See What I Mean? Photography as Nonverbal Communication in Cross-Cultural Psychology." In F. Poyatos (ed.) *Cross-Cultural Perspectives in Nonverbal Communication* (pp.240–290). Toronto: C.J. Hogrefe.

Weiser, J. (1999) *Phototherapy Techniques: Exploring the Secrets of Personal Snapshots and Family Albums*. Vancouver, BC: PhotoTherapy Centre.

Weiser, J. (2001) "Phototherapy techniques: Using clients' personal snapshots and family photos as counseling and therapy tools." *Afterimage*, 3, 10–15.

Weiser, J. (2004) "PhotoTherapy techniques in counseling and therapy: Using ordinary snapshots and photo-interactions to help clients heal their lives." *The Canadian Art Therapy Association Journal*, 17(2), 23–53.

Weiser, J. (2015) *PhotoTherapy, Therapeutic Photography & Related Techniques* [online]. Canada: Wordpress.com. Available from http://phototherapy-centre.com, accessed 1 January 2015.

Weiser, J. (2016) *Comparisons* [online]. Canada: Wordpress.com. Available from http://phototherapy-centre.com/comparisons, accessed 7 March 2016.

White, M. and Epston, D. (1990) *Narrative Means to Therapeutic Ends*. London: W.W. Norton.

White, V. (1995) "Commonality and diversity in feminist social work." *British Journal of Social Work*, 25(2), 143–156.

Wiles, R. *et al.* (2008) *Visual Ethics: Ethical Issues in Visual Research*. Southampton: ESRC National Centre for Research Methods.

Wilson, N. *et al.* (2007) "Engaging young adolescents in social action through photovoice: The Youth Empowerment Strategies (YES!) Project." *The Journal of Early Adolescence*, 27(2), 241–261.

Winnicott, D.W. (1965) *The Maturational Process and the Facilitating Environment*. London: Hogarth Press.

Winnicott, D.W. (1971) *Playing and Reality*. New York, NY: Basic Books.

Worden, J.W. (2008) *Grief Counseling and Grief Therapy: A Handbook for the Mental Health Practitioner*. New York, NY: Springer Publishing Company.

Wortman, C.B. and Silver, R.C. (2001) "The Myths of Coping with Loss Revisited." In: M.S. Stroebe *et al.* (eds) *Handbook of Bereavement Research: Consequences, Coping and Care* (pp.405–429). Washington DC: American Psychological Association.

Yalom, I.D. and Leszcz, M. (2005) *The Theory and Practice of Group Psychotherapy*. New York, NY: Basic Books.

Yerushalmi, H. and Yedidya, T. (1997) "The family album." *American Journal of Family Therapy*, 25(3), 261–269.

Yohani, S.C. (2008) "Creating an ecology of hope: Arts-based interventions with refugee children." *Child and Adolescent Social Work Journal*, 25(4), 309–323.

Young, B. (2004) "Rebirth at 40: Photographs as transitional objects." *International Journal of Applied Psychoanalytic Studies*, 1(2), 158–181.

Zhang, S., Jiang, H. and Carroll, J.M. (2010) "Social identity in Facebook community life." *International Journal of Virtual Communities and Social Networking*, 2(4), 66–78.

Ziller, R.C. (1990) *Photographing the Self: Methods for Observing Personal Orientations*. London: Sage.

Subject Index

Author Index